COLLINS GEM

WINE

Text by David Rowe
Consultant: Paul Abbott

HarperCollins*Publishers*

HarperCollins Publishers
P O Box, Glasgow G4 0NB

First published 1991

Reprint 10 9 8 7 6 5 4 3 2 1

ISBN 0 00 459113 5

Printed in Great Britain by
HarperCollins Manufacturing, Glasgow

Contents

Introduction

The Gem Guide to Wine provides an extensive and easy-to-use introduction to the world's wines. The compact, pocket-size format makes it easy to consult at the supermarket or wine merchant, in a restaurant, or on holiday in wine-producing regions.

The bulk of the book consists of an A–Z section, which gives definitions for many of the terms found on wine labels. The entries are designed to help the newcomer to wine, faced with an unfamiliar bottle, to find out more about it – what grapes it is made from, what it is going to taste like. The introduction also explains how to store and serve wine, and which wines to drink with various foods.

The entries are thoroughly cross-referenced (cross-references appear in **bold** lettering), so it is possible to start with any term on a wine label. The label on a bottle of Rioja, from Spain, for instance, might say Rioja Reserva Denominación de Origen, Cosecha 1978, Produce of Spain. By looking up Rioja, the entry will give information on the wines of that region, how they are made, from which grape varieties, and what they taste like. Equally, the reader could start with *reserva*, *denominacion de origen*, *cosecha*, or even Spain, and be led to the same information via the cross-references.

There has not been room to cover every

possible wine-label term. If there is no entry for the first term chosen try, starting elsewhere on the label. This dictionary does not cover the names of individual wine-producing companies, or their trademarks.

The A–Z section also explains unfamiliar words used by wine writers in newspapers and the specialist wine press. Wine writers have their own vocabulary for describing wines, with many common words used in a special context. There are separate entries for the most commonly used tasting terms. There are also definitions of many of the specialist terms used by winemakers to describe special techniques and equipment.

A Definition of Wine

Wine is the fermented juice of the grape. A simple definition because wine, basically, is the simplest and most natural of alcoholic drinks. The presence of wild yeasts on the skin and the sugar-rich juice of the grape, only required the skin to be broken and to wait. However, within that simple definition there are apparently infinite variations. The fascination and enjoyment of wine has endured through the centuries because no two wines are ever the same. All that is written and spoken about wine derives from the analysis of the factors that make one wine different from another.

Nearly all wine is made from the grapes of the *Vitis vinifera* species of vine, native to Europe and central Asia, but now widely planted throughout the world. Within this species, there are thousands of different grape varieties (or, more properly, vine varieties), each producing wines with distinctively different tastes and characteristics. The choice of grape, either a single variety or a blend of several, has a profound effect on the taste of the wine produced. However, there are also many other factors at work.

The Pinot Noir grape variety, for instance, is planted in Burgundy, California and Romania (to name just three areas); and the wine produced in each region tastes appreciably different. Further, a wine made from grapes grown on a particular slope in Burgundy can be distinguished from one that has its origins only a few hundred yards away. So natural factors, such as regional climate, soil type, drainage and exposure of the vineyard to the sun, all have an effect on the taste of wine, as does the local climate (microclimate) of an individual vineyard site.

In many regions, the climate is not identical from year to year, and so the vintage can also have an effect on the taste of wine produced.

Then there is the effect of the methods of production used by the wine-producer. Growers can allow each vine to produce as many grapes as possible, in which case the wine will taste relatively thin, or dilute. Or they can restrict the yield from each vine, so that the flavour and the nutrients from the soil are concentrated in fewer bunches of grapes, thereby producing a more flavourful and concentrated wine.

Once the grapes are harvested, growers can exert the most profound influence on the taste of the wine while it is in the wine-making cellar. They can make indiscriminate use of all the grapes available, or they can select only the ripest and most healthy. They can squeeze every last drop of juice out of the grapes, or use only the best-quality juice from a light pressing. Growers may allow yeasts that occur naturally on the grape skins to do their work, or use yeasts cultivated in a laboratory. They can also control the temperature of the fermentation. In some regions where grapes are deficient in natural sugar, more sugar may be added to achieve a satisfactory alcohol content.

Once the wine is made, the winemaker has the option of making a blend of wine from different grape varieties, or different parts of the vineyard.

How Wine is Made

The juice of nearly all grapes is white (the colour of red wines derives largely from the skins of red grapes). In making white wine, the first step is to press the grapes, to extract the colourless juice, which is then usually kept separate from the skins. The unfermented grape juice, or must, is then sometimes clarified to remove unwanted solids, either by chilling it, or by using a centrifuge. Yeast can then be added to the must, to begin its work of the converting sugar in the grape juice into alcohol. The two major by-products are carbon dioxide gas and heat.

Carbon dioxide is normally allowed to escape into the atmosphere. The heat produced during fermentation can be a problem. If uncontrolled it can mar the taste of the wine produced. Wine-makers often go to great lengths to keep the fermenting must cool. Various methods may be used, from leaving the cellar door open, to more sophisticated methods involving stainless-steel tanks with computer-controlled cooling systems.

Gradually, the sugar is converted into alcohol, and the must becomes wine. In the case of dry wines, all the sugar is converted. In the production of sweet wines, the fermentation is stopped before all the sugar is fermented out, either naturally (once the alcohol content reaches a certain level), or by human intervention, such as chilling, filtering, or by adding brandy.

After the first, alcoholic, fermentation is complete, the wine may undergo another transformation, called the malolactic fermentation. In this complex process, tart malic acid is converted into the smoother, softer lactic acid. Winemakers may encourage the malolactic fermentation, by warming the cellar, or they may avoid it altogether, depending on the style of wine desired.

Before it is bottled, the wine may undergo some period of maturation. This can range from storing the wine in huge stainless-steel vats, to ageing it in small oak barrels. All wine is aged to some extent, although the duration can vary from a few days in bottle (e.g. Beaujolais Nouveau), to decades in oak casks (e.g. Tawny Port). Ageing in oak barrels results in a controlled oxidation of the wine. If the barrels are small, and relatively new, the ageing process can also impart flavours and tannins to the wine, improving its potential to age further in bottle.

To make red and rosé wine, the unfermented grape juice must be kept in contact with the skins. The grapes are just lightly crushed, and the mixture of skins and juice is placed in a fermentation vat. The length of skin contact, or maceration, varies widely: it may be short – only a few hours in the case of pale pink wines – or several weeks in the case of a full-flavoured red. As well as colour, the juice also picks up tannin from the skins and pips, an essential component of a well-balanced red wine. If some or all of the stalks are also included in the fermentation vat, the wine will pick up more tannin and bitterness.

When the winemaker has achieved the desired degree of maceration, the skins are separated from the fermenting juice, and pressed. Some or all of the wine extracted from this pressing, which is usually more bitter and tannic, may be added back into the vat, or it may be disposed of separately.

Once the alcoholic fermentation is complete, red wines may also undergo malolactic fermentation. A period of ageing is then usual, more than with whites, before the red wine is bottled.

Sparkling wines are usually made by inducing a

second fermentation in still wine. This occurs in a closed vessel so that the carbon dioxide gas produced cannot escape. In the case of Champagne, and other quality sparkling wines, the process is achieved by adding sugar and yeast to a still wine in bottle, and then securing it with a tight-fitting closure. The yeast turns the added sugar into alcohol and carbon dioxide, but the gas cannot escape this time; it is retained in the wine as bubbles. Once the second fermentation is complete, a deposit of dead yeast cells forms in the bottle. This is removed by slowly shaking and turning the bottle over a period of weeks, while gradually moving it to a vertical, upside-down position in a specially designed rack. The yeast cells gather in the neck of the bottle. This is then plunged, still upside-down, into freezing brine, and a plug of wine and sediment freezes in the neck of the bottle. The cork is then removed, and the plug flies out under pressure, leaving a clear sparkling wine. After topping up, the bottle is re-stoppered, with a secure wired cork.

Alternatively, the second fermentation can take place in bulk, in a sealed vat, and the sparkling wine is bottled under pressure.

Bottle Ageing

Even after a wine is bottled, it is still developing and changing. Indeed, one of the hallmarks of a fine wine is that it has the potential to improve as it grows older.

Bottle ageing is a complex process, not fully

understood. In the case of a red wine, the simple tannins of a young, purple red join together to form progressively longer chains, and the colour changes through shades of red and orange, eventually to brown. At the same time, the flavours soften and blend to produce a harmonious taste. After reaching its peak, which it may maintain for several years, a wine will go into irreversible decline if it is allowed to age further.

It is impossible to generalize about the correct length of time to age a wine. Full-bodied reds which are often found to improve with bottle age include the top wines of Bordeaux, Burgundy, Barolo, Brunello di Montalcino, New World Cabernets and Vintage Ports. The best Champagnes often benefit from a year or two in bottle, and Sauternes and sweet whites from the Loire and Germany can benefit from prolonged ageing.

At a less grand level, even humble table wines, especially reds, can benefit from a few months' ageing to soften them. However, beware of losing the freshness of crisp, light white wines, which are their very attraction.

Storing Wine

Most people buy wine as and when it is needed; a couple of bottles for a dinner party the same day, or simply to drink while enjoying a relaxing evening at home. Storage is not really an important factor.

Once people get really interested in wine,

however, they soon start to build up a 'cellar', often without even realizing it at first. You may start by buying two bottles, one to drink straight away, another to keep in reserve. Or you may decide to save a bit of money by buying a case of your favourite wine from the local wine merchant or wine warehouse, instead of buying by the bottle. And if you want to enjoy wines such as mature Vintage Port and fine Claret, you may have to buy them young and lay them down for years, if you are to enjoy them at their peak. Before you know it, your stocks will outgrow the wine rack in the kitchen, or in the cupboard under the stairs.

If you are going to keep wine for any length of time – more than a few months – storage conditions become important. If you have a basement or cellar, this is a great asset. You can fit it out with wine racks from a DIY store, or improvise using wooden pallets, or old book-cases. The important thing is to keep the wine in an environment where the temperature is at least stable, and preferably cool. A cellar is ideal, because the temperature is probably cool, and fairly constant. Humidity may be a problem: too dry, and the corks will shrink; too damp, and all your labels may fall off (although this will not effect the condition of the wine).

Most modern houses do not have cellars, so it is necessary to look for alternatives. A spiral cellar can be built into the living-room floor, but this is an expensive option, and is only suitable for those who are sure that they are not going to move house in the foreseeable future. Instead use somewhere in the house – a broom-cupboard, or a spare room, for instance – where your wine can be left undisturbed, away from central heating and bright lights. Certainly, wine should never be stored near radiators; there is nothing it dislikes more than being regularly heated up and cooled down. For the same reason the loft, although it may seem an attractively large and under-used space, is also a danger.

If your wine collection does outgrow the house, then the only option may be to entrust it to a commercial cellar or wine merchant – of course you will have to pay for this privilege. In this case, make sure that your wine is insured, at the full replacement cost.

Wherever you store your wine, make sure that the bottles are lying flat, because this will help to stop the cork from drying out and letting deadly oxygen into the bottle.

Serving Wine

The first essential when it comes to serving wine is temperature. Most people have at least a vague idea that white wine should be served cold, and red wine at room temperature. The full enjoyment of wine – in restaurants as well as private homes – is often marred by serving it at the wrong temperature.

For most white wines, one hour in the fridge is quite sufficient, although the same effect can be achieved in under 15 minutes in an ice bucket. If using an ice bucket, be sure to fill it with a mixture of ice and water, as this will chill the wine far more efficiently than ice alone. Less expensive wine often tastes better when it is very cold, while good-quality wine can lose some of its complexity if it is over chilled.

Tradition has it that red wine should be served *chambré*, or at room temperature. However, rooms in most houses are warmer now than they used to be, and red wine is usually served too warm rather than too cold. If you store your wine in a cool area, then bring it into a warm room about one hour before serving. Never plunge it in boiling water, microwave it, or put it by the fire. If anything, err on the side of serving red wine too cool. It will soon warm up in the glass; cooling it down in the glass is more difficult.

Some red wines, such as light Beaujolais and Loire reds, can taste better if lightly chilled; maybe 20 minutes or half an hour in the fridge. The same goes for Tawny Port.

Much nonsense is written and spoken about decanting. The main reason for decanting a wine is to separate it from any sediment that may have developed – which mainly effects red wines that have been in bottle for a considerable time. Some people decant wine 'to let it breathe', but it will aerate much more efficiently once it is poured into glasses.

Generally only Vintage Port and mature Claret, or similar old reds, really need to be decanted.

Let the bottle stand upright for 24 hours. Take the cork out without moving the bottle more than is necessary. Then gently pour the contents into a decanter or carafe, always keeping an eye on the sediment gathering in the shoulder of the bottle. Only stop pouring when there seems to be a danger of some sediment coming out. If you wish, it is possible to filter the sediment using coffee-machine filter paper in a clean plastic or glass funnel.

The choice of glass is all too often neglected. For Champagne, use a flute, not a saucer-shaped glass. For chilled *fino* Sherry use the traditional Spanish *copita*. The appreciation of both reds and whites will be enhanced if you can see and smell the wine, as well as taste it. So avoid decorative cut glass, and choose a plain, generously sized glass, preferably tapering inwards towards the top, to concentrate the aroma, and do not fill it right up to the brim. Needless to say, the glass should be clean. However, any residual traces of detergent will kill the fizz in any sparkling wine, so use as little as possible, and rinse the glass thoroughly.

Wine with Food

The hard and fast rule about matching wine with food is that there is no hard and fast rule. The great thing is to experiment. Do not be afraid to drink red wine with fish – it can be delicious. On the other hand, avoid making it too difficult for a fine wine by matching it with a vindaloo curry.

Apart from such obvious pitfalls as a curry, some apparently innocuous foods can pose problems. Eggs, for example, deaden the palate and spoil the appreciation of the subtleties of a fine wine. Certain green vegetables, such as artichokes, sorrel and spinach, can prove difficult to match. Their flavours react with the wine, producing an undesirable, metallic taste. Vinegar in large amounts will kill the taste of any good wine, causing the wine itself to taste vinegary. If a salad is to be served dress it with oil and wine, or prepare a viniagrette with a sparing measure of mellow balsamic vinegar. Similarly citrus fruit should also be avoided if a wine is to be fully appreciated.

An aperitif should freshen the palate, and start the gastric juices running. Champagne, or another sparkling wine, is a good bet. So is *fino* Sherry. Or you can serve any bone-dry, light white wine.

In matching wine with food, there are two schools of thought: matching like with like (a rich pâté of foie gras with a rich, sweet Gewürztraminer or Sauternes); and providing contrast (rich, fatty meat, cut by the acidity of a lean, bone-dry, fruity white). Both can be successful, and you can use both within the same meal. Avoid overwhelming delicate dishes with powerful wines, and vice versa.

Light soups, or consommés, can be partnered by fresh, light whites, or dry Sherry or Madeira, and the latter can cope with really strong and spicy tastes. Seafood needs crisp whites with plenty of acidity: Muscadet and oysters is a great combination. Delicate fish calls for delicate wine: a dry, gently flavoured Riesling, for example. Stronger tasting fish can cope with fuller whites, or even light reds.

With poultry, the choice of wine depends partly on the method of cooking. Chicken poached in white wine can be enjoyed with the same wine as was used for cooking (never cook with a wine you would not drink). With poultry cooked in red wine, on the other hand, you could try a red Burgundy, or a Pinot Noir from the New World. Red Burgundy and Claret also go well with roast birds, particularly turkey, and with well-hung game.

Pork, like veal, provides an accommodating background for both reds and whites. The acidity of a light, fresh red, with plenty of zest, or a fruity white, such as German Riesling or Loire Chenin Blanc, will help offset any fattiness.

Red meat dishes are generally well-matched by smooth red Burgundy, which has the necessary power to cut through any creamy sauce. The firmer, more tannic reds of Bordeaux marry better with the direct flavours of a plain roast. Game or casseroles are best with an equally warming, robust red, such as a Rhône or Italy's Barolo. The permutations are endless, but the basic object is to match wine and food of compatible weight and intensity of flavour.

Cheese can be a great friend and a great enemy. There is a saying in the wine trade, 'Buy on apples, sell on cheese', meaning that tasting a wine after having eaten a tart, green apple exaggerates its faults; tasting the same wine after having eaten a lump of cheese hides them. In general, all but the mildest cheeses will overwhelm a fine red wine. Sweet whites, such as Sauternes and sweet Loire whites made from the Chenin Blanc grape, can make a perfect match for salty, strong cheeses, like Roquefort. And the combination of Port with fine Stilton or Cheddar is a marriage made in heaven.

Puddings are a great danger. The term 'dessert wine' for sweet whites is a bit of a misnomer, because they are rarely a match for sweet food. And if there is chocolate around, it is difficult to find any wine to match.

Price Guide

The entries for individual wine types include a broad guide as to the expected retail price (except for wines rarely or never encountered outside their region of production). Price band A means under £4 per bottle; B £4–£7; C £7–£10; D £10–£15; E over £15; E+ well over £15.

List of maps

abboccato A term found on Italian labels meaning 'medium-sweet'. It is used particularly for **Orvieto** wines, which may be **secco** (dry) or *abboccato*. See also **amabile**; **dolce**.

abocado A term found on Spanish table wine labels meaning 'medium-sweet'. See also **dulce**; **seco**.

Abruzzi The wild and mountainous wine region in the east of central Italy. The region's best red is the deep, fruity Montepulciano d'Abruzzo (not to be confused with **Vino Nobile di Montepulciano**). The white wine of the region, **Trebbiano d'Abruzzo**, is usually no better than a good, if rather neutral, quaffing wine.

AC (appellation contrôlée) A part of the French system that guarantees the origin of a wine from a demarcated area; its specific purpose is to guarantee authenticity. The wines are placed into three main categories, of which AC is the highest. Within regions there can be a hierarchy of appellations; in **Bordeaux**, for instance, there are generic ACs (e.g. AC Bordeaux), sub-regional ACs (e.g. AC **Médoc**), and, at the top, village ACs (e.g. AC **Pauillac**). In general, the laws of any AC control the following: the area entitled to the name; permitted **grape** varieties; density of vine plants; minimum alcohol levels; yields. The wine must be analysed and tasted before the AC documents are granted.

acetaldehyde (also called **ethanal**) A chemical substance formed in wine by the **oxidation** of **alcohol**. It is desirable in **Sherry**, but undesirable, if it can be tasted, in table wines. Acetaldehyde can be further oxidized to **acetic acid**.

acetic A tasting term used to describe a wine that is sharp, sour and tastes of vinegar. See also **acetic acid**.

acetic acid (also called **ethanoic acid**) A chemical substance formed in wine by the **oxidation** of **alcohol**. It is present in most wines in trace quantities, and is sometimes referred to as the **volatile acidity**. Too much acetic acid is a fault, and gives the wine an unpleasant, **acetic** taste.

acidity An integral component of a wine, which greatly affects its taste. The total acidity of a wine is the sum of its **volatile acidity** and fixed acidity. Volatile acidity refers to the undesirable presence of **acetic acid**, and fixed acidity is mainly composed of citric, tartaric and malic acid; see **acids**.

It is also used as a complimentary tasting term, particularly used to describe a dry white wine with a refreshing crispness on the palate. It is also desirable as a foil to the sweetness in **dessert wines**. See also **flabby**.

acids Essential components in all wines. The 'fixed' acids, such as tartaric, malic and citric, come largely from the grape. Malic acid is transformed into the softer lactic acid during the **malolactic fermentation** that occurs in many wines after the alcoholic fermentation. These acids give a wine crispness and bite and can aid cellaring potential. See also **acetic acid**.

adega A Portuguese term for a wine-making cellar, similar to the Spanish **bodega**.

Affental A light, red wine from certain villages in **Baden**, Germany, made from the **Spätburgunder** grape. Affental means 'monkey valley', and some Affentaler Spätburgunder Rotwein is sold in bottles embossed with the image of a monkey.

aftertaste A tasting term that describes the sensation, pleasant or otherwise, that is left in the mouth after the wine has been swallowed (or spat out). The intensity and duration of the aftertaste is described as the **length**. A long and pleasant aftertaste is one of the hallmarks of a great wine.

ageing All wine is 'aged' to some extent, although the duration can vary from a few days in bottle, e.g. **Beaujolais Nouveau**, to decades in oak casks, e.g. **Tawny Port**. Ageing in oak **barrels** results in a controlled **oxidation** of the wine. If the barrels are relatively new, the ageing process can also impart flavours and **tannins** to the wine, improving its potential to age further in bottle.

Bottle ageing is a more complicated process. In

the case of a red wine, the simple tannin molecules of a young, purple red join together to form progressively longer chains, and the colour changes through shades of red and orange, eventually to brown. At the same time the flavours soften and meld to produce a harmonious taste. The tannins and colouring matter eventually precipitate out in the form of sediment. After reaching its peak a wine will go into irreversible decline with further ageing.

It is impossible to generalize about the correct length of time to age a wine. Full-bodied reds that are often found to improve with bottle age include the top wines of **Bordeaux**, **Burgundy**, **Barolo**, **Brunello di Montalcino**, New World **Cabernets** and **Vintage Ports**. The best **Champagnes** often benefit from a year or two in bottle, and **Sauternes** and sweet whites from the **Loire** can also benefit from prolonged ageing.

aggressive A tasting term, usually pejorative, that describes the effect of excessive **tannin** or **acidity** on the palate. However, a red wine that is aggressive in its youth, may become more mellow with age. White wines, e.g. Loire, Champagne or German, may also soften and improve with age.

Aglianico A top-quality, red grape variety of southern Italy, used to make **Taurasi** in Campania, and **Aglianico del Vulture** in Basilicata.

Aglianico del Vulture A full-bodied, red **DOC** Italian wine made from the **Aglianico** grape in the hills surrounding the Monte Vulture, **Basilicata**. The wine can be excellent, but, unfortunately, rarely is. PRICE BAND: B.

aguardente The neutral grape spirit (77% alcohol) used to fortify **Port**. *Aguardiente*, with an 'i', is the Spanish term for grape spirit.

Ahr The northernmost and second-smallest wine region, or **Anbaugebiet**, in Germany. Two-thirds of its production is of light, red wines, which may be dry or sweet, made from the **Spätburgunder** and **Portugieser** grapes. The remainder is largely taken up with whites from **Riesling** and **Müller-Thurgau**. There is one **Bereich** and one **Grosslage**, Klosterberg, covering the region.

Airén The most widely planted grape variety of Spain. It is found particularly in **La Mancha**, where it is used to produce vast quantities of rather ordinary white wine, and it is also blended with local reds. However, with the use of modern wine-making techniques it can make fresh, fruity whites.

Aix-en-Provence See **Coteaux d'Aix-en-Provence**.

Ajaccio An AC wine of **Corsica** that may be red, white, or rosé. The reds are based on the Sciacarello grape variety, and the whites on Malvoisie de Corse.

Alameda A wine-producing county in **California** to the east of San Francisco, whose most important **AVA** is the **Livermore Valley**. It produces mainly good-quality white **varietals**.

Alba A town in **Piedmont**, Italy, and the region where **Barolo**, **Barbaresco**, **Nebbiolo d'Alba**, Barbera d'Alba (see **Barbera**) and Dolcetto d'Alba (see **Dolcetto**) are produced.

Albalonga A German grape variety that is a **cross** of **Sylvaner** and Rieslaner (itself a cross of **Riesling** and Sylvaner). It is grown mainly in the **Rheinhessen**, where it produces fruity, zesty white wines.

Albana A native Italian grape variety grown mainly in **Emilia-Romagna**, where it is used to produce the white **DOCG** wine **Albana di Romagna**.

Albana di Romagna A white Italian **DOCG** wine, produced in **Emilia-Romagna**. It can be dry or medium-sweet, still or sparkling. At its best it is creamy and nutty. However, its quality is variable, and the granting of the DOCG – the first for a white wine – was controversial. PRICE BAND: B.

Albariño A Spanish variety of white grape, grown in **Galicia**, which produces fresh, crisp whites. See also **Alvarinho**.

albariza The finest of the three soil types of the **Sherry** region around the town of Jerez de la Frontera, near Càdiz in Spain. The white colour of this chalky soil helps the grapes to ripen by reflecting sunlight, and the chalk has good water-retention properties.

Alcamo (also called **Bianco Alcamo**) A dry white Italian **DOC** wine produced in western Sicily around the town of Alcamo, from the **Catarratto** grape. PRICE BAND: B.

alcohol (also called **ethanol**) A colourless, flammable liquid. It is naturally present in all wine, and is produced by the action of yeast on sugar from the grapes (**fermentation**). Although alcohol is colourless and odourless, it does have a slightly sweet taste in its pure form. But the main tasting sensation from alcohol is a warm, even hot, feeling in the mouth.

alcohol content The amount of **alcohol** present in a wine, usually expressed as a percentage by volume. '12% Vol' means that 12% of the volume of the wine is pure alcohol. A glass of Port, at 20% alcohol by volume, will have twice the intoxicating effect of the same sized glass of table wine, at 10%. For comparison, the most common spirits are 40% or 43%.

aldehydes A class of organic chemical compounds sometimes found in wine, of which the most commonly found is **acetaldehyde**.

Aleatico A native Italian variety of red grape

used to make dark, rich, sometimes sweet wines in **Latium** (e.g. Aleatico di Gradoli) and **Apulia** (e.g. Aleatico di Puglia). It is also found on the island of **Elba**, around the villages of Portoferraio and Lacona. Outside Italy, it is also planted in Chile, Australia, and California.

Alella A **DO** wine from north of Barcelona in Catalonia, Spain. Mainly white wine is produced, but some red and rosé is also made. The whites largely come from **Garnacha** Blanca and **Xarel-lo** grapes, together with some varieties new to the region, including **Chenin Blanc** and **Chardonnay**. The whites may be dry (*seco*) or medium-sweet (*semi-seco*). Much of the former vineyard area has been built on, and the wines are rarely better than dull. PRICE BAND: B.

Alentejo A vast demarcated wine region in southern **Portugal**. It produces strong white wines, from the Roupeiro grape, and full-bodied reds, mainly from **Periquita**. The quality of the wines, particularly of the reds, is increasing fast. PRICE BAND: A–B.

Alexander Valley An **AVA** of **Sonoma** county, California.

Alezio A small **DOC** region around Gallípoli in **Apulia**, Italy. It produces mainly red and some **rosato** wines from the **Negroamaro** and **Malvasia** Nera grapes. The *rosato* can rank along with the best rosé wines of Italy, and overall quality is improving rapidly.

Algarve The southernmost, coastal wine region in Portugal. It produces mainly low-quality, high-alcohol reds from **Tinta Negra Mole**, Trincadeira and **Periquita** grapes. It has recently been demoted from **Região Demarcada** status.

Algeria North Africa's major wine-producing country. Under French occupation Algeria made vast quantities of full-bodied, red wine, some of it ending up in French bottles. Today, with the French gone, the vineyard area has been reduced. However, what is left can produce acceptable reds made from **Cinsault**, **Grenache**, **Mourvèdre**, **Syrah**, **Carignan**, **Alicante Bouschet** and **Cabernet Sauvignon**. The whites, from **Ugni Blanc** and **Clairette**, are undistinguished. The main wine regions are in Alger (Ain-Bessem Bouira, Medea and Côtes de Zaccar) and Oran (Mostagenem, Mascara, Haut-Dahra, Monts du Tessalah and Côteaux du Tlemcen).

Alicante A **DO** region on the west coast of Spain. The DO includes the town of Alicante, although most of the vineyards are just inland, in the Upper Vinalopo hills. Most of the wine produced is deep-coloured, high-alcohol red from the **Monastrell** grape, which is better used for blending than drinking on its own. Sweet white wine is produced from the **Moscatel** grape, and dry white from Merseguera and **Airén**.

Alicante Bouschet A **teinturier**, red-fleshed grape, produced from a crossing of **Grenache** and

Petit Bouschet (itself a crossing of **Aramon** and Teinturier du Cher). It is widely planted in the Midi, France, as well as in North Africa and California (although its use has dwindled since the Prohibition era). In France it is mainly used to add colour to pale reds made from the Aramon grape.

Aligoté A white-wine grape variety of **Burgundy**, playing second fiddle to **Chardonnay**. It produces fresh, lemony, often sharp wines, traditionally used in kir, and is usually planted on the poorer sites in Burgundy and sold as **AC** Bourgogne Aligoté. The best examples come from **Bouzeron**, the northernmost village of the Côte Chalonnaise, and from the villages of **Saint-Bris-le-Vineux** and Chitry-le-Fort near Chablis. Aligoté **varietals** from **Bulgaria** have recently come on the UK market. PRICE BAND: B.

Allier A forest in France where some of the best oak is grown for making **barrels** used for ageing wine. The oak's dense, narrow-grained wood has a high phenol content, which imparts a straw flavour; it has a particular affinity with **Cabernet Sauvignon**. See also **Limousin**; **Nevers**.

almacenista A small-scale maturer of **Sherry**, who buys wine from small producers, ages it, and then sells it, usually to a larger **bodega**, for blending. Emilio Lustau is a *bodega* that specializes in bottling individual, unblended wines bought from *almacenistas*.

Almansa A **DO** region of southeast Spain, near **La Mancha**, that produces mainly full-bodied red wine from Garnacha Tintorera (a red-juiced **teinturier** variety) and **Monastrell** grapes. Its white wines, from the Merseguera grape, are of low quality.

almond A tasting term that can be complimentary when referring to a pleasant almond-paste smell in white wines (often Italian), or perjorative when the smell is of bitter almonds, which usually indicates a wine-making fault.

almude A unit of measurement in the **Port** trade, equal to 25.4 litres. One **pipe** is equivalent to 21 *almudes*, and there are about 12 **canadas** (of 2.1 litres) in one *almude*. The origin of these strange measures is said to have been that an ox-cart could pull a *pipe*, an *almude* could be carried on a man's head and a *canada* was the right amount for a man to drink.

Aloxe-Corton A village and *appellation* at the northern end of the **Côte de Beaune**, Burgundy. It produces mainly red wine from the **Pinot Noir** and some white from **Chardonnay**. It can produce among the finest of red Burgundies, although the very best wines do not bear the name Aloxe-Corton.

The two **grands crus** are **Corton** and **Corton-Charlemagne**, both producing rich, top-quality, long-lived reds. These *grands crus* are shared

with the neighbouring villages of Pernand-Vergelesses and Ladoix-Serrigny, and the latter also
includes some vineyards classified as Aloxe-
Corton **premier cru**. The *premiers crus* are not of
the same depth and richness as the *grands crus*,
but they can be fine and elegant, while the
communal wines, sold as AC Aloxe-Corton, have
less style. PRICE BAND: GRAND CRU, D–E; ALOXE-
CORTON AND PREMIER CRU, C–D.

Alsace A region in northwest France, between
the Vosges mountains and the Rhine, which was
once part of Germany. It produces mainly white
wines from single grape varieties. The best are
Riesling and **Gewürztraminer**, followed by **Pinot
Blanc**, **Tokay-Pinot Gris**, **Muscat**, **Sylvaner**, **Auxerrois** and **Chasselas**. The reds, usually light, are
made from **Pinot Noir**. The whites range from
dry, scented wines to rich, intense **vendanges
tardives**, made from late-harvested grapes, and
Sélection de Grains Nobles, made from grapes
affected by **botrytis**.

Most Alsace wines are plain **AC** Alsace,
although a classification of **grands crus**, specially
selected and supposedly superior sites, is being
introduced. **Edelzwicker** is a blend of several of
the lesser white-wine grape varieties. Quality can
be sublimely good for the top Rieslings and
Gewürztraminers, and it is rare to find a poor
bottle of any Alsace wine on export markets.
There is, however, a large volume of cheap,

inferior Alsatian wine on sale in French supermarkets. PRICE BAND: A–E.

Alsheim A village between Worms and **Oppenheim**, in the **Rheinhessen**, Germany. It produces high-quality white wines from the **Riesling** grape. The best, sloping vineyard sites are in the **Grosslage** Rheinblick, and its best-known **Einzellage** is Frühmesse. The flatter land is in the Krötenbrunnen *Grosslage*.

Altenbamberg A village in the Burgweg **Grosslage** of the **Nahe**, Germany, on the River Alsenz (a tributary of the Nahe). It produces excellent white wines from the **Riesling** grape.

Altesse (also called **Roussette**) A grape-variety found mainly in **Savoie**, France, which produces dry, full-bodied, spicy, aromatic whites. It is the basis of the still and sparkling AC **Seyssel** wines. It is entitled to the Roussette de Savoie *appellation*, under which it may be blended with other varieties including **Chardonnay.** Altesse is also grown in **Bugey**.

Alto Adige (also called **Südtirol**) The most northern wine region of Italy. It was formerly part of Austria, and is known to its German-speaking population as Südtirol (South Tyrol). More than half the wine produced is red, much of it from the native **Schiava** (Vernatsch) grape, which gives light, scented wines with a soft fruity taste. French red grapes are also important here, particularly the **Cabernet** and **Merlot**, which produce herbaceous reds with ageing potential, and **Pinot Nero** which is usually less successful.

The crisp, dry whites of Alto Adige are made from French and German varieties, including **Pinot Grigio** (Rülander), **Chardonnay**, **Pinot Bianco** (Weissburgunder), Riesling Renano (**Rhine Riesling**), **Sylvaner**, **Müller-Thurgau**, and **Traminer**. For the other **DOC**s of the region see **Colli di Bolzano**; **Lago di Caldaro**; **Meranese di Collina**; **Santa Maddalena**; **Terlano**; **Valle Isarco**.

Alvarelhão A Portuguese variety of red grape. It produces light, but balanced, red table wines, which mainly come from the Tras-os-Montes and **Douro** regions, but also from the Minho and **Dão**. It is also found occasionally in **Galicia**, Spain.

Alvarinho A Portuguese variety of white grape, probably the best of the **Vinho Verde** region. It is grown in and around Monção, near the Spanish border in the north of the region, where it produces the Vinho Verde's only single-variety wine. It is known as **Albariño** in Spain.

amabile A term found on Italian labels. It indicates a sweet wine, sweeter and fuller-bodied than **abboccato**.

Amador County A county in the Sierra Foothills region of eastern **California**. It produces mainly rich, heady red wines from the **Zinfandel** grape, together with smaller quantities of **Cabernet Sauvignon**, **Sauvignon Blanc**, **Chardonnay**

and **Chenin Blanc**. There are two **AVA**s, **Fiddletown** and **Shenandoah Valley**.

Amarone An unusual bitter-sweet and heady red wine from **Valpolicella**, Italy. Its more correct, full name is Recioto della Valpolicella Amarone. About 10 days before the normal vintage, carefully selected grapes (of the usual Valpolicella varieties), are laid out on straw mats, in a dry, airy room. They are allowed to dry until January, when the shrivelled grapes are crushed and fermented slowly. Some barrels stop fermenting at around 13% alcohol with some residual sugar, and become Recioto della Valpolicella. Others continue to ferment to dryness, reaching around 16% alcohol, producing the strong, bitter-sweet Amarone. The wines are produced in very limited quantities; their quality can be stunningly good, with a long ageing potential. PRICE BAND: E.

Ambrato di Comiso An unusual amber-coloured wine from **Sicily**, made mainly from the red Frappato di Vittoria grape, and cooked **must**. Its taste ranges from medium-sweet to sweet.

American Oak A wood used in the manufacture of **barrels**. It has a high porosity and a medium phenol content. The barrels made from American Oak impart a distinctive sweet flavour with a scent of vanilla and sawn wood.

amontillado A name given to a completely dry, nutty **Sherry**, with an amber colour. It results when a **fino** is allowed to mature without being refreshed with younger wines. Less-expensive, medium-sweet Sherries are often described as *amontillado*, but in fact these are sweetened blends containing only a small amount of true *amontillado*. PRICE BAND: C.

amoroso A sweet **oloroso**, similar to **Cream Sherry**, made by adding **PX** and **vino de color**. The term is rarely used today.

Ampurdán-Costa Brava A **DO** region of Catalonia, in northeastern Spain. It produces very ordinary **rosado** wine from the **Cariñena** and **Garnacha** grapes, mainly for consumption by holiday-makers on the Costa Brava. Sweet, **fortified** red wines are also produced, together with heavy reds and semi-sparkling and sparkling whites.

Amtliche Prüfungsnummer See **AP Nr**.

añada A term used in **Sherry** production for a wine in its first year, before the **solera** ageing process has begun.

Anbaugebiet A term used in German wine law to indicate the 11 major quality regions: **Ahr**, **Baden**, **Franken**, **Hessiche Bergstrasse**, **Mittelrhein**, **Mosel-Saar-Ruwer**, **Nahe**, **Rheingau**, **Rheinhessen**, **Rheinpfalz** and **Württemberg**. The name of the *Anbaugebiet* must appear on the label of a quality wine. Each can be further subdivided into **Bereich**, **Grosslage** and **Einzellage**. See **QbA**.

Andalusia 1. The southern region of Spain, where **Sherry**, **Montilla-Moriles** and **Málaga** are produced. 2. A wine region of **South Africa**, about 80 km north of Kimberley, which produces mainly sweet white wines.

Anderson Valley An **AVA** of **Mendocino** county, **California**. A cool wine region, that is well-suited to growing **Pinot Noir**, **Chardonnay**, **Gewürztraminer** and **Riesling**. It is rapidly gaining a reputation as a good area for sparkling wine produced from Pinot Noir and Chardonnay.

Añina A region of the **Sherry** production area, with **albariza** soil.

Anjou-Saumur A region of the **Loire** valley, France. Most of the production is of rosé wine, from **Grolleau** (e.g. AC **Rosé d'Anjou**) or from **Cabernet Franc** grapes (e.g. AC **Cabernet d'Anjou**). There are also large quantites of red and white AC Anjou made from **Gamay** or Cabernet Franc (reds) or **Chenin Blanc** (whites).
   The Anjou-Villages *appellation* applies to 46 villages in Anjou. They produce red wines made from Cabernet Franc and **Cabernet Sauvignon**, and the quality is generally better than straight AC Anjou Rouge. The greatest wines of the region are, however, dry whites (e.g. **Savennières**), sweet whites (e.g. **Coteaux du Layon**, **Quarts de Chaume** and **Bonnezeaux**) made from Chenin Blanc, and fine reds from Cabernet Franc in the **Saumur-Champigny** *appellation*.

The production of the Loire's finest **méthode champenoise** white wine, **Saumur** – made chiefly from Chenin Blanc but increasingly featuring **Chardonnay** – is centred around the town of Saumur.

annata An Italian term meaning the year of the vintage.

AOC (Appellation d'Origine Contrôlée) See **AC**.

AP Nr (Amtliche Prüfungsnummer) A number given to quality German wines which indicates that they have undergone an official blind tasting and chemical analysis. Although all quality wines must undergo the AP test, it is very rare for any to fail, so it is of limited use as a system of quality control.

appellation contrôlée See **AC**.

apple A tasting term used to indicate the smell or taste of apples. It may describe the tartness of green apples, as in an immature wine, or the old-apple smell of some mature whites.

Approved Viticultural Area See **AVA**.

Apremont A **cru** of the **Vin de Savoie** *appellation*. The wines are mainly dry, biting whites, made from the **Jacquère** and **Chardonnay** grapes.

Aprilia A **DOC** region south of Rome, in

Latium, Italy. It produces reasonable quality, soft reds from the **Merlot** grape, dull reds from **Sangiovese** and dull, dry whites from **Trebbiano**.

Apulia (also called **Puglia**)   A region in southern **Italy**, which produces a vast quantity of table wine, and only 2% **DOC** wine. In the Salento peninsula, in the south of the region, the main grapes are **Negroamaro** and **Malvasia** Nera, which are used to make red and rosé DOC wines and **vino da tavola**. The DOCs based on these two grapes include **Alezio**, **Brindisi**, **Copertino**, **Leverano** (which are also whites), **Matino**, **Salice Salentino** and **Squinzano**.

In the north, the Uva di Troia grape is the most important for reds, often blended with **Sangiovese** and **Bombino** Nero. The best DOCs are **Castel del Monte** (red, white and rosé) and Rosso di Cerignola (red). Cacc'e Mmitte di Lucera, Rosso Barletta and Rosso Canosa are rarely good.

The **Primitivo** grape is used to make **Primitivo di Manduria**, a **big**, deep red which may be dry or sweet and may be **fortified.** A curious red dessert wine, which may or may not be fortified, is made throughout Apulia from the **Aleatico** grape. The best white DOC of the region is **Locorotondo** made from the Verdeca and **Bianco d'Alessano** grapes. These wines are dry and fruity, and can be still or sparkling. DOC **Martina Franca** is similar, and the white DOC wine Gravina is based on the Verdeca grape. Some adventurous producers have made successful wines from French grapes, particularly **Chardonnay**, **Cabernet Franc**, **Pinot Noir** and **Pinot Blanc**.

Aquileia A **DOC** region of **Friuli-Venezia Giulia** in Italy. It produces fruity, soft, good-quality reds from the native **Refosco** grape, and light, but less-successful reds from **Merlot** and the two **Cabernet** (Franc and Sauvignon) grapes. Fairly ordinary whites are made from **Pinot Grigio**, **Pinot Bianco** and **Riesling Renano**, as well as delicate, light whites from native varieties of **Tocai Friulano**, **Traminer** and **Verduzzo Friulano**. A light, dry **rosato** is also produced, mainly from the Merlot grape.

Aramon A very high yielding red grape, extensively grown in the **Midi**, France. When yields are high, it produces a very thin, pale wine, which must be blended with **teinturier** varieties. At low yield it can make a respectable rosé.

Arbin A **cru** of the **Vin de Savoie** *appellation*. The **Mondeuse Noire** grape is planted in the vineyards of Arbin, and can produce good quality, smoky, beefy reds.

Arbois 1. An **AC** wine of the **Jura** region of France. It may be red, white, or rosé, still or sparkling. The most important grape variety for the reds is **Trousseau**, which produces distinctive, flavourful wines of a good quality. Also used are **Pinot Noir** and **Poulsard**, which produce more delicate reds. **Savagnin** is the local white variety, occasionally softened with **Chardonnay**, which makes distinctive sweet-sour whites. See also **vin jaune**. 2. A white grape variety (also known as Menu Pineau) grown in the **Loire** valley, France, where it is used to make the white wines of **Valençay** and as part of the blend in **Cheverny**.

are A unit of area, equal to 100 m². There are 100 ares in 1 hectare (2.47 acres).

arena One of the three soil types of the **Sherry** region in Spain. It literally means 'sand'. Although it is suitable for growing the **Moscatel** grape, *arena* is the least reputed of the soil types because it produces coarser wines.

Argentina The highest-volume wine-producing country of South America. Most of the wine is consumed by the home market. Although there may be the potential to produce wines as fine as those of **Chile**, this has yet to be realized. Most of the vineyards are situated in the foothills of the Andes, mainly in Mendoza. Other important regions are San Juan and Rio Negro.

The country's wine industry had its origins in the 16th century, when the Jesuits planted **Vitis vinifera** vine varieties. The country's most widely planted grapes today, **Criolla** and **Cereza**, are thought to be descended from *vinifera*, and Criolla may be the same as Chile's **Pais**. It yields basic, ordinary table wine. 'Foreign' varieties are increasingly important, however, particularly **Cabernet Sauvignon**, **Chardonnay**, **Chenin Blanc**, **Malbec**, **Merlot** and **Pinot Noir**.

Arinto A white-wine grape variety of **Portugal**, and the main component of **Bucelas**. It yields wines of high acidity and little flavour when young, although complexity can develop with age.

Arneis A white grape variety grown in **Piedmont**, Italy. It produces dry, nutty, full-bodied white wines of increasingly good quality, which are best drunk young. It makes a **DOC** wine in Arneis dei Roero.

aroma A tasting term used loosely to mean the smell of the wine, and more correctly to describe the smells deriving from the grape and from the fermentation process. See also **bouquet**.

aromatic A tasting term used to indicate a fragrant-smelling wine, particularly one made from grapes such as **Muscat** and **Gewürztraminer**.

arrope A Spanish term for a dark-coloured, caramelized grape concentrate, made by boiling grape juice. It is mixed with more **must** and then fermented to make **vin de color**, which is the colouring agent in brown **Sherry** and **Málaga**.

Arroyo Grande Valley An **AVA** in the **San**

Luis Obispo area of **California**. It is important for the production of sparkling wines from **Chardonnay**, **Pinot Noir** and **Pinot Blanc**.

Arroyo Seco An **AVA** in **Monterey** county, **California**, stretching from Soledad south to Greenfield. The soil, containing large, grapefruit-sized stones, produces some of the county's finest **Chardonnay** and **Riesling**. **Cabernet Sauvignon** and **Sauvignon Blanc** are also planted, and the region is also a source of grapes for making sparkling wine.

Arvine A white grape of the **Valais** district of Switzerland, best suited to producing sweet wines.

Asprinio See **Asprino**.

Asprino (also called **Asprinio**) A white grape used to make a dry, white, **frizzante** wine of the same name in **Basilicata** and **Campania**, southern Italy. The wine lacks character, and is mainly gulped down as a thirst-quencher in the bars of Naples.

assagio The Italian term for 'a tasting'.

assemblage A French term used to describe the process of blending wines. It is particularly used in **Bordeaux**, where vats of wine from different parts of the vineyard, and different grape varieties, are blended to 'assemble' the wine before **ageing** in oak barrels. The exclusion of inferior vats from the *assemblage*, or 'selection', is one of the keys to producing great red Bordeaux.

Assmannshausen A village in the **Rheingau**, Germany, situated in the **Grosslage** of Steil. It is famous for its red wines produced from **Spätburgunder (Pinot Noir)**, which may be dry or sweet.

Assyrtiko A good-quality, high-acid, white grape variety from **Greece**. It is grown on the island of Santorini, where it is one of the main ingredients in the island's white wine. The high acidity is sometimes exploited by blending Assyrtiko with the low-acidity Savatiano, the main grape of **Retsina**.

Asti Spumante A sweet sparkling white wine of **Piedmont**, Italy. It is made from the **Moscato** grape, grown in the Langhe and Alto Monferrato hills. The grape juice is allowed to ferment to 4–5% alcohol and then chilled to stop fermentation. The fermentation is re-started in sealed stainless-steel tanks, so that the bubbles of carbon dioxide produced are trapped in the wine, and it is then bottled under pressure. The resulting wine is low in alcohol (7.5–9%), delicately sweet, aromatic, grapey and thirst-quenching. It is ideal for drinking outdoors on a summer day. PRICE BAND: A.

astringent A tasting term for a dry, mouth-puckering feeling on the palate. It is caused by excess **tannin** or **acidity**, usually encountered in young red wines. A young wine may become less astringent as it matures.

Aszú A Hungarian term for grapes affected by **botrytis**, and used specifically in the production of Tokaji Aszú (see **Tokaji**).

Attica The region around Athens, **Greece**, which is the source of the best **Retsina**, made from the Savatiano grape.

Aube The southernmost region of **Champagne**. Its vineyards are planted mainly with **Pinot Noir** and **Chardonnay** grapes. The resulting rich and fruity wine is often considered inferior to that obtained from the Marne, farther north. Much of it is sold by growers to the Champagne houses for blending, although some Aube growers bottle their own Champagne.

Aubun (also called **Counoise**) A red grape variety grown mainly in the southern **Rhône**, France. It is one of the permitted grape varieties, although not often used, in **Châteauneuf-du-Pape**, where it is called Counoise.

Ausbruch A rich and raisiny white wine category peculiar to **Austria**, with a **must weight** of 138° *Oechsle* (between **Beerenauslese** and **Trockenbeerenauslese**). The rich grapes, which are affected with **botrytis**, are moistened with **Spätlese** juice before pressing.

Auslese A **German** and **Austrian** quality white

wine category, meaning 'selected harvest'. Individual bunches of very ripe grapes (which may be affected by **botrytis**) are selected after the **Spätlese** harvest. Unripe or diseased grapes must be removed from the bunches. The minimum **must weight** is 83–105° *Oechsle* in Germany and 105° in Austria. The wines are usually rich, sweet and honeyed, although **trocken** (dry) *Auslesen* do exist. See also **QmP**.

austere A tasting term, not necessarily uncomplimentary, which describes a tough, severe or reserved taste on the palate.

Australia An important wine-producing country, with a relatively recent reputation for good-quality **varietal** wines and blends made from varieties including **Chardonnay**, **Cabernet Sauvignon**, **Sauvignon Blanc**, **Shiraz**, **Sémillon**, **Rhine Riesling**, **Muscat** and **Marsanne**.

The first **Vitis vinifera** grapes were planted towards the end of the 18th century, but until the 1960s wine production concentrated on **fortified wines** and inferior reds. Then there was a winemaking revolution, with the introduction of new varieties, techniques and equipment, so that today Australian winemakers are considered among the most technically advanced in the world.

The main wine-producing regions are concentrated in the southeastern part of the continent, in **New South Wales**, **Victoria** and **South Australia**, and around Perth in **Western Australia**.

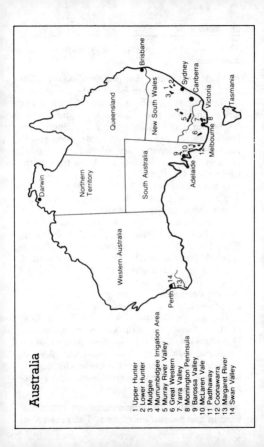

Australia

1 Upper Hunter
2 Lower Hunter
3 Mudgee
4 Murrumbidgee Irrigation Area
5 Murray River Valley
6 Great Western
7 Yarra Valley
8 Mornington Peninsula
9 Barossa Valley
10 McLaren Vale
11 Padthaway
12 Coonawarra
13 Margaret River
14 Swan Valley

There are also vineyards in **Queensland** and **Tasmania**.

Austria A country that produces mainly white wine. The vineyards are found in the eastern part of the country, north and south of Vienna and along the Hungarian, Czechoslovak and Yugoslav borders. The major regions are **Burgenland** (sweet whites and the best reds), **Niederösterreich** (predominantly dry whites), Steiermark (reds and very dry whites) and Wien (mainly the white wine Heurige).

Grüner Veltliner is the most important white grape variety planted. It produces largely dry whites, high in acidity, which are good as an accompaniment to fatty Austrian food. Other white grapes are **Müller-Thurgau**, **Welschriesling**, **Pinot Blanc** (Klevner), **Neuburger**, and Muskat-Ottonel (see **Muscat**). There are also small plantings of **Chardonnay**. The light-bodied red wines of Austria are produced mainly from **Blauer Portugieser**. Some producers are now experimenting with **Cabernet Sauvignon**.

The quality designations are similar to those used in Germany, with **Tafelwein**, **Landwein**, **Qualitätswein**, **Kabinett**, **Spätlese**, **Auslese**, **Beerenauslese**, **Eiswein** and **Trockenbeerenauslese**. In addition, Austria operates the **Ausbruch** category, which comes between *Beerenauslese* and *Trockenbeerenauslese* in **must weight**.

autovinificator A **fermentation** vat sometimes used in the production of **Port**. The pressure of

carbon dioxide produced during fermentation is used to force the **must** to circulate, to extract the maximum colour and **tannin** from the grape skins. This was formerly achieved by treading the grapes by foot in a stone vat. Some producers still use this traditional method.

Auxerrois 1. A low to medium quality white grape variety grown in **Alsace**, France, where it is mainly blended with other varieties to make **Edelzwicker**. 2. A local name for the **Malbec** grape in **Cahors**, France. 3. A term for the area of vineyards around Auxerre and **Chablis** in **Burgundy**, particularly the villages of **Irancy**, **Saint-Bris-le-Vineux**, Chitry-le-Fort and **Epineuil**.

Auxey-Duresses A village and *appellation* of the **Côte de Beaune**, Burgundy. Two-thirds of the wine it produces is red, made from the **Pinot Noir** grape, and one-third white, from **Chardonnay**. The best reds are pleasant, fairly light, good-value, cherry-scented wines, while the **premiers crus**, which include Les Duresses, La Chapelle and Clos du Val, have more body. The whites are more variable in quality. The best have a biscuity flavour reminiscent of nearby **Meursault**. All should be drunk young.

AVA (Approved Viticultural Area) An American term, roughly equivalent to the French **AC**. There are 58 AVAs in **California**, generally subdivisions within a county, and more are expected. The boundary of each has been drawn up according to natural features, soil type and climate. If a label bears the name of an AVA, then 75% of the wine must come from that area. If the label additionally bears a vineyard name, then 95% of the wine must come from that vineyard.

Avelsbach A village in the **Grosslage** of Römerlay near Trier in the **Mosel-Saar-Ruwer** region of Germany. Its vineyards are planted with a very high proportion of **Riesling**. The best **Einzellage** sites are Altenberg, Herrenberg and Hammerstein.

azienda agricola The Italian term for a wine estate producing its own grapes.

Bacchus A German white grape variety. It is a cross between **Müller-Thurgau** and Silvaner-Riesling, another cross. It is widely planted in the **Rheinhessen**, and produces a full-bodied wine low in acidity, which is often blended into **Liebfraumilch**. It is also a popular variety in the vineyards of **England**.

Bacharach A town and **Bereich** in the **Mittelrhein**, Germany. It produces steely white wines of a reasonable quality from the **Riesling** grape.

Baco Blanc A **hybrid** grape variety planted in Gascony, France, where the wine it produces is distilled to produce the brandy Armagnac. However, it is considered inferior to Ugni Blanc (**Trebbiano**) for Armagnac production.

Baco Noir A **hybrid** grape variety that is a crossing of **Folle Blanche** with *Vitis riparia*. It is grown in the eastern United States and produces fruity red wines, often described as **foxy**.

Bad Dürkheim A spa town in the **Rheinpfalz**, Germany. It produces good-quality white wines from **Riesling** and other white grape varieties, as well as some less-distinguished reds. The vineyards are in three **Grosslagen**: Feuerberg, Hochmess and Schenkenböhl. The wines do not have 'Bad' in their names, so a wine would be labelled, for example, 'Dürkheimer Feuerberg'.

Baden The most southerly **Anbaugebiet** in Germany. It produces mainly white wine, as well as some red and rosé. The majority of the whites are made from the **Müller-Thurgau**, **Ruländer** and **Gutedel** grapes, and are more full-bodied than the wines of other regions. The reds are made mainly from the **Spätburgunder** grape, as is the rosé **Weissherbst**. The rosé **Badisch Rotgold** is made by mixing Spätburgunder and Ruländer.

The co-operative cellars in the region account for the majority of the wine production. There are seven **Bereiche**, including **Bodensee, Kaiserstuhl-Tuniberg, Markgräflerland** and **Ortenau**.

Bad Kreuznach A spa and main city of the

Nahe region of Germany. Some of the finest whites of the Nahe are produced in the **Grosslage** of Kronenberg, and these are labelled 'Kreuznacher Kronenberg'.

Badisch Rotgold A rosé wine from **Baden**, Germany, which is made by mixing **Spätburgunder** and **Ruländer** grapes.

Baga The most widely planted red grape variety of **Portugal**, and the dominant variety used to produce red **Bairrada**. It can produce rich fruity wines, but traditionally it is fermented with the stalks, producing an **astringent** wine.

Bairrada A **Região Demarcada** (RD) wine of **Portugal**, usually red but occasionally white, or sparkling. The reds, which are made mainly from the **Baga** grape, are traditionally full and fruity, but with an **astringent** taste. Modern winemaking techniques, however, have produced softer, smoother wines, which rank among the best of Portugal's red table wines. The whites are made largely from the Maria Gomes grape.

balanced A tasting term that indicates whether the component parts of a wine (i.e. fruit, **acid**, **tannin**, sugars and alcohol) are present in the right proportions.

Balbaina A district of the **Sherry** region, Spain, which has **albariza** soil and is highly rated.

balthazar A large **Champagne** bottle of 12

litres capacity, equivalent to 16 bottles of the normal size (75 cl).

Bandol An AC wine from the vineyards around the town of Bandol in **Provence**, France. It may be red, white, or rosé, but the finest – and the largest quantity produced – is red. The main grape for the red is **Mourvèdre** (at least 50%), supported by the **Grenache**, **Cinsault** and **Syrah** grapes. The red wine must be aged at least 18 months in barrel, and at its best is long-lived, rich and fragrant, although quality is extremely variable. The rosés, based on Mourvèdre, can be extremely fine, but the dry whites, made from **Clairette**, **Ugni Blanc**, **Sauvignon** and **Bourboulenc**, are usually bland and expensive.

Banyuls A sweet, fortified AC wine from the foothills of the Pyrenees, in the **Midi**, France. It may be red or tawny in colour. Banyuls is based on **Grenache** (at least 50%), and is similar, but inferior, to **Port**. Banyuls Grand Cru has a higher proportion of Grenache (75%), and is matured in wooden barrels for 30 months. Banyuls that is allowed to age for longer acquires a **rancio**, oxidized flavour and a tawny colour.

Barbacarlo A red **frizzante** wine within the DOC **Oltrepò Pavese** in **Lombardy**, Italy. It is made from several grapes, including **Barbera**, **Croatina**, **Uva Rara** and Ughetta. A long-lived, deep, robust wine, it is usually dry but can be

amabile. It ranks among the best of Italy's sparkling reds.

Barbaresco A **DOCG** red wine from **Piedmont**, Italy. It is grown around the villages of Barbaresco, Neive and Treiso, to the north of Alba. It is made exclusively from the **Nebbiolo** grape. The wine is aged for at least two years (one year in cask) before release; some producers age Barbaresco in small oak **barriques**. As in **Barolo**, several labels bear a single vineyard, or **cru** name, but these are not officially regulated. The wines can be tough and tannic in their youth, with a good ageing potential, often developing a complex, exquisite, truffly aroma. Quality is variable, but the best Barbarescos rank among the great Italian reds.

Barbarossa A rare red grape variety grown only at the Fattoria Paradiso estate in **Emilia-Romagna**, Italy. It yields a fine, deep, red wine, tannic in its youth, but capable of developing great complexity with age.

Barbera A red grape variety planted widely in Italy, particularly in **Piedmont**, **Oltrepò Pavese** and **Emilia-Romagna**. It is an up-and-coming variety, and the most encouraging results have been achieved in Piedmont. Much of the Barbera grown there is sold simply as Barbera del Piemonte, but the best wines are the **DOC**s Barbera d'Alba and Barbera d'Asti. They are a deep, purply red, with spicy, leathery fruit and a high acidity, which can make them a good match for food. They have a great quality potential. PRICE BAND: A–E.

Bardolino A popular dry red or rosé **DOC** wine, made around the village of Bardolino on Lake Garda in the **Veneto**, Italy. It is made from **Corvina**, **Rondinella**, **Molinara** and **Negrara** grapes. The red is light and grapey, with a slight bitterness in the background, and has the potential to age three or four years. The rosé, or *chiaretto*, is cherry pink and light-bodied.

Barolo A **DOCG** red wine of **Piedmont**, Italy, that ranks among the finest red wines of the world. It is made in the Langhe hills southeast of Alba, exclusively from the **Nebbiolo** grape. The wine must be aged for at least three years in barrel before release, and is austere and tannic in its youth. It develops great complexity and depth with age, developing an exquisite aroma of truffles and a rich, full-bodied taste. Some producers now age Barolo in small oak **barriques**, much to the annoyance of traditionalists.

As in **Barbaresco**, many labels now bear the name of a vineyard, or **cru**, but these are not yet officially regulated. Fine Barolo from a good vintage needs long ageing in bottle before it reaches its peak.

Barolo Chinato A curious red drink, based on **Barolo** wine flavoured with quinine.

Baroque A white grape, used particularly to

make the white wine **Tursan** (which must contain 90% Baroque grape). It was also once found in the rare white wines of **Béarn**. Baroque produces strong, flavourful wines with little aroma.

Barossa Valley A district in **South Australia**, northeast of Adelaide. The region originally produced mainly **fortified** and **dessert wines**. Today, however, it produces some fine **varietal** table wines from grapes including **Rhine Riesling**, **Shiraz**, **Grenache**, **Cabernet Sauvignon** and **Chardonnay**. Original plantations were on flat land, but excellent results have been achieved from cooler, high-altitude vineyards.

barrel A cylindrical container of various sizes, usually made of wood, used to store and mature wine. Traditionally, barrels were made from several different types of wood, but today most are made of **oak**. A new barrel imparts **tannin** and a vanilla flavour to wine, and the smaller the barrel, the more marked is this effect. An old barrel, if it is clean, will impart no flavour but it will allow a slow, controlled **oxidization** of the wine. See also **ageing**; **barrique**.

barrique An oak **barrel** of 225 litres capacity, originally used in Bordeaux, and now found in many wine regions throughout the world.

barro One of three soil types of the **Sherry** region in Spain; the other two are **albariza** and **arena**. *Barro* is a clay soil, and wines produced from it do not have the finesse of those from the white, chalky *albariza*.

Barsac One of the five communes of the AC **Sauternes** in **Bordeaux**, France. It produces sweet, white wines of high quality and complexity. Barsac also has its own **AC**, although its wines may be labelled Sauternes, or Sauternes-Barsac. The wine is produced from the **Sémillon**, **Sauvignon Blanc** and **Muscadelle** grapes. Its distinctively rich balance between fruit and acidity derives from the action of **botrytis** on the grapes. PRICE BAND: C–E+.

Basilicata A wine region of southern **Italy**, which produces only one **DOC** wine, **Aglianico del Vulture**. Other wines from the region include the fizzy white **Asprino**, dry or sweet white wines from the **Malvasia** grape, sweet golden whites from the **Moscato** and red table wines from the **Montepulciano** grape.

Bastardo A red grape variety of **Portugal**, once frequently used in the production of **Port** and **Madeira**, but now mainly used in the red table wines of **Dão** and **Bairrada**. See also **Trousseau**.

Bâtard-Montrachet A **grand cru** vineyard in the villages of **Puligny-Montrachet** and **Chassagne-Montrachet** in the **Côte de Beaune** region of **Burgundy**. It produces rich, mouth-filling white wines of classy bouquet and flavour from the **Chardonnay** grape. However, it is generally reckoned to be inferior to the neighbouring *grands crus* of **Le Montrachet** and **Chevalier-Montrachet**.

Baumé A French scale for measuring the concentration of sugar in grape **must** (1° *Baumé* equals 17–18 g of sugar in 1 litre of water). A reading of, for example, 12° *Baumé* indicates that the must would yield a wine of 12% alcohol by volume, if it were fermented to complete dryness.

Bay of Plenty A tiny wine growing region on the North Island of **New Zealand**. It is planted mainly with **Chardonnay** and **Sauvignon Blanc** grapes.

Béarn An **AC** wine from three separate areas of southwest **France**, east of Biarritz. It includes the ACs of **Madiran** and **Jurançon**, and the towns of Bellocq and Salies-de-Béarn. The majority of the wine produced is red and made from **Tannat**, **Cabernet Franc** and **Cabernet Sauvignon** grapes. A light fruity rosé is made from either the pure Tannat grape or the Cabernet Franc. A white is also produced, but only in tiny quantities and from many permitted grape varieties, including Raffiat de Moncade, **Manseng** and **Courbu**.

The producers of AC Jurançon can also label their red wine as AC Béarn, and in AC Madiran rosé wines use the Béarn *appellation*.

Beaujolais An **AC** wine and a region of

Burgundy, which produces mainly red wines from the **Gamay** grape, and some whites from the **Chardonnay**. **Beaujolais Nouveau** is designed for early drinking (possibly chilled) in the year of the vintage. Most of the wine is labelled Beaujolais or Beaujolais-Villages, and is a simple, fruity, easy-drinking wine. The best wines of the regions are **cru** wines from 10 specified areas: **Brouilly**, **Chénas**, **Chiroubles**, **Côte de Brouilly**, **Fleurie**, **Juliénas**, **Morgon**, **Moulin-á-Vent**, **Régnié** and **Saint-Amour**, the names of which appear on labels. Each wine has its own special character, and all have more complexity and ageing potential than the ordinary Beaujolais.

Beaujolais Nouveau (also called **Beaujolais Primeur**) A light, easy-drinking red **AC** wine of **Burgundy** made from the **Gamay** grape. It is marketed on the third Thursday of November after the vintage. It never has the complexity of the **cru** wines of **Beaujolais**, but it is not intended to. Its success has been as a marketing tool, to create public interest in Beaujolais. The drawback has been the early-drinking, quaffing-wine image that has resulted, to the detriment of serious, *cru* Beaujolais producers. PRICE BAND: A–B.

Beaujolais Primeur   See **Beaujolais Nouveau**.

Beaulieu-sur-Layon   See **Coteaux du Layon**.

Beaumes-de-Venise   A village in the **Côtes du Rhône**, France, which is entitled to the **AC**

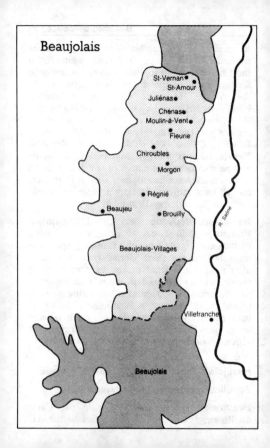

Côtes du Rhône-Villages for its red wines. It is, however, more famous for its **Muscat de Beaumes-de-Venise**, a **vin doux naturel**, a white, **fortified wine** made from the **Muscat** grape.

Beaune A town and an **AC** wine in the **Côte d'Or** region of **Burgundy**. It gives its name to the **Côte de Beaune**, the southern section of the Côte d'Or, as well as to the wines of its own vineyards. Mainly red wines are produced from the **Pinot Noir** grape, as well as some whites from the **Chardonnay**.

The best Beaune wines, from the **premier cru** vineyards of Les Marconnets, Teurons and Grèves (to name but a few), can be of a high quality, with a great ageing potential. The straight Beaune reds are less complicated and can be enjoyed within five years of the vintage, and the whites, too, are generally best drunk young. The town of Beaune is home to many of Burgundy's **négociants**.

Beauroy A **premier cru** vineyard of **Chablis**.

Beerenauslese A German and Austrian quality white wine category, literally meaning 'selected grapes'. Individually selected overripe grapes, probably affected by **botrytis**, are cut from the bunches and carefully pressed. In Germany the minimum **must weight** is 110–128° **Oechsle**. The wines are yellow gold in their youth, turning to deep amber with age. They are exceedingly rare, luscious and quite sweet, but with a balancing acidity. The most successful are made from the **Riesling** grape. See also **QmP**.

beery A tasting term used to describe an undesirable yeasty smell, which is caused by secondary **fermentation** in bottle.

Bellet An **AC** of **Provence**, France, which produces small quantities of good quality red, white and rosé wine. The white is made mainly from the **Chardonnay** and **Rolle** grapes, and is quite full-bodied and flavourful. The red is made mainly from the Folle Noire and Braquet grapes, and occasionally the **Cinsault**. It is light and elegant, but is capable of ageing well. Most of the production is consumed locally by holiday-makers on the Riviera.

Bereich A German wine law term used to describe a wine-growing district. The 11 larger **Anbaugebiet** regions are divided into a total of 35 *Bereich* districts. Each *Bereich* is a combination of sites in neighbouring villages, which, theoreti-cally, produce wines of similar character. The *Bereich* usually takes its name from the most famous village, for example *Bereich* **Bernkastel**. A *Bereich* may be further subdivided into several **Grosslagen**, combinations of vineyards.

Bergerac An **AC** wine and a region in the southwest of France, to the east of **Bordeaux** on the Dordogne River. AC Bergerac may be red or white; the red is produced (like Bordeaux) from the **Cabernet Sauvignon**, **Cabernet Franc** and

Merlot grapes; the white, which is labelled Bergerac Sec, is made from **Sauvignon Blanc**, **Sémillon** and **Muscadelle**. The reds are similar to red Bordeaux in taste, and they can be of a good quality, although they never reach the heights of the great wines of the **Médoc**. The whites are clean and fruity and should be drunk young.

The Bergerac region includes the ACs **Monbazillac**, **Montravel**, **Pécharmant** and **Rosette**.

Bernkastel   A **Bereich** in the **Mosel-Saar-Ruwer** region of Germany, covering the **Mittelmosel** area. Wines sold as *Bereich* Bernkastel, which are made from the **Müller-Thurgau** grape, should be crisp and fresh, and are best drunk young. Those made from the **Riesling** grape should be of a higher quality and more complex. The top wines of the area are sold under their own vineyard or **Einzellage** names.

Bernkastel-Kues   A village on the banks of the Mosel river in the **Mosel-Saar-Ruwer** region of Germany. Many of the finest vineyards of the *Bereich* **Bernkastel** are concentrated around the village, in two **Grosslagen**, Badstube and Kurfürstlay. The Doktor vineyard is the most famous **Einzellage**, it produces some of Germany's top **Rieslings**.

bianco   The Italian for white.

Bianco Alcamo   See **Alcamo**.

Bianco Capena   See **Capena**.

Bianco d'Alessano A white grape variety grown in the **Apulia** region of southern Italy. It is blended with Verdeca, to make the **DOC** wine **Locorotondo**.

Bianco dei Colli Maceratesi A white **DOC** wine from the **Marches** region of Italy, made from the **Trebbiano** Toscano and Maceratino grapes. This delicate, dry white should be drunk young.

Bianco della Lega A white table wine from **Tuscany**, Italy, made from **Trebbiano** and **Malvasia** grapes. It is light and dry, and can be pleasantly fruity.

Bianco della Val d'Arbia A white **DOC** wine from the Arbia valley between Radda and Montalcino in **Tuscany**, Italy, made from **Trebbiano** and **Malvasia** grapes. It is a dry, clean and, at its best, fruity wine which should be drunk young. The DOC also applies to sweet **vin santo** from the same area.

Bianco della Valdinievole A white wine from **Tuscany**, Italy, made from **Trebbiano** grapes grown around the towns of Montecatini Terme and Pescia. It is light and dry, and is best drunk young. A sweet DOC **vin santo** exists, but is rarely produced.

Bianco di Custoza A white **DOC** wine from around Lake Garda in the **Veneto** region of Italy, made mainly from the **Trebbiano** Toscano,

Garganega Tocai grapes. It is a dry wine and, at its best, softly fruity, somewhat similar to **Soave**. A **spumante** version also exists, which is made by the **Charmat method**.

Bianco di Gravina A white **DOC** wine from around Gravina in the **Apulia** region, southern Italy, made from the Verdeca grape. A medium-weight, dry wine that should be drunk young.

Bianco di Pitigliano A white **DOC** wine from southern **Tuscany**, Italy, made mainly from the **Trebbiano** and **Grechetto** grapes. A clean, fruity, if somewhat neutral wine that should be drunk young.

Bianco di Scandiano A white **DOC** wine from around Scandiano in the **Emilia-Romagna** region of Italy, made from **Sauvignon**, **Malvasia** and **Trebbiano** grapes. This soft, sparkling white can be dry or medium-dry and **frizzante** or **spumante**.

Bianco Pisano San Torpè A white **DOC** wine from **Tuscany**, Italy, southeast of Pisa, made from **Trebbiano**, **Canaiolo** Bianco and **Malvasia** grapes. It is a light, dry wine which should be drunk young.

Bianco Vergine della Valdichiana A white **DOC** wine from the Chiana valley between Arezzo and Chiusi, in **Tuscany**, Italy. It is made mainly from the **Trebbiano** grape together with **Malvasia** and **Grechetto**. A soft, dry and pleasantly fruity wine, better than many other Tuscan whites.

Bical A white grape variety with good acidity and a fine fruit aroma, used for the production of white wines in the **Bairrada** and **Dão** regions of **Portugal**.

Bienvenues Bâtard-Montrachet A **grand cru** vineyard in the village of **Puligny-Montrachet** in the **Côte de Beaune** region of **Burgundy**. It produces rich, mouth-filling white wines of classy bouquet and flavour from the **Chardonnay** grape. The vineyard is virtually an enclave of **Bâtard-Montrachet** and its wines are similar in quality and taste.

Biferno A **DOC** wine from the **Molise** region of Italy. It can be red or rosé, made from the **Montepulciano** grape, or white, made from **Trebbiano**.

big A tasting term which can be used to describe a wine's intensity of colour, smell, taste or **finish**.

Bingen A town in the **Rheinhessen** area of Germany, which also gives its name to one of the Rheinhessen's three **Bereiche**. The vineyards around Bingen come under the Sankt Rochuskapelle **Grosslage** and produce some of the region's finest **Rieslings**. The best-known **Einzellage** is Binger Scharlachberg.

bite A tasting term used to describe the attack

of **acidity** (and sometimes **tannin**) on the palate. Desirable in a young wine destined for ageing, it can mellow with time.

bitter A tasting term, usually pejorative, which describes a sharp taste on the palate or **finish**. A slight bitterness on the finish of some light red wines can be attractive.

blackcurrant A tasting term that describes the smell and taste of blackcurrant fruit, which is often a characteristic of the **Cabernet Sauvignon** grape. Some tasters use the French equivalent, *cassis*.

Blagny A village and **AC** wine between **Puligny-Montrachet** and **Meursault** in the **Côte de Beaune**, Burgundy. The AC is given for the reds only. They are earthy, gamey wines made from the **Pinot Noir** grape. The whites from the Blagny vineyards are entitled to the Puligny-Montrachet or Meursault ACs.

blanc The French for white.

blanc de blancs A term used on labels, mainly in France, to indicate a white wine made from white grapes. Thus nearly all white wines could be described as *blanc de blancs*. The term is only truly relevant in **Champagne**; most white Champagne is made from both red (**Pinot Noir** and **Pinot Meunier**) and white (**Chardonnay**) grapes, but *blanc de blancs* Champagne is pure Chardonnay.

Blanc de la Salle A dry white table wine made in the **Valle d'Aosta** region of Italy, to the southeast of Mont Blanc. It is clean and delicately flavoured, made from the Blanc de Valdigne grape and grown at an altitude of 1000 m. A sparkling **méthode champenoise** version is also produced. Both wines are best drunk young.

Blanc de Morgex A dry white table wine made in the **Valle d'Aosta** region of Italy, from the Blanc de Valdigne grape. Light and high in acidity, it is best drunk young. It is a similar wine to **Blanc de la Salle**.

blanc de noirs A term used on labels, mainly in France, to indicate a white wine made from 'black' grapes. Nearly all grapes yield white juice when pressed and it is the grape skin that gives the colour of red wines. The term is used mainly in **Champagne**, where it usually means a white Champagne made exclusively from the black **Pinot Noir** grape.

Blanc Fumé de Pouilly See **Pouilly-Fumé**.

Blanchots One of the seven **grand cru** vineyards of **Chablis**.

blanco The Spanish for white.

Blanquette de Limoux A **méthode champenoise** sparkling white **AC** wine, produced around the town of Limoux, southern France.

The wine is made mainly from the **Mauzac Blanc** grape (called Blanquette locally), together with **Chardonnay** and **Chenin Blanc**. It is dry and can be quite complex. Its quality can be extremely good, but without reaching the heights of top **Champagne**. There is a move to rename the wine Crémant de Limoux. PRICE BAND: B.

Blauburgunder The German name for the **Pinot Noir** grape, also used in German-speaking parts of Italy. See also **Spätburgunder**.

Blauer Portugieser (also called **Portugieser**) A grape variety that produces light red wines of a very ordinary quality. It is the most widely planted red variety in **Austria**, and is also found in Germany, Yugoslavia, Hungary and (only rarely) France.

Blaufränkisch A grape variety that produces light-bodied, quite acidic red wines of a very ordinary quality. It is the second most widely planted red variety in **Austria**, and is also found in Germany (where it is called Blauer Limberger), Bulgaria, Yugoslavia and Hungary (where it is called Kékfrankos).

Blaye See **Premières Côtes de Blaye**.

bleichert A German term for a rosé wine.

blush A term used, mainly in the United States, to indicate a pale pink wine made from red grapes. Thus white **Zinfandel** is in fact a pale pink, or 'blush'. Lesser quality blush wines have been made by blending red and white wine. See also **rosé**.

Bobal A red grape variety extensively planted in **Spain**, especially **Utiel Requena**, as well as **Alicante** and **Cariñena**. It can produce good-quality wines with good acidity, and relatively low alcohol.

Boca A dry red **DOC** wine from the Novara Hills near Boca in the **Piedmont** region of Italy, made mainly from **Nebbiolo**, together with **Bonarda** and Vespolina. The wine can be of a fine quality, solid and tough in its youth and ageing well, but it is rarely seen outside Piedmont.

bocksbeutel A squat, flagon-shaped bottle of green glass. It is used in Germany for the quality wines of **Franken** and some wines of north **Baden**. A similar shape is sometimes used in Portugal and Chile.

bodega The Spanish for wine cellar. It is also used as a term to indicate a place where wine is made or matured, or, more loosely, a wine-producing company.

Bodensee The German name for Lake Constance, and one of the seven **Bereiche** of the **Baden** region of Germany; some vineyards also lie within **Franken** and **Württemburg**. The wine produced is sometimes known as Seewein, because of the lake's warming influence on the climate. The main grapes are **Müller-Thurgau** and **Spätburgunder**. The latter is often made into the rosé **Weissherbst**.

body A tasting term used to describe the weight of a wine in the mouth. High **alcohol content** and high **extract** make for more body.

Bolgheri A white and rosé **DOC** wine from Bolgheri in **Tuscany**, Italy. The **rosato** is made from **Sangiovese** and **Canaiolo** grapes, and can be of good quality. The white is made from **Trebbiano** and **Vermentino**.

Bombino Red and white grape varieties, grown mainly in the **Apulia** region of Italy. Bombino Nero is used to make red and rosé **Castel del Monte**. Bombino Bianco is widely planted, and is used to make the white Castel del Monte and **San Severo** in Apulia. In **Abruzzi**, Bombino Bianco is known as **Trebbiano d'Abruzzo**.

Bommes One of the villages entitled to the **AC** of **Sauternes**.

Bonarda (also called **Croatina**) A red grape variety used to make **varietal** wines in the **Oltrepò Pavese** region of Italy and for blending with other varieties, notably **Barbera**, in **Emilia-Romagna**. It produces a dark-coloured, fruity wine, often quite tannic. See also **Bonarda Piemontese**.

Bonarda Piemontese A red grape variety related to, but distinct from **Bonarda**, which produces a lighter, more supple wine. As its name suggests it is planted in **Piedmont**, Italy, particularly around Turin.

Bonnes Mares A **grand cru** vineyard divided between the villages of **Chambolle-Musigny** and **Morey-St-Denis** in the **Côte de Nuits** area of **Burgundy**. It produces one of the finest reds of Burgundy, a fat wine with a remarkable bouquet.

Bonnezeaux A sweet white **AC** wine in the **Coteaux du Layon** area of **Anjou-Saumur** in the **Loire** valley, France. The wines, made only from the **Chenin Blanc** grape, are of a very high quality, rich and luscious, with their sweetness balanced by **acidity** and are very long-lived.

Bordeaux A city and major wine region of **France**, perhaps the most famous and celebrated in the world. The greatest wines are from the **Médoc**, where some of the world's finest reds are produced from **Cabernet Sauvignon**, **Cabernet Franc**, **Merlot**, **Malbec** and **Petit Verdot** grapes. On the right bank of the Gironde estuary the emphasis is mainly on **Merlot**, and great red wines are made in **Saint-Emilion** and **Pomerol**, as well as slightly lesser wines in **Fronsac**, **Canon-Fronsac**, the **Côtes de Bourg** and the **Premières Côtes de Blaye**.

South of the Médoc, great reds and dry whites are made in the **Graves**, especially in the separate **AC** of **Pessac-Léognan**. Some of the most celebrated sweet white wines are made in **Sauternes**

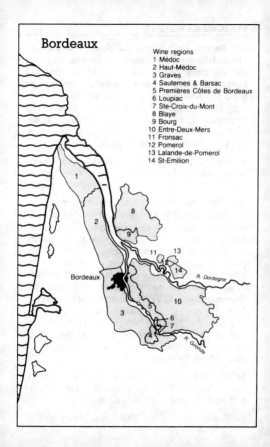

Bordeaux

Wine regions
1 Médoc
2 Haut-Médoc
3 Graves
4 Sauternes & Barsac
5 Premières Côtes de Bordeaux
6 Loupiac
7 Ste-Croix-du-Mont
8 Blaye
9 Bourg
10 Entre-Deux-Mers
11 Fronsac
12 Pomerol
13 Lalande-de-Pomerol
14 St-Emilion

Bordeaux

R. Dordogne

R. Gironde

and **Barsac**, from **Sauvignon Blanc**, **Sémillon** and **Muscadelle** grapes affected by **botrytis**. Between the Garonne and Dordogne rivers, the vast **Entre-Deux-Mers** region produces increasingly good dry whites from the same varieties used in Sauternes, although occasionally from 100% Sauvignon Blanc. **Loupiac** and **Sainte-Croix-du-Mont** produce wines similar in style to Sauternes, but of a distinctly inferior quality.

Bordeaux mixture A fungicide spray based on copper sulphate, used to treat vines against oidium, mildew, anthracnose and other diseases.

botrytis (also called **botrytis cinerea**) The fungus responsible for the creation of 'noble rot' (Fr. *pourriture noble*) on grapes. This allows water to evaporate from the grape juice, leading to an increased concentration of sugar. The presence of this beneficial rot is the key to the production of the great sweet wines of **Sauternes**, **Monbazillac** and **Anjou-Saumur** in France, the **Beerenauslese** and **Trockenbeerenauslese** wines of Germany and Austria, and of **Tokaji** in Hungary. In most other regions, botrytis is undesirable and can lead to the development of grey rot, which causes the grapes to spoil. Botrytis is called *edelfäule* in German.

botte The Italian name for a large **barrel**, usually made of oak or chestnut, used to store and mature wine. See also **ageing**.

Botticino A dry red **DOC** wine from east of

Brescia in the **Lombardy** region of Italy. It is made from the **Barbera**, **Marzemino**, **Schiava** and **Sangiovese** grapes. It is usually bright red in colour, quite sturdy and develops well after three to four years in bottle.

bottle age A tasting term used to describe the mature **bouquet** and flavour that a wine develops after spending some time in bottle. See also **ageing**.

bottle sickness (also called **bottle shock**) A tasting term used to describe a temporary deterioration in a wine tasted shortly after it has been bottled.

bottle stink The smell of stale air, trapped in a wine bottle, which is sometimes detectable when the cork is drawn. It usually fades quickly.

Bouchet An alternative name for the **Cabernet Franc** grape, used in **Saint-Emilion**.

Bougros One of the seven **grand cru** vineyards of **Chablis**.

bouquet A tasting term, used loosely to describe the smell of the wine, and more correctly to describe the characteristics of smell that develop as the wine matures in bottle.

Bourboulenc A white grape variety, one of the 13 permitted in the red wine of **Châteauneuf-du-Pape** in the **Rhône** valley, France. On its own it produces a thin, neutral wine.

Bourg See **Côtes de Bourg**.

Bourgogne The basic **AC** wine of **Burgundy**. Its wines are red, made from the **Pinot Noir** grape, or white from **Chardonnay**.

Bourgueil A red **AC** wine of the **Touraine** region of the **Loire** valley, France, made mainly from the **Cabernet Franc** grape (called Breton locally). It is one of the finest-quality red wines of the Loire, with a grassy, raspberry fruit flavour, and capable of long ageing. **Saint-Nicolas-de-Bourgueil** is similar, but has its own AC. PRICE BAND: B–C.

Bouvier (also called **Bouviertraube**) A white grape variety grown usually for eating, but cultivated for wine mainly in the **Burgenland** and Styria regions of **Austria**, **Yugoslavia** (where it is known as Ranina) and **Hungary**. It produces wine of very ordinary quality, mostly used for blending with more characterful varieties, but it can have good **must weight**.

Bouzeron A village in the **Côte Chalonnaise** in **Burgundy**. It produces one of the best white wines from the **Aligoté** grape.

Bouzy A village of **Champagne**. Its vineyards, rated 100%, are planted with the **Pinot Noir** grape. Most of this is made into Champagne, but some still Bouzy Rouge is bottled, and some is used to give blended pink Champagnes their colour.

Bozner Leiten The German name for **Colli di Bolzano**.

Brachetto A red grape variety grown mainly in **Piedmont**, Italy and in **Bellet**, Provence (where it is known as Braquet). In Piedmont it makes medium-sweet to sweet sparkling wines, either **frizzante** or **spumante**, with a fruity strawberry flavour. The wine is **DOC** in Brachetto d'Acqui and Brachetto d'Asti.

Bramaterra A dry red **DOC** wine grown in the hills around the village of the same name in **Piedmont**, Italy. It is made mainly from the **Nebbiolo** grape, together with **Croatina**, **Bonarda Piemontese** and Vespolina. It is a fairly full-bodied, robust red with a good ageing potential.

branco The Portuguese for white.

Brauneberg A small village within the **Grosslage** of Kurfürstlay, in the **Mosel-Saar-Ruwer** region of Germany. Its vineyards are planted with a high proportion of **Riesling** grapes, which can produce fine-quality, rich, full-bodied wines. The best, and best-known, **Einzellage** is Juffer.

Brazil A large wine-producing country in South America. Most of the vines are not **Vitis vinifera**, and so are unsuitable for quality wine production. This is slowly changing and *vinifera* varieties planted now include **Cabernet Sauvignon**, **Chardonnay**, **Johannisberg Riesling**, **Merlot**, **Pinot Noir**, **Sauvignon Blanc**, **Sémillon** and **Trebbiano**. These are planted mainly in the vineyards of Santana do Livramento in the southern state of Rio Grande do Sol, which borders Uruguay.

Breganze A **DOC** wine from the **Veneto** region of Italy, north of Vicenza. It comes in seven versions: Bianco, a dry, delicate white from the **Tocai Friulano** grape; Rosso, a pleasant, grapey red based on **Merlot**; Cabernet, an excellent dry red of high quality made mainly from **Cabernet Franc**; **Pinot Bianco** and **Pinot Grigio**, both fresh and smooth dry whites; **Pinot Nero**, which is light but fruity; and Vespaiolo, which is a dry white with a citrus flavour.

Breisgau One of the seven **Bereiche** of the **Baden** region of Germany.

Breton An alternative name for **Cabernet Franc**, used in the **Loire** valley, France.

Brindisi A **DOC** wine grown inland from the port of the same name in the **Apulia** region of Italy. Dry red and rosé versions are produced, both based on the **Negroamaro** grape. The red can achieve quite a good quality and has a good ageing potential.

British wine A drink prepared in the UK from imported grape powders or concentrates. It is not to be confused with **English** wine, which is made from grapes grown out of doors in England.

Brouilly A **cru** of **Beaujolais**, with the largest area of vineyards. The wines are among the finest of Beaujolais, fruity, supple and full of flavour.

Brunello di Montalcino A **DOCG** wine of **Tuscany**, Italy, made only from the Brunello grape, a superior clone of **Sangiovese**. This dry red wine is among Italy's finest. It is deep-coloured, powerful, structured, tannic and very long-lived.

brut A French term meaning 'very dry', usually found on the labels of **Champagne** and other sparkling wines, not necessarily from France.

Bual A grape variety grown on the island of **Madeira**, where it gives its name to a category of wine. It is sweet and smoky and can rank among the best of all Madeiras.

Bucelas A white **RD** wine of **Portugal**, made chiefly from the **Arinto** grape, plus **Cercial**, Esgana Cão, and Rabo d'Ovelha. Dry, but rich, it is one of the few Portuguese whites that can improve with age.

Bugey A **VDQS** wine region between Savoie and Lyon, France. It produces light red, white and rosé wines, which may be still, semi-sparkling, or sparkling. The reds are made mainly from the **Pinot Noir**, **Gamay** and **Mondeuse Noire** grape varieties. The whites are made from **Altesse** (also called Roussette) and, increasingly, **Chardonnay**.

Bulgaria An important eastern European wine-producing country, and the one that has most successfully tailored its wine-making to the tastes of the West. Traditionally, the vineyards were planted with native varieties. Since World War II, noble west-European varieties have taken over, principally **Cabernet Sauvignon**, **Merlot** and **Pinot Noir** among the reds, and **Chardonnay**, **Aligoté**, **Sauvignon Blanc**, **Riesling**, **Gewürztraminer** and **Pinot Gris** among the whites.

The top-quality wines come from defined *controliran* areas, of which there are 24. 'Reserve' wines are aged in oak, two years for whites and three for reds. The wines tend to lack any great complexity, but they are good value.

Burgenland A region of **Austria**, in the east of the country near the Hungarian border. It produces mainly sweet white wines. There are four subregions: Neusiedlersee, Neusiedlersee-Hügelland, Mittelburgenland and Südburgenland.

Burgundy A region of France, and one of the major wine areas of the world which produces some of the finest white and red wines. From north to south, it includes the subregions of **Chablis**, **Côte de Nuits**, **Côte de Beaune**, **Côte Chalonnaise**, the **Mâconnais** and **Beaujolais**. The dominant grape varieties are **Chardonnay** for the

Burgundy

Chablis

Wine regions
1 Chablis
2 Côte de Nuits
3 Côte de Beaune } Côte D'Or
4 Côte Chalonnaise
5 Mâconnais
6 Beaujolais

Dijon

Beaune

Chagney

R. Saône

Chalon-sur-Saône

Tournus

Mâcon

Villefranche

R. Rhône

Lyon

whites and **Pinot Noir** for the reds, with **Aligoté** and **Gamay** playing important secondary roles.

butt A barrel used for ageing **Sherry**, with a capacity of 500 litres.

buttery A tasting term that describes the smell and taste of butter, often found in mature, oak-aged white wines, especially those made from the **Chardonnay** grape.

Buzet An **AC** area of southwest France, which produces mainly red wines, similar in style to those of **Bordeaux**. The reds are made from the **Cabernet Sauvignon**, **Cabernet Franc** and **Merlot** grapes, and the few whites are mainly from **Sémillon**. Quality is good, and the wines usually represent good value for money. PRICE BAND: A.

Cabardès A **VDQS** wine produced around the town of Carcassonne, in southwest **France**. The wine can be red or rosé, and is made mainly from the **Carignan**, **Cinsault**, **Grenache**, **Mourvèdre** and **Syrah** grape varieties. PRICE BAND: A.

Cabernet d'Anjou A rosé **AC** wine produced in **Anjou-Saumur** in the **Loire** valley. It is similar to **Rosé d'Anjou**, but better in that it is made from the **Cabernet Franc** grape, and is usually drier, with fresh, grassy, fruit flavours. PRICE BAND: A–B.

Cabernet de Saumur A rosé **AC** wine produced in **Saumur** in the **Loire** valley. It is similar to **Cabernet d'Anjou**, but usually slightly off-dry. It is made mainly from the **Cabernet Franc** grape, with occasionally some **Cabernet Sauvignon** added. PRICE BAND: A–B.

Cabernet Franc A red grape variety, planted in **Bordeaux** and the **Loire** valley, France, and in the **Friuli-Venezia Giulia**, **Trentino-Alto Adige**, and **Veneto** regions of northeast **Italy**.

In Bordeaux, Cabernet Franc is very much in the shadow of **Cabernet Sauvignon**, and in most regions it contributes only a minor part to the blend. However, **Saint-Emilion** and **Pomerol** are exceptions, where Cabernet Franc (here known as **Bouchet**) plays a more important role, along with **Merlot**.

In the **Loire**, Cabernet Franc (alias Breton) has a chance to shine, in the great red wines of **Bourgueil**, **Saint-Nicolas-de-Bourgueil**, **Chinon** and **Saumur-Champigny**, and the pleasant rosé wines **Cabernet d'Anjou** and **Cabernet de Saumur**.

In northeast Italy, Cabernet Franc is **DOC** in many zones, either as a **varietal** or as a blend with Cabernet Sauvignon. Some Cabernet Franc is also planted in **California**, mainly in **Napa Valley** and **Sonoma**. It is mainly used for Bordeaux-style blends with Cabernet Sauvignon and Merlot. In **Chile**, it is sometimes vinified along with Cabernet Sauvignon.

Cabernet Sauvignon A red grape variety, one of the most important and distinctive. It is planted widely throughout the wine-producing world. It is the most important ingredient in nearly every red wine from **Bordeaux** (with a handful of notable exceptions in Saint-Emilion and Pomerol), usually blended with **Cabernet Franc** and **Merlot**. Cabernet Sauvignon is also widely planted in other French regions, especially the **Loire** valley, **Languedoc-Roussillon** and Bordeaux's satellites.

In terms of quality, it is the most important red variety of most New World wine-producing countries; in **California**, **Australia** and **New Zealand** it makes fine **varietal** wines, as well as blends (notably with Cabernet Franc and Merlot in California, and with **Shiraz** in Australia). It is also planted in **Chile** and **South Africa**, and **Bulgaria**, where it founded the modern wine industry on sales of varietal Cabernet Sauvignon to the West.

In northeast **Italy**, in **Friuli-Venezia Giulia**, **Trentino-Alto Adige** and the **Veneto**, Cabernet Sauvignon is **DOC** in many zones, either as a varietal, or blended with Cabernet Franc. In **Tuscany**, Cabernet is found in **Carmignano**, and can play a minor role in the blend for **Chianti**. There are also many fine **vini da tavola** made from pure Cabernet, or a blend of Cabernet and **Sangiovese**.

Cabernet Sauvignon wines have a distinctive blackcurrant aroma and taste, capable of developing great complexity with age. They marry beautifully with oak flavours derived from **ageing** in **barrique**.

Cadillac A white **AC** wine of **Bordeaux**, produced at the southern end of the **Premières Côtes de Bordeaux** area, from the **Sémillon**, **Sauvignon Blanc** and **Muscadelle** grape varieties. The wine is good-value, light and sweet, but without any of the richness, elegance and concentration of **Sauternes** or **Barsac**. PRICE BAND: B.

Cahors A red **AC** wine of southwest **France**, produced on the banks of the river Lot, around the town of Cahors, from the **Malbec** (known locally as **Cot**, or sometimes **Auxerrois**), **Merlot** and **Tannat** grape varieties. It is a dark, deep wine, with plummy richness and blackcurrant flavours, capable of long ageing. Quality can be very good. PRICE BAND: A–C.

Cairanne See **Côtes du Rhône**.

Calabrese An alternative name used, confusingly, for the **Canaiolo** Nero, Nero d'Avola and **Sangiovese** grape varieties. In **Sicily**, the names Calabrese and Nero d'Avola are interchangeable for the island's finest red variety, which makes robust, good-quality wines on its own, and is also useful in blends. In dialect, it is known as Calavrisi.

Calabria A region of southern **Italy**, at the 'toe' of the peninsula. Pale, light red wines are produced in the mountainous west, mainly from the **Gaglioppo** grape variety (see **Donnici** and **Pollino**). The most famous wines are **Cirò**, white, red and **rosato**, and the white Greco di Bianco (see **Greco**). **Melissa** is similar to Cirò, but generally of lower quality. See also **Mantonico di Bianco**.

Caldaro (also called **Kalterer**; **Kalterersee**; **Lago di Caldaro**) A red **DOC** wine of the **Alto Adige** region of northeast **Italy**, produced around the lake of the same name, from the **Schiava** grape variety. An easy-drinking, slightly bitter, pale red wine, it is best drunk young and fresh.

California The most important wine-producing state of the **United States**, with a wide variety of climatic conditions. It produces high-quality **varietal** wines from grape varieties as diverse as **Cabernet Sauvignon**, **Chardonnay**, **Chenin Blanc**, **Gewürztraminer**, **Merlot**, Petite Sirah, **Pinot Noir**, **Riesling**, **Sauvignon Blanc** and **Zinfandel**, among others, as well as large quantities of medium-quality 'jug' wine, usually from unspecified grape varieties. California is also a source of high-quality **méthode champenoise** sparkling wines. The most important regions are **Napa Valley** and **Sonoma**. See **Alameda**; **Alexander Valley**; **Amador County**; **Anderson Valley**; **Arroyo Grande Valley**; **Arroyo Seco**; **Dry Creek Valley**; **Edna Valley**; **Fiddletown**; **Guenoc Valley**; **Howell Mountain**; **Knights Valley**; **Lake County**; **Livermore Valley**; **Madera**; **McDowell Valley**; **Mendocino**; **Monterey County**; **Paso Robles**; **Potter Valley**; **Russian River Valley**; **San Luis Obispo**; **Solano County**; **York Mountain**.

California

Anderson Valley

Napa Valley

Napa

Sonoma

El Dorado

Livermore
Valley

Santa Cruz
Mountains

Monterey

Chalone
Arroyo Seco

San Joaquin Valley

Paso Robles

San Luis Obispo

Edna Valley

Santa Maria
Valley

Santa Ynez Valley

Santa Barbara

PACIFIC OCEAN

Los Angeles

Caluso See **Erbaluce di Caluso**.

Calvi See **Vin de Corse**.

Campania A region of southern **Italy**, centred on the town of Naples. Good Campanian wines are few and far between, with very few quality winemakers. The best wine is probably the red **Taurasi**, produced in the hills surrounding the village of the same name, mainly from the **Aglianico** grape variety. It has deep colour and good ageing potential, although austere **tannins** can mask the fruit flavours when young. **Asprino** is a fairly characterless, fizzy white thirst-quencher, while the red **Falerno** is fruity and full-bodied, and better than the white version. The white **Fiano di Avellino** can have a pleasant nuts and pears aroma at its best, but quality varies enormously. The white Greco di Tufo (see **Greco**) can have a good fruity and crisp flavour, and the island of **Ischia** produces fine white **vini da tavola** and less interesting **DOC** wines. **Lacryma Christi del Vesuvio**, which can be dry red, **rosato**, or white, still or sparkling, is rarely as interesting as its name.

Campidano di Terralba A dry red **DOC** wine produced on the Italian island of **Sardinia**, mainly from the Bovale and **Monica** grape varieties. It is a medium, deep red, but lacks depth and body, best drunk when young and fresh.

Campo de Borja A **DO** wine produced in a

region to the south of **Rioja** and **Navarra**, in northeast **Spain**. The wine can be red or **rosado**, based mainly on the **Garnacha** grape variety, plus a little **Macabeo**. Traditionally, they have been very high in alcohol, and lacking in acidity, but there are signs of a move towards lighter, more approachable reds.

Canada A minor wine-producing country of north America, traditionally a producer of wines from native, non-**Vitis vinifera** vines. In recent decades there has been a move towards planting **hybrids** and true *vinifera* varieties (especially **Chardonnay**, **Riesling** and **Cabernet Sauvignon**). Most of the vineyards are in British Columbia and Ontario, and the Niagara Peninsula area looks particularly promising.

canada A unit of measurement in the **Port** trade, equal to 2.1 litres. One **pipe** is equivalent to 21 **almudes**, and there are about 12 *canadas* in one *almude*. A *canada* was traditionally thought to be the right amount of Port for a man to drink.

Canaiolo A red grape variety of **Italy**, and a minor part of the blend for **Chianti**, to which it adds colour. It is also planted in **Umbria**, **Latium** and the **Marches** regions.

Canary Islands Wine-producing islands belonging to **Spain**. **Tenerife** produces light, astringent reds; Lanzarote produces dry and medium-sweet white wines from the **Malvasia** grape. The wine-making techniques are rustic, and quality is often poor.

Cannellino An unusual type of medium-sweet **Frascati**, made from very dry grapes, preferably affected by **botrytis**.

Cannonau The version of the **Garnacha** grape variety grown in **Sardinia**. It is **DOC** in Cannonau di Sardegna, which can be red or **rosato**, dry or **amabile**, and also **fortified**. All are quite high in alcohol (reds, minimum of 13.5% vol.), and the best and most popular are the dry reds.

Canon-Fronsac An **AC** wine of **Bordeaux**, made in the heart of the **Fronsac** region, producing chunky, deep red-coloured wines, which are well-flavoured and tannic, requiring more bottle age than plain Fronsac. The main grape varieties are **Cabernet Franc**, **Cabernet Sauvignon**, **Merlot** and **Malbec**. Quality is improving and the wines are deservedly becoming better known. PRICE BAND: B–C.

Canterbury A cool-climate, wine-producing region of **New Zealand's** South Island. The climate is best suited to white **varietal** wines, made from **Chardonnay**, **Gewürztraminer** and **Riesling** grapes. A little red wine is also made, from **Pinot Noir**.

cantina The Italian term for a cellar or winery.

cantina sociale The Italian term for a co-operative winery.

Cape Riesling A white grape variety (no relation to **Riesling**), grown widely in **South Africa**, where it makes dry, rather neutral, gently aromatic, easy-drinking wines. Its true name is Crouchen Blanc.

Capena (also called **Bianco Capena**) A white **DOC** wine produced in the hills north of Rome, in the **Latium** region of Italy, from the **Malvasia**, **Trebbiano** and **Bombino** grape varieties. A pleasant, easy-drinking dry, or off-dry white.

Capriano del Colle A **DOC** wine produced in the **Lombardy** region, northwest **Italy**. Most of the production is of lively, easy drinking red, made from the **Sangiovese**, **Marzemino** and **Barbera** grape varieties. There is also a small production of varietally labelled, crisp dry white wine from the **Trebbiano** grape.

caratello A small barrel, of approximately 50 litres capacity, traditionally used for ageing **Vin Santo**.

carato An Italian term for a barrel, of a similar capacity to the **barrique**.

carbon dioxide A colourless, odourless and incombustible gas. In winemaking it is produced during **fermentation**, when grape sugar is converted into **alcohol**. Normally carbon dioxide is lost to the atmosphere. When fermentation takes place in a closed vessel (either a pressurized tank or during secondary fermentation in bottle), the carbon dioxide is trapped in the wine, until it is released as bubbles when the bottle is opened.

carbonic maceration A technique sometimes used in **fermentation** of **Beaujolais** and other red wines intended for early drinking. Uncrushed grapes are fermented in vat under a blanket of inert **carbon dioxide**. The process promotes bouquet and fruit flavours (ideal for the **Gamay** grape), and minimizes the extraction of **tannin**.

Carema A red **DOC** wine made in tiny quantities in the northern **Piedmont** region of Italy, from the **Nebbiolo** grape variety. A light, lean and elegant dry red, the quality of which can be very good. PRICE BAND: C.

Carignan A red grape variety widely planted in **France**, in **Languedoc-Roussillon** and **Provence**, and as an ingredient for much **vin de table**. In Spain it is known as **Cariñena**, and contributes to the blend for the **DO** wine of that name as well as for many other DO wines of the northeast. In **Rioja** it surfaces as Mazuelo, a minor blending ingredient. Carignan is sometimes bottled as a **varietal**, but is chiefly valued for the deep colour and structure it can give to a blend.

Cariñena A **DO** wine of northeast **Spain**. Most of the production is of red wine, the best of it full and soft, made mainly from the **Garnacha** and **Tempranillo** grape varieties, plus a little Cariñena (which originally comes from this region), **Bobal**

and **Monastrell**. White and **rosado** wines are also made.

Carmignano A fine red **DOCG** wine of **Tuscany**, similar to **Chianti** in that it is made from **Sangiovese** and **Canaiolo**, but differing in that it must also contain between 6 and 10% of **Cabernet Sauvignon** and/or **Cabernet Franc**. Some **rosato** is also produced, based on the same grape varieties. PRICE BAND: B–C.

Carneros An **AVA** wine-producing region of **California**, shared by the **Napa Valley** and **Sonoma** regions. The relatively cool climate makes for fine **varietal** wines, especially from **Pinot Noir** as well as **Chardonnay**. Carneros also has a rapidly growing reputation for fine **méthode champenoise** sparkling wines.

Carso A **DOC** wine of the **Friuli-Venezia Giulia** region of northeast **Italy**. Carso and Terrano del Carso are assertive, sturdy dry reds, both based on the native Terrano grape (a variety of Refosco, or **Mondeuse Noire**). Malvasia del Carso is a dry, vibrant white, sometimes with a honeyed, almond note. All are intended for drinking young.

Cassis An **AC** wine of **Provence**, produced around the port of the same name. The fruity, fresh white is one of the most celebrated of the region, produced from the **Ugni Blanc**, **Clairette** and **Marsanne** grape varieties (plus sometimes **Sauvignon Blanc**). Red and rosé are both made, from **Grenache**, **Cinsault** and **Mourvèdre**, but are rarely as good as the white version. PRICE BAND: C.

cassis A tasting term, used to indicate a blackcurrant aroma or taste. It is particularly characteristic of wines made from the **Cabernet Sauvignon** grape variety.

Castel del Monte A DOC wine of the **Apulia** region of southern **Italy**, produced in rocky, hilly vineyards in the centre of the region. The **bianco** is a neutral, inoffensive dry white, based on the Pampanuto grape variety. The dry **rosato** is more characterful, based on the **Bombino Nero**. Best of all is the **rosso**, made from **Uva di Troia** plus **Sangiovese**, **Montepulciano**, **Aglianico** and **Pinot Nero**, deep in colour and flavour and with good ageing potential.

Casteller A red DOC wine produced throughout the **Trentino** region of northern **Italy**, based on the **Schiava** grape variety. Most of it is light, easy drinking, dry red, best drunk young. There is also an **amabile** version.

cat's pee (also called **piss**) A tasting term, used to describe the pungent, yet fruity, aroma which connoisseurs look for in a good wine made from the **Sauvignon Blanc** grape.

Catalan An alternative name, used in France, for the **Carignan** grape variety.

Catarratto A white grape variety native to

Sicily, where it goes to make the **DOC** wines of **Alcamo** and **Etna**, as well as contributing to the blends for many of the island's **vini da tavola**. It is among the grapes used for the fortified wine **Marsala**.

Catawba A **hybrid** grape variety widely planted in the eastern **United States**, producing cheap white and rosé wines, often sparkling.

Cava A sparkling **DO** wine of **Spain**, produced mainly in the **Penedès** region by the **méthode champenoise**, from the **Macabeo**, **Parellada** and **Xarel-lo** grape varieties, plus, increasingly, **Chardonnay**. For **rosado** Cavas, **Garnacha** and **Monastrell** add the colour. Quality can be very good and, from some producers, is steadily getting better, especially where some Chardonnay is used to add class and fruit and improve the ageing potential. PRICE BAND: B–C.

cave coopérative The French term for a co-operative wine-making cellar. Growers, often without their own wine-making equipment, and without the capacity to bottle and market their own production, send their grapes to a central vinification centre. Here, their grapes are usually lost in a blend that is sold under the co-op's label, but some co-ops produce special **cuvées** from individual members' vineyards. See also **cantina sociale**.

cedar A tasting term, used to indicate the

cedar-wood aroma often found in fine, mature red **Bordeaux**, a characteristic of the **Cabernet Sauvignon** grape variety.

Cellatica A red **DOC** wine produced in the **Lombardy** region of northwest **Italy**, from the **Schiava**, **Barbera** and **Marzemino** grape varieties. A dry, light red, with a characteristic bitter **finish**, it is best drunk young.

Cencibel An alternative name, used in **La Mancha**, for the **Tempranillo** grape variety.

cépage The French term for grape variety.

Cerasuolo di Vittoria A dry red **DOC** wine of **Sicily**, produced from the **Calabrese**, Frappato and **Nerello** Mascalese grape varieties. In fact it is more like a dark rosé than a red, but is surprisingly full-flavoured. Best drunk young.

Cérons A sweet white **AC** wine produced in the communes of Cérons and Illats, within the **Graves** region of **Bordeaux**. The same varieties for **Sauternes** are used: **Sémillon**, **Sauvignon Blanc** and **Muscadelle**. But the wines, soft and fairly sweet, never have the same richness and depth as Sauternes. Most producers now make dry white wine, which they can sell as AC Graves.

Cerveteri A **DOC** wine produced in the north of the **Latium** region of **Italy**. The fairly bland, dry white version is made from a wide variety of grape varieties, including **Trebbiano** and **Malvasia**. The red is better, based on the **Sangiovese** and **Montepulciano** grape varieties.

Cesanese A red grape variety of the **Latium** region of **Italy**. In the Ciociaria hills, it is **DOC** in three wines: Cesanese di Olevano Romano, Cesanese di Affile and Cesanese del Piglio. Traditionally they were sweet, sparkling red wines; today, thankfully, they are warm, fleshy, dry red wines.

Chablais See **Switzerland**.

Chablis A white **AC** wine of northern **Burgundy**, produced in vineyards around the town of Chablis from the **Chardonnay** grape variety. Chablis has a bone dry, steely taste, which distinguishes it from the more opulent Chardonnays from farther south in Burgundy. With bottle age, it can develop wonderful complexity of aroma and flavour, especially if it is from one of the **premier cru** or **grand cru** vineyard sites. Some producers age, and even ferment, Chablis in new oak barrels, especially for *premier cru* and *grand cru* wines. Other producers maintain that the true taste of Chablis is masked by oak flavours, and use only stainless steel. Superb wines are to be found in both styles. The name Chablis has been usurped by producers outside Europe, who use it as a generic term for white wine. PRICE BAND: B–C; PREMIER CRU: C–D; GRAND CRU: D–E.

chai A French term, used particularly in **Bordeaux**, for an 'overground cellar' used for storing wine in cask.

Chalk Hill An **AVA** of **Sonoma** county, **California**. Its chalk soil is especially suited to production of **varietal** wines from **Chardonnay**.

Chalone An **AVA** of **Monterey County, California**. Its high-altitude vineyards produce some fine **varietal** wines, particularly from **Chardonnay** and **Pinot Noir**.

Chambertin A **grand cru** vineyard – arguably the best – of **Gevrey-Chambertin** in the **Côte de Nuits** area of **Burgundy**. It produces one of the greatest red Burgundies, combining finesse and elegance with power and depth of flavour.

Chambertin-Clos de Bèze A **grand cru** vineyard of **Gevrey-Chambertin** in the **Côte de Nuits** area of **Burgundy**. It produces one of the best red Burgundies, of very similar quality to **Chambertin**.

Chambolle-Musigny A red **AC** wine of the **Côte de Nuits** region of **Burgundy**, made from the **Pinot Noir** grape variety. At its best, the wine is light, classy, delicately perfumed, particularly from the **grand cru** vineyards of **Bonnes Mares** and **Musigny** (even if the latter hasn't always lived up to the top *grand cru* standards in recent vintages). PRICE BAND: C–D.

chambré The French term for the temperature

at which red wine should be served. Literally, it means room temperature, although modern rooms are often warmer than the ideal 15–17° C intended.

Champagne A sparkling **AC** wine of northeast **France**, produced around the towns of Reims, Epernay and Chalons-sur-Marne, from the **Chardonnay**, **Pinot Noir** and **Pinot Meunier** grapes. Champagne is certainly the world's finest and most highly prized sparkling wine. It is made by the **méthode champenoise**, which invovles a second, bubble-forming **fermentation** in bottle, followed by ageing on the **lees**, then **remuage** and **dégorgement**.

The most important vineyard areas are the **Côte des Blancs**, planted mainly with Chardonnay; the **Montagne de Reims**, mainly Pinot Noir; and the **Vallée de la Marne**, mainly Pinot Noir and Pinot Meunier. The **Aube** is the southernmost outpost, planted mainly with Pinot Noir and Chardonnay.

Champagne is nearly always a blend of different grape varieties from different areas, and in the case of non-vintage different years. **Blanc de Blancs** is made entirely from Chardonnay, however, and **Blanc de Noirs** is white Champagne made from the red grapes Pinot Noir and Pinot Meunier. Vintage Champagne is wine from a single year, but it is not necessarily superior to non-vintage. Pink, or rosé, Champagne is made either by allowing a short, controlled **maceration**

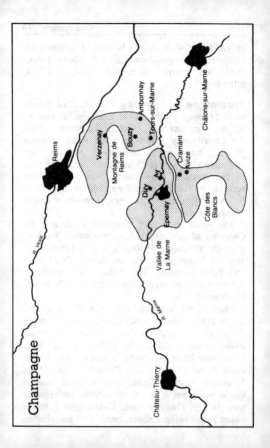

Champagne

Reims

R. Vesle

Verzenay

Montagne de Reims

Ambonnay

Bouzy

Tours-sur-Marne

Dizy

Épernay

Vallée de La Marne

R. Marne

Cramant

Avize

Côte des Blancs

Châlons-sur-Marne

Château-Thierry

of the fermenting wine on the skins of the Pinot Noir; or by adding a little still red wine, often from **Bouzy**, to the white before the second fermentation. PRICE BAND: D–E++.

Chapelle-Chambertin A **grand cru** vineyard of **Gevrey-Chambertin** in the **Côte de Nuits** area of **Burgundy**.

chaptalization The practice of adding sugar to **must** before **fermentation**, in order to increase the final **alcohol content**. It is permitted in many northern regions, where grapes do not always have a sufficient level of natural sugar. The amount of sugar that can be added is controlled by law, since excess detracts from quality.

Chardonnay A white grape variety, one of the most important and widely planted in the world. Chardonnay is planted in almost every wine-producing country.

In **France**, it produces some of the world's finest white wines in **Burgundy**, particularly in **Chablis** and the **Côte d'Or**. It is an important part of the blend in the world's greatest sparkling wine, **Champagne** (where it is usually blended with **Pinot Noir** and **Pinot Meunier**, but is sometimes vinified alone to make a **blanc de blancs**).

Chardonnay produces fine **varietal** wines in **California**, **Australia** and **New Zealand**. In **Italy** it is **DOC** in the **Alto Adige**, **Trentino**, **Friuli-Venezia Giulia** and **Veneto**, and also contributes to the blend for many sparkling wines. In Spain it is increasingly important as part of the blend for the sparkling wine **Cava**, and for the still wines of **Penedès**.

Chardonnay and **oak** is a marriage made in heaven, and it is probably the white grape variety most suited to oak **ageing**. Although both oaked and unoaked Chardonnays have their fans.

Charmat method (also called **cuve close**) A method of producing sparkling wines in bulk by second **fermentation** in tank. A still base wine is produced in the normal way. Sugar and yeast are then added to the base wine, in a sealed tank. A second fermentation takes place, and the added sugar is converted into alcohol and **carbon dioxide**. Because the tank is sealed, the carbon dioxide cannot escape, and is dissolved in the wine. The sparkling wine can then be bottled under pressure. This is a less expensive and less time-consuming method than the **méthode champenoise**, in which the second fermentation takes place in bottle, but it undoubtedly results in wines of a lesser quality.

Charmes-Chambertin A **grand cru** vineyard of **Gevrey-Chambertin** in the **Côte de Nuits** area of **Burgundy**.

Chassagne-Montrachet An **AC** wine of the **Côte de Beaune** region of **Burgundy**. Good quality white wine is produced from the **Chardonnay** grape variety, ranging from superb, from the **grand cru** sites of **Le Montrachet**, **Bâtard-Montrachet** (both shared with **Puligny-Montrachet**) and Criots-Bâtard-Montrachet, to very good from the **premier cru** sites. In fact, more than half of the production is red wine, made from **Pinot Noir**, but it is rarely as good as the white.

Chasselas A white grape variety of **Switzerland**, also planted to a limited extent in **Germany** and **Alsace**. In general, it produces rather light, neutral wine; at its best, in the Valais and Vaud regions of Switzerland and **Baden** in Germany, it can produce a wine with a flinty, smoky aroma. In Switzerland it is sometimes known as Fendant and in Germany as Gutedel.

château The French word for castle. In **Bordeaux**, the term is used to indicate a wine estate, whether or not it possesses a castle or mansion.

Château-Grillet A white **AC** wine produced in a tiny vineyard in the northern **Rhône**, from the **Viognier** grape variety. The wine has a delicious and distinctive apricot-and-cream aroma and taste. It is rare and consequently expensive. PRICE BAND: E.

Château-Chalon An **AC** wine of the **Jura** region. Only **vin jaune** is produced, from the **Savagnin** grape variety, with its distinctive dry, assertive, nutty flavour. PRICE BAND: D–E.

Châteauneuf-du-Pape An **AC** wine of the

southern **Rhône**, produced in vineyards around the town of the same name. Although 13 grape varieties are permitted (eight red and five white), most producers use fewer. The majority of the production is of red wine, based on **Grenache**, **Syrah** and **Mourvèdre**. At its best it is a deep, plummy, spicy wine, packed with red fruit flavours, and capable of long ageing.

White Châteauneuf-du-Pape is much less common. Based on Grenache Blanc, **Clairette** and **Bourboulenc**, it can be highly aromatic in its youth, with fresh, spicy fruit balanced by a refreshing cut of acidity. PRICE BAND: B–E.

Châtillon-en-Diois   An **AC** wine of the **Rhône**. Very small quantities of white are produced, from the **Aligoté** and **Chardonnay** grape varieties, and red and rosé from **Gamay**, **Syrah** and **Pinot Noir**.

Chénas   A red **AC** wine, the smallest of the 10 crus of the **Beaujolais** region of **Burgundy**, made from the **Gamay** grape. The wine is rich and chocolaty, similar to that of **Moulin-à-Vent**. Quality is usually very good, among the best, if perhaps the least characteristic, of all Beaujolais. PRICE BAND: B.

Chenin Blanc   A white grape variety planted especially in the **Anjou-Saumur** and **Touraine** areas of the **Loire** valley. Chenin is highly versatile. It can make high-quality, bone-dry wines in **Savennières** and **Jasnières** and luscious sweet, dessert wines in **Coteaux du Layon**, **Bonnezeaux** and **Quarts de Chaume**. In **Vouvray** and **Montlouis**, it can be dry, medium dry, or sweet and still, **pétillant**, or fully sparkling. In **Saumur**, Chenin is the base for **mèthode champenoise** sparkling wines. It has been adopted by many other wine-making countries, including **South Africa** (where it is known as **Steen**), **Australia** and **California** (where it makes **varietal** wines for drinking young).

Chevalier-Montrachet A **grand cru** vineyard of **Puligny-Montrachet** in the **Côte de Beaune** area of **Burgundy**. It produces white wine of superb quality and richness from the **Chardonnay** grape variety, perhaps second only to **Le Montrachet**. Its colour begins as a greenish yellow, deepening to gold with age, as the dry but honeyed taste and aromas develop. The wine is rich and mouth-filling, and needs at least 10 years to reach peak maturity. PRICE BAND: E.

Cheverny A **VDQS** wine produced in **Touraine** in the **Loire** valley. A harsh, unpleasant white is made based on the Romarantin grape variety; fresh, crisp, fruity whites from **Arbois**, **Chardonnay**, **Chenin Blanc** and **Sauvignon Blanc** are much better. The light, somewhat astringent reds of Cheverny are based on **Cabernet Franc**, **Cabernet Sauvignon**, **Gamay** and **Pinot Noir**. The same varieties are used to make light, attractive rosé, all best drunk young. PRICE BAND: A–B.

Chianti A red **DOCG** wine of **Tuscany**, produced mainly from the **Sangiovese** grape, plus **Canaiolo**, **Trebbiano**, **Malvasia**, and up to 10% of other varieties (sometimes **Cabernet Sauvignon**). There are seven subregions within the DOCG: Classico and Rufina (the best two), plus Colli Aretini, Colli Fiorentini, Colli Senesi, Colline Pisane and Montalbano. Quality varies enormously, from very ordinary to superb (especially in Classico and Rufina, which produce some of Italy's finest red wines). In the past Chianti has suffered from overproduction, blending with wines from other regions, over-prolonged wood ageing and the use of inferior clonal material in the vineyard. Now Classico and Rufina in particular have addressed these problems, and overall quality is constantly improving.

Chianti is a versatile wine. The basic non-*riserva*, or *normale*, is a limpid, purple red, with delicious cherry flavoured fruit. *Riserva*, aged for three years before bottling, can be much deeper and more concentrated, with a full, fruity flavour supported by a tannic backbone. Most of the ageing is done in large oak or chestnut **botti**, but some producers make limited use of small oak **barriques**. The use of Cabernet in the blend is controversial: some producers say it enhances the structure and ageing potential of Chianti; others hold that, even at a maximum of 10%, it can begin to mask the attractive fruit flavour of Sangiovese. PRICE BAND: A–C. See also **governo**.

chiaretto The Italian term for a light, rosé style wine. See also **Bardolino**.

Chignin See **Vin de Savoie**.

Chile An important wine-producing country of South America. The vine was brought here by the Spanish, and for many years the main variety grown was **Pais**, a high-yielding vine producing thin, poor wines, both red and white, which were purely for domestic consumption. In recent years, producers have planted more noble varieties, particularly **Sémillon**, **Sauvignon Blanc**, **Chardonnay**, **Cabernet Sauvignon** and **Merlot**, to produce wines for export. Good results have already been obtained with reds made from Cabernet, and refreshing, fleshy Merlots for early drinking. Fine crisp, white Sauvignon is also beginning to appear as producers adopt more modern wine-making techniques, although much of what is sold as Sauvignon is in fact made from the Sauvignonasse variety, so the wines lack some of the juicy fruit intensity of top Sauvignons from the **Loire** and **New Zealand**. Wines made from Sémillon have so far been undistinguished, largely owing to the extraordinarily high yields obtained. Chile's vineyards are free from **phylloxera**, and so are planted with ungrafted vines.

Chinon A red **AC** wine of the **Touraine** area of the **Loire** valley, produced from the **Cabernet Franc** grape variety. It is one of the finest-quality red wines of the Loire, with grassy, raspberry fruit flavours, and capable of long ageing. Rosé and white Chinons exist, but are extremely rare. PRICE BAND: B–C.

Chiroubles A red **AC** wine, one of the 10 **crus** of the **Beaujolais** region of **Burgundy**, made from the **Gamay** grape. The wine is light and delicate, with delicious strawberry-flavoured fruit, best drunk young. PRICE BAND: B–C.

chocolate A tasting term, used to describe a rich, sweet, thick, chocolate-like aroma, found particularly in some wines made from the **Gamay** grape variety, such as **cru Beaujolais**.

Chorey-lès-Beaune An **AC** wine of the **Côte de Beaune** region of **Burgundy**. Most of the wine is red, made from the **Pinot Noir** grape variety: soft, fruity, good value for money, and best drunk relatively young. Many producers use the alternative **AC** of **Côte de Beaune-Villages**. An insignificant quantity of white wine is also made. PRICE BAND: B–C.

Chusclan See **Côtes du Rhône**.

Cinqueterre A white **DOC** wine produced in the **Liguria** region of northwest **Italy**, from the Bosco, Albarola and **Vermentino** grape varieties. Dry, light and fragrant in their youth, the wines oxidize easily and are best drunk young. A mildly sweet version, Schiacchetrà, is made from dried grapes.

Cinsault (also called **Cinsaut**) A red grape variety, widely planted in the south of **France**. When harvested at low yields, it can produce moderately deep-coloured wine with a beefy, full flavour and high acidity. It is much used as an ingredient in **vins de table** and **AC** wines of **Languedoc-Roussillon**, in some of the red wines of **Provence**, and in the southern **Rhône** (it is one of the 13 permitted varieties in **Châteauneuf-du-Pape**). It produces small quantities of **varietal** wine in **South Africa**, where it is known as 'Hermitage'.

Cirò A **DOC** wine produced in the **Calabria** region of southern **Italy**. The dry **bianco** is made from the **Greco** Bianco grape, plus some **Trebbiano**. The strong, dry **rosso** and **rosato** are based on **Gaglioppo**. Quality rarely rises above the ordinary.

Clairette A white grape variety grown in southern **France**, as an ingredient for blended **vin de table**, in the **AC** wines of **Provence**, and in the southern **Rhône** (it is one of the permitted varieties for **Châteauneuf-du-Pape**). On its own, it produces rather dull **AC** wine in Clairette de Bellegarde and Clairette du Languedoc, both in **Languedoc-Roussillon**. Its finest expression is in the sparkling Rhône wine Clairette de Die: the **brut** version is pure Clairette, while 'Tradition' is a blend of **Muscat** and Clairette, a delicious, light, fresh, grapey sparkling wine, and very good value for money. PRICE BAND: B.

Clare Valley A wine-producing region of **South Australia**. Fine **varietal** wines are produced, particularly white **Riesling**, and red **Cabernet Sauvignon** and **Shiraz** (plus good blends of Cabernet and Shiraz).

Claret The English term for any red **Bordeaux**.

clarete The Spanish term for pale red wine. See also **tinto**.

classico An Italian term, sometimes appended to **DOC** and **DOCG** wine names, to indicate that the wine comes from a designated subregion within the DOC, often the historical or central area of production.

Clevener In **Alsace**, a wine made by blending the **Pinot Blanc** and **Auxerrois** grape varieties.

climat A French term, used particularly in **Burgundy**, to indicate an individual vineyard site.

clone A sort of subvariety, within the family of a single grape variety. The **Sangiovese** grape, for instance, has many clones, some producing better wines than others, some suited to particular soil types and local climates.

clos A French term used to describe a vineyard that is (or was once) surrounded by a wall.

Clos de Vougeot An **AC**, **grand cru** red wine of the **Côte de Nuits** area of **Burgundy**, produced from the **Pinot Noir** grape variety grown in the largest *grand cru* of the **Côte d'Or**. Because of its size, and the large number of growers who own a tiny slice of it, quality is variable, not always up to *grand cru* standard. At its best, it can be fleshy, rich and chocolaty, sometimes with smoke and liquorice flavours on the long finish. PRICE BAND: D–E.

CM (coopérative-manipulant) The letters found on **Champagne** labels, indicating that it comes from a co-operative cellar. The numbers following the letters identify the co-op.

co-operative A wine-making cellar owned by a group of growers. Co-operatives are common in most European wine-producing countries. See **cantina sociale; cave coopérative**.

Colares An **RD** wine produced in central **Portugal**, from vines not affected by **phylloxera** grown in sand-dune vineyards on the coast, near Lisbon. Most of the wine made is red, from the Ramisco grape, and is very tough and tannic in its youth. It takes ten years to become drinkable. White Colares is made from **Malvasia**. PRICE BAND: A–B.

Colheita Port A **Tawny Port** with a date of harvest. Port of a single year is aged in wood, sometimes for decades, before being bottled. The label must bear the year of bottling, as well as the harvest date.

Colli Albani A white **DOC** wine produced in the **Latium** region of **Italy**, from the **Malvasia**

and **Trebbiano** grape varieties. Similar to, but not as good as the best of, **Frascati**. PRICE BAND: A–B.

Colli Altotiberini A DOC wine of the **Umbria** region of **Italy**. **Bianco** is made from **Trebbiano** and **Malvasia**; easy-drinking and best while fresh and young. **Rosso**, made from **Sangiovese** with a touch of **Merlot**, can be softly fruity, and the same grapes make a good, dry **rosato**.

Colli Aretini See **Chianti**.

Colli Bolognesi A DOC wine of the **Emilia-Romagna** region of **Italy**. The **bianco** is a dry white (sometimes **amabile**) based on the **Albana** grape variety. The four **varietal** whites are Pignoletto, **Pinot Bianco**, **Riesling Italico** and **Sauvignon**. The three red varietals are **Barbera** (the best), **Cabernet Sauvignon** (also very good) and **Merlot**.

Colli del Trasimeno A DOC wine produced in the **Umbria** region of **Italy**. The **bianco** is a dry, refreshing white, based on the **Trebbiano** grape variety. The **rosso**, supple, fresh and fruity, is based on **Sangiovese** and **Gamay**.

Colli di Bolzano (also called **Bozner Leiten**) A dry red **DOC** wine, produced in the hills around Bolzano, in the **Alto Adige** region of northern **Italy**. It is based on the **Schiava** grape variety, and is a simple, easy-drinking wine.

Colli di Luni A DOC wine produced in the **Liguria** region of northwest Italy. **Bianco** is a blend of the **Vermentino** and **Trebbiano** grape varieties, and there is also a **varietal** Vermentino. **Rosso** is a blend based on **Sangiovese**.

Colli di Parma A DOC wine of the **Emilia-Romagna** region of Italy. A dry **rosso** (sometimes **frizzante**) is based on the **Barbera** and **Bonarda** grape varieties. **Malvasia** is a dry or **amabile** white (sometimes **spumante**), a blend of Malvasia and **Moscato**. **Sauvignon** is a dry **varietal** white, sometimes **frizzante**.

Colli Euganei A DOC wine of the **Veneto** region of Italy. The **bianco** is a blend based on **Garganega** and the **rosso** is a blend of **Merlot**, **Cabernet Sauvignon** and **Cabernet Franc**, plus some **Barbera**. Both can be dry or **amabile**, still or sparkling. In addition there are **varietal** whites from Tocai Italico and **Pinot Bianco** (both usually dry), and **Moscato** (sweet, and sometimes sparkling). The red varietals are **Cabernet** (Cabernet Sauvignon and/or Cabernet Franc) and **Merlot**.

Colli Fiorentini See **Chianti**.

Colli Lanuvini A white **DOC** wine produced in the **Latium** region of Italy, from the **Malvasia** and **Trebbiano** grape varieties. Similar to, but not as good as the best of, **Frascati**. PRICE BAND: A–B.

Colli Martani A **DOC** wine produced in the **Umbria** region of Italy. There are two **varietal** whites, **Grechetto** and **Trebbiano**, and one varietal red made from **Sangiovese**.

Colli Orientali del Friuli   A **DOC** wine produced in the **Friuli-Venezia Giulia** region of northeast **Italy**. Excellent light whites, and reds which can take moderate ageing, are produced in 20 different styles. The whites are **varietals** made from **Chardonnay**, **Malvasia**, **Pinot Bianco**, **Pinot Grigio**, **Ribolla**, **Riesling Renano**, **Sauvignon**, **Tocai Friulano**, **Traminer Aromatico** and **Verduzzo Friulano** (all dry), plus the sweet whites Ramandolo (made from Verduzzo) and **Picolit**. Red varietals are Cabernet (**Cabernet Sauvignon** and/or **Cabernet Franc**), **Merlot**, **Pinot Nero**, Refosco dal Peduncolo Rosso (a clone of **Refosco**) and Schioppettino. Dry **rosato** is based mainly on **Merlot**.

Colli Perugini   A **DOC** wine produced in the **Umbria** region of **Italy**. The **bianco** is based on the **Trebbiano** grape variety, the **rosso** and **rosato** on **Sangiovese**. None is very exciting.

Colli Piacentini   A **DOC** wine produced in the **Emilia-Romagna** region of **Italy**. There are four sub-zones: Gutturnio (dry red, sometimes sweet, sometimes sparkling, made from **Barbera** and **Bonarda**); Monterosso Val d'Arda, Trebbiano Val Trebbia, and Val Nure (all three, dry or **amabile**, sometimes sparkling, based on **Malvasia** and **Trebbiano**). There are three **varietal** reds (Barbera, Bonarda and **Pinot Nero**) and four varietal whites (Malvasia, Ortugo, **Pinot Grigio** and **Sauvignon**).

Colli Senesi See **Chianti**.

Colli Tortonesi A DOC wine of the **Piedmont** region of northwest **Italy**. Red **varietal** wine, made from the **Barbera** grape variety, is dry and often lightly fizzy. Varietal white is made from **Cortese**, and is dry and often lightly sparkling or fully **spumante**.

Colline Pisane See **Chianti**.

Collio (also called **Collio Goriziano**) A DOC wine of the **Friuli-Venezia Giulia** region of northeast **Italy**. Excellent light whites, and reds that can take moderate ageing, are produced in 11 different styles. Collio Bianco is a white blend of the **Ribolla**, **Malvasia** and **Tocai Friulano** grapes. Then there are seven white **varietals** made from Malvasia, **Pinot Bianco**, **Pinot Grigio**, **Riesling Italico**, **Sauvignon**, Tocai Friulano and **Traminer**; and three red varietals, **Merlot**, **Pinot Nero** and **Cabernet Franc**.

Collioure A red **AC** wine of the **Languedoc-Roussillon** region of **France**, produced from the **Grenache**, **Mourvèdre**, **Carignan** and **Cinsault** grape varieties. Assertive and full-bodied in its youth, it is capable of long ageing. PRICE BAND: B.

Colombard A white grape variety, which was traditionally grown for distillation into Cognac. Recently it has enjoyed a revival, making good, ordinary quality varietal wines in **California** and in the **Côtes de Gascogne** in France.

Commandaria A deep-coloured dessert wine produced in **Cyprus** from semi-dried grapes. The best, sold as '100 years old', lives up to its legendary reputation; much of the modern, commercial product does not.

complex A tasting term, used to indicate a wine with many layers of aroma and flavour; one of the hallmarks of a great wine.

Concord A red non-**Vitis vinifera** grape variety, native to America, and widely grown in the east of the **United States**. It is used to make usually sweet, often sparkling red wine, with the curious **foxy** flavour of the *labrusca* vine. It is also grown in **Brazil**.

Condrieu A white **AC** wine of the northern **Rhône**, produced from the **Viognier** grape variety. The wine has a delicious and distinctive apricot-and-cream aroma and taste. It is rare, although by no means so rare as **Château-Grillet**, and is consequently somewhat less expensive. PRICE BAND: C–E.

consejo regulador The Spanish regulatory body (there is one for each **DO** wine region), which enforces the DO regulations and monitors production and movement of wines within the region.

consorzio The Italian term for a voluntary consortium of producers, within a given region, which can supervise its members' production, or help to promote and market their wines.

Coonawarra An important wine-producing region of **South Australia**. It produces superb **varietal** and blended red wines, among Australia's best and longest-lived, from **Cabernet Sauvignon**, **Shiraz** and **Merlot**. Good whites are also made, largely from **Chardonnay** and **Riesling**.

Copertino A **DOC** wine produced in the **Apulia** region of southern **Italy**. Full-bodied red and dry **rosato** wines are made mainly from the **Negroamaro** grape variety.

copita The Spanish term for the smallish, quite narrow, tapering glass from which **Sherry**, particularly chilled **fino**, should be drunk.

Corbières An **AC** wine of the **Languedoc-Roussillon** region of southern **France**. Most of the production is of full-bodied, consistently good-value, meaty, spicy reds, based on the **Grenache**, **Cinsault** and **Carignan** grape varieties. The small amount of white wine produced, mainly from **Bourboulenc** and **Clairette**, is less interesting, and is at best clean and refreshing. PRICE BAND: A–B.

Cori A **DOC** wine produced in very small quantities in the **Latium** region of **Italy**. The **bianco** is based on the **Malvasia** and **Trebbiano** grape varieties, and the **rosso** is produced mainly from **Montepulciano** and **Cesanese**.

cork The best substance yet found for keeping

wine in the bottle, and the air out. Cork is made from the bark of the cork oak tree, and Portugal is the major centre of production.

corked (also called **corky**) A tasting term, used to describe a wine that is 'off', with a stale woody smell and taste, possibly accompanied by **oxidation**.

Cornas An **AC** wine of the northern **Rhône**, France, produced from the **Syrah** grape variety. It is deep-coloured and tannic in its youth, developing a splendid depth of flavour and complexity with age, with delicious spicy, leathery red fruit. PRICE BAND: C–D.

Corsica See **Vin de Corse**.

Cortese A white grape variety, grown mainly in **Piedmont**, northwest **Italy**; it is also found in **Oltrepò Pavese** and the **Veneto**. In Piedmont, it is **DOC** in Cortese dell'Alto Monferrato (a fine dry white, occasionally **frizzante** or **spumante**) and Cortese di Gavi, one of Italy's finest white wines, gently aromatic, fairly full, and with a good cut of refreshing acidity. PRICE BAND: B–E. Cortese is also used in Piedmont to produce white Colli Tortonesi.

Corton A **grand cru** vineyard of the **Côte de Beaune** region of **Burgundy**, shared by the villages of **Aloxe-Corton**, **Pernand-Vergelesses** and **Ladoix-Serrigny**. A rich, top-quality, long-lived red Burgundy of the highest quality. A very

small quantity of white Corton is also produced.
PRICE BAND: D–E.

Corton-Charlemagne A **grand cru** vineyard
of the **Côte de Beaune** region of **Burgundy**,
shared by the villages of **Aloxe-Corton Pernand-
Vergelesses** and **Ladoix-Serrigny**. A rich, buttery,
long-lived white Burgundy of the highest quality.
PRICE BAND: D–E.

Corvina A red grape variety of the **Veneto**
region of **Italy**. It is the best quality ingredient in
the blends for **Valpolicella** and **Bardolino**, especially prized for the **recioto** and **Amarone** wines
of Valpolicella.

cosecha The Spanish term for vintage.

Costers del Segre A **DO** wine of northeast
Spain, producing high quality red and white
wines from a mixture of native varieties (including **Tempranillo**, **Garnacha**, **Parellada**, **Macabeo**,
Xarel-lo and **Cariñena**) and foreign varieties
(mainly **Cabernet Sauvignon**, **Merlot**, **Pinot Noir**
and **Chardonnay**).

Costières-du-Gard An **AC** wine of the **Languedoc-Roussillon** region of southern **France**.
Most of the wine produced is simple, beefy reds
(and some fresh rosé) based on the **Carignan**,
Grenache and **Syrah** grape varieties. A relatively
small amount of fresh white wine, for early
drinking, is based on **Bourboulenc**, **Clairette** and
Ugni Blanc.

Cot A red grape variety of **France**, grown mainly in **Bordeaux** (where it is called **Malbec**, or **Pressac** in **Saint-Emilion**) where it is a very minor component in much of the red wine, particularly in the **Côtes de Bourg** and the **Premières Côtes de Blaye**. It is a more important ingredient in **Cahors** (where it is sometimes also known as **Auxerrois**), and for Touraine Tradition in the **Loire**. In **Spain** Cot is found in **Ribera del Duero**, and in **Italy**, in **Rosso Barletta** from **Apulia**.

côte The French term for hill or slope, often extended to designate a region.

Côte Blonde See **Côte Rôtie**.

Côte Brune See **Côte Rôtie**.

Côte Chalonnaise A wine-producing region of **Burgundy** in **France**, producing white wine from the **Aligoté** and **Chardonnay** grape varieties, and red from **Pinot Noir** and **Gamay**. There are five **AC** wines. **Bouzeron** is one of the best white wines from the Aligoté grape. **Givry** makes mainly dry red wines from Pinot Noir, and a small amount of white from Chardonnay. **Mercurey**, produced around the village of the same name, is mostly red Pinot Noir plus a small amount of Chardonnay. **Montagny** produces good Chardonnay, especially with oak **ageing**. **Rully** produces soft, medium-bodied, nutty Chardonnay, sometimes with a touch of **oak**; reds, from Pinot Noir, are lighter bodied, and less successful.

Côte d'Or The heart of the **Burgundy** region, where some of the world's finest red, from **Pinot Noir**, and white wines, from **Chardonnay**, are produced. The Côte d'Or ('golden slope'), stretches in a thin band from **Marsannay** in the north to **Santenay** in the south, including the two subregions of the **Côte de Nuits** and the **Côte de Beaune**.

Côte de Beaune The southern of the two subregions of the **Côte d'Or** area of **Burgundy**. See **Aloxe-Corton**; **Auxey-Duresses**; **Beaune**; **Blagny**; **Chassagne-Montrachet**; **Chorey-lès-Beaune**; **Ladoix-Serrigny**; **Les Maranges**; **Meursault**; **Monthélie**; **Pernand-Vergelesses**; **Pommard**; **Saint-Aubin**; **Saint-Romain**; **Savigny-lès-Beaune**.

Côte de Beaune-Villages An AC wine from one or more of 16 villages in the **Côte de Beaune**. Producers can declassify from the more specific village *appellation*, if they want to blend wine from more than one village AC, or for commercial reasons, for instance if the village AC name is not well known. PRICE BAND: B–C.

Côte de Brouilly A red AC wine, one of the 10 **crus** of the **Beaujolais** region of **Burgundy**, made from the **Gamay** grape. The wine is full and perfumed, with juicy, ripe sweetness, and strawberry flavours. The quality is usually very good, among the best of all Beaujolais. PRICE BAND: B–C.

Côte de Nuits The northern of the two subregions of the **Côte d'Or** area of **Burgundy**. See

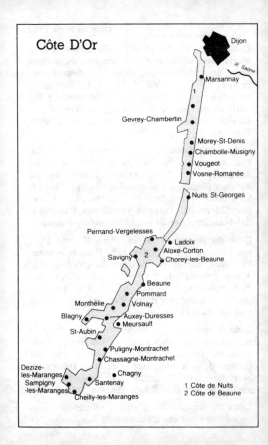

Côte D'Or

Dijon

R. Saône

Marsannay

1

Gevrey-Chambertin

Morey-St-Denis
Chambolle-Musigny
Vougeot
Vosne-Romanée

Nuits St-Georges

Pernand-Vergelesses

Ladoix
Aloxe-Corton
2
Savigny
Chorey-les-Beaune

Beaune
Pommard
Monthélie
Volnay
Blagny
Auxey-Duresses
Meursault
St-Aubin

Puligny-Montrachet
Chassagne-Montrachet

Dezize-
les-Maranges
Chagny
Sampigny
-les-Maranges
Santenay
Cheilly-les-Maranges

1 Côte de Nuits
2 Côte de Beaune

Fixin;   **Flagey-Echézeaux**;   **Gevrey-Chambertin**;
Marsannay; **Morey-St-Denis**; **Nuits-Saint-Georges**;
Vosne-Romanée; **Vougeot**.

Côte de Nuits-Villages   An AC wine of the **Côte
de Nuits** region of **Burgundy**, produced in the
villages of Brochon, Corgoloin, Comblanchien,
Prissey and **Fixin** (Fixin can also be sold under its
own AC). Most of the wine produced is good-value,
red Burgundy, from the **Pinot Noir** grape variety,
and is best drunk fairly young. PRICE BAND: B–D.

Côte des Blancs   A vineyard area in the **Champagne** region of **France**. It is planted almost
entirely with the white grape variety **Chardonnay**, hence the name.

Côte Rôtie   A red **AC** wine of the northern
Rhône, produced mainly from the **Syrah** grape
variety, with just a touch of the white **Viognier**.
At its best, the wine is scented, fine and
concentrated, with spicy, curranty fruit, capable
of long ageing. The two best slopes are Côte
Blonde and Côte Brune, occasionally vinified and
bottled separately. PRICE BAND: C–E.

coteau   A French term for a slope or hillside.

Coteaux Champenois   A still **AC** wine of the
Champagne region. It can be white, made from
the **Chardonnay** grape variety, or red, from **Pinot
Noir** and **Pinot Meunier**. Both wines are usually
rather thin, harsh and acidic. See also **Bouzy**.

Coteaux d'Aix-en-Provence   An **AC** wine of

Provence in southern **France**. The best wines are reds, made from the **Grenache** and **Syrah** grape varieties and, increasingly, **Cabernet Sauvignon**, rich and fruity, and capable of moderate ageing. Good fresh rosé is made from the same grape varieties. Small quantities of fairly neutral dry white wine are also made, from varieties including **Ugni Blanc**, **Sauvignon Blanc** and **Sémillon**. The subregion of Coteaux des Baux-en-Provence makes some high-quality red wines, mainly from **Grenache** and **Syrah**. PRICE BAND: A–C.

Coteaux d'Ancenis A VDQS wine of the **Loire** valley, mainly light-bodied red and rosé from the **Gamay** and **Cabernet Franc** grape varieties, plus a little sharp white from **Chenin Blanc** and **Pinot Gris**.

Coteaux de l'Aubance A white AC wine of the **Loire** valley, made from the **Chenin Blanc** grape. A delicate and medium-sweet wine, it is best drunk young. PRICE BAND: B.

Coteaux des Baux-en-Provence See Coteaux d'Aix-en-Provence.

Coteaux du Cap Corse See **Vin de Corse**.

Coteaux du Giennois A VDQS wine of the **Loire** valley. Dry, fairly acidic white is made from the **Sauvignon Blanc** and **Chenin Blanc** grape varieties; ordinary red and quite decent rosé are made from **Gamay** and **Pinot Noir**.

Coteaux du Languedoc An AC wine of the

Languedoc-Roussillon region of southern **France**. The region produces good, fresh, fruity red and rosé wines, from the **Carignan**, **Cinsault**, **Grenache**, **Syrah** and **Mourvèdre** grape varieties, among others. PRICE BAND: A.

Coteaux du Layon A sweet white **AC** wine produced in the **Anjou-Saumur** area of the **Loire** valley, made from the **Chenin Blanc** grape variety. The wine is sweet and fresh, and in exceptional years the grapes can be affected by **botrytis**. However, Coteaux du Layon seldom approaches the luscious richness of **Bonnezeaux** and **Quarts de Chaume**. Seven villages in Layon are entitled to the AC Côteaux du Layon-Villages: Beaulieu sur Layon; Chaume; Faye d'Anjou; Rablay sur Layon; Rochefort sur Loire; Saint Aubin de Luigné; and Saint Lambert de Lattay. They are one degree higher in alcohol, and have longer ageing potential. PRICE BAND: B.

Coteaux du Lyonnais An **AC** wine of **Burgundy**, produced in vineyards south of Lyon. Mostly red is produced, light, **Beaujolais**-like wine made from the **Gamay** grape variety. A little rosé is also produced from Gamay, plus a small amount of white, from **Chardonnay** and **Aligoté**.

Coteaux du Tricastin An **AC** wine of the southern **Rhône**. Mostly red and rosé wines are produced, from the **Grenache**, **Cinsault**, **Mourvèdre** and **Syrah** grape varieties. They are light,

fresh and fruity, for good-value early drinking.
Quality is steadily improving. A small amount of
white is made from **Bourboulenc** and **Marsanne**.
PRICE BAND: A–B.

Coteaux du Vendômois A **VDQS** wine of
the **Loire** region, produced along the banks of
the **Loir** tributary. Dry, quite austere white is
produced from the **Chenin Blanc** and **Chardonnay** grape varieties. Light, dry reds and rosés are
based on **Pineau d'Aunis** and **Gamay**, with the
possible addition of **Pinot Noir**, **Cabernet Sauvignon** and **Cabernet Franc** for the red.

Coteaux Varois A **VDQS** wine produced in
the **Provence** region of southern France. Light
reds and fresh, dry rosés are produced from the
Grenache, **Syrah**, **Mourvèdre** and **Cinsault** grape
varieties and, increasingly, **Cabernet Sauvignon**.
PRICE BAND: A–B.

Côtes d'Auvergne A **VDQS** wine produced
in vineyards near to Clermont-Ferrand, in the
upper **Loire** valley. Most of the production is of
red wine, light, fresh and **Beaujolais**-like, made
from the **Gamay** and **Pinot Noir** grape varieties.
Light, dry rosés are produced from the same
grape varieties. Virtually no white wine is
produced.

Côtes de Bergerac An **AC** wine of the
Bergerac region of southwest France. The red
wines are simply a higher-alcohol, lower-yield

version of red Bergerac. White Côtes de Bergerac is bigger and higher in alcohol than Bergerac Sec, and Côtes de Bergerac-Moelleux is the AC for the sweet whites of the region.

Côtes de Blaye A white **AC** wine of **Bordeaux**, produced on the east side of the Gironde estuary, facing the Haut-Médoc. Red Blaye comes under the AC of **Premières Côtes de Blaye**. The wine is light, softly fruity white, usually dry, made from the **Sauvignon Blanc** and **Sémillon** grape varieties, plus a touch of **Colombard**.

Côtes de Bourg An **AC** wine of **Bordeaux**, produced on the east side of the Gironde estuary, just south of the **Premières Côtes de Blaye**. Nearly all of the production is of red wine, from the classic Bordeaux grape varieties, **Cabernet Sauvignon**, **Cabernet Franc** and **Merlot**, with the emphasis on Merlot. These are fresh, fruity, easy-to-drink wines, best drunk relatively early. PRICE BAND: B.

Côtes de Castillon An **AC** wine of **Bordeaux**, produced in vineyards just to the east of **Saint-Emilion**. Nearly all of the production is red, from the classic Bordeaux grape varieties, **Cabernet Sauvignon**, **Cabernet Franc** and **Merlot**, with the emphasis on Merlot. These are fresh, fruity, easy-to-drink wines, best drunk relatively early. PRICE BAND: B.

Côtes de Duras An **AC** wine of southwest

France, just outside the **Bordeaux** area, and using much the same grape varieties. Good quality, fresh white wine is produced mainly from **Sauvignon Blanc**, plus some **Sémillon** and **Muscadelle**. Soft, fresh, good-value reds, best drunk young, are made from **Cabernet Sauvignon**, **Cabernet Franc** and **Merlot**. PRICE BAND: A.

Côtes de Francs   An **AC** wine of **Bordeaux**, produced in vineyards just to the east of **Saint-Emilion**. Nearly all of the production is of red wine, from the classic Bordeaux grape varieties, **Cabernet Sauvignon**, **Cabernet Franc** and **Merlot**, with the emphasis on Merlot. These are excellent, good-value wines, deep, fruity, with a good tannic backbone to provide structure and ageing potential. PRICE BAND: B.

Côtes de Gascogne   A **vin de pays** of southwest France, producing excellent, good-quality, good-value whites, particularly from the **Colombard** grape variety, as well as **Ugni Blanc** and **Sauvignon Blanc** whites. A small amount of rather thin red is also produced, from **Cabernet Sauvignon**, **Cabernet Franc**, **Merlot** and **Tannat**. PRICE BAND: A.

Côtes de Montravel   A sweet, white **AC** wine produced in the west of the **Bergerac** region, from the **Sauvignon Blanc**, **Sémillon** and **Muscadelle** grape varieties. It lacks the richness of the great sweet wines of **Bordeaux**, and is declining in popularity, so production is switching to dry wines.

Côtes de Provence An **AC** wine of **Provence** in southern **France**. Most of the production is of fresh, fruity, fairly full rosé wine, made mainly from the **Grenache** and **Cinsault** grape varieties, and fruity, herby reds based on **Mourvèdre**, **Syrah** and **Cabernet Sauvignon**, among others. Smaller quantities of rather dull white are made from **Sémillon**, **Rolle**, **Ugni Blanc** and **Clairette**. PRICE BAND: B–C.

Côtes de Saint-Mont A VDQS wine of southwest **France**. Good, light and fruity red (and a little rosé) wine is produced from the **Cabernet Sauvignon**, **Cabernet Franc**, **Merlot** and **Tannat** grape varieties. Dry white is made from the two **Manseng** varieties, plus Arrufiac and Petit Courbu. PRICE BAND: A.

Côtes du Forez A VDQS wine of the upper reaches of the **Loire** valley, not far from Lyon. Mainly red wine is produced from the **Gamay** grape variety, similar to a very pale version of **Beaujolais**.

Côtes du Frontonnais An **AC** wine produced near the town of Fronton in southwest **France**. Most of the production is of good-quality, fruity red wine, best drunk young, based on the **Négrette** grape variety, plus **Cabernet Franc** and **Cabernet Sauvignon**. A little rosé is produced from the same grape varieties.

Côtes du Jura An **AC** wine of the **Jura** region of eastern France. Most of the production is of white wine, based on the **Savagnin** and **Chardonnay** grape varieties. It can be still and dry, a **méthode champenoise** sparkler, or a **vin jaune**. A small amount of light red and rosé is produced from **Trousseau**, **Poulsard** and **Pinot Noir**. Wines from the subregion of **Arbois** show more distinction.

Côtes du Lubéron An **AC** wine of the southern **Rhône**. Lightweight reds and rosés, best drunk young, are produced from **Grenache**, **Syrah**, **Cinsault** and **Mourvèdre**. Fresh, fruity whites are based on **Ugni Blanc** and **Clairette**. PRICE BAND: A.

Côtes du Marmandais A **VDQS** wine of southwest **France**, mainly soft, fruity red from the classic **Bordeaux** grapes plus the local Abouriou and **Fer**, and a very small quantity of white, from **Sauvignon Blanc**, **Sémillon**, **Muscadelle** and **Ugni Blanc**. PRICE BAND: A.

Côtes du Rhône An **AC** wine of the **Rhône** region of France. This AC covers most of the Rhône's basic production, nearly all of it spicy, fruity red wine, based on the **Grenache**, **Syrah**, **Cinsault** and **Mourvèdre** grape varieties. Côtes du Rhône-Villages comes from one or more of 17 selected villages of the Southern Rhône, and generally has more depth and character to it. The villages are **Beaumes-de-Venise**, Cairanne,

Chusclan, **Laudun**, **Rasteau**, Roaix, Rochegude, Rousset-les-Vignes, Sablet, Saint-Gervais, Saint-Maurice-sur-Eygues, Saint-Pantaléon-les-Vignes, Séguret, Vacqueyras, Valréas, Vinsobres and Visan.

White Côtes du Rhône (and Côtes du Rhône-Villages) is produced from the **Clairette**, **Marsanne** and **Roussanne** grape varieties; it is rarely impressive. PRICE BAND: A–B.

Côtes du Roussillon An AC wine of the **Languedoc-Roussillon** area of southern **France**. Good-value, robust, fruity red and rosé, for early drinking, are made from the **Carignan**, **Cinsault**, **Grenache** and **Mourvèdre** grape varieties. A very small quantity of white is made, mainly from **Macabeo**. Red wines from selected sites, such as Caramany, are entitled to the Côtes du Roussillon-Villages AC, and they are usually superior. PRICE BAND: A.

Côtes du Ventoux An **AC** wine of the southern **Rhône**. Most of the production is of full-flavoured, fruity red made from the **Carignan**, **Cinsault**, **Grenache**, **Mourvèdre** and **Syrah** grape varieties. Only a tiny amount of white wine is produced. PRICE BAND: A–B.

Côtes du Vivarais A VDQS wine of the southern **Rhône**. Most of the production is of lively, fruity red (and some rosé) made from the **Grenache**, **Mourvèdre** and **Syrah** grape varieties. Only a tiny amount of white wine is produced.

Counoise See **Aubun**.

Courbu A minor white grape variety of **France**, used as part of the blend to make **Jurançon**.

Cramant An important wine-producing village in the **Côtes des Blancs** region of **Champagne**.

Cream Sherry A popular style of sweet **Sherry**, made by sweetening an **oloroso**. PRICE BAND: A–B. See also **Pale Cream**.

crémant The French term for a sparkling wine (particularly from **Alsace**, **Burgundy** and the **Loire**) or, in **Champagne**, a slightly less than fully sparkling wine.

Crémant d'Alsace A **méthode champenoise** sparkling **AC** wine from **Alsace**. It is usually white, based mainly on **Pinot Blanc**, sometimes with **Riesling** and **Auxerrois**. PRICE BAND: B.

Crémant de Bourgogne A **méthode champenoise** sparkling **AC** wine from **Burgundy**. It is made mainly from the **Chardonnay** grape variety, sometimes with **Aligoté** and **Pinot Noir**. Quality has improved a great deal lately, making this a good-value alternative to Champagne. Some good rosé is also made from Pinot Noir. PRICE BAND: B.

Crémant de Limoux See **Blanquette de Limoux**.

Crémant de Loire A **méthode champenoise** sparkling **AC** wine of the Loire. It is similar to sparkling **Saumur**, except that it can come from anywhere in the **Anjou** and **Touraine** regions, and permitted yields are lower: quality should therefore be better. Most of the production is white, based on the **Chenin Blanc**, **Chardonnay** and **Cabernet Franc** grape varieties. Some rosé is produced, from Cabernet Franc and **Gamay**. PRICE BAND: B–C.

Crépy   A white **AC** wine of the **Savoie** region of France. Very delicate white wine is produced, sometimes slightly **pétillant**, from the **Chasselas** grape. Rarely seen outside the region.

criadera   See **solera**; **Sherry**.

crianza   See **Rioja**.

Criolla   An alternative name, used in South America (particularly Argentina), for the **Mission** grape.

crisp   A tasting term, used to describe a pleasantly assertive, fresh wine, usually white, with a good level of balancing **acidity**.

Croatina   See **Bonarda**.

cross   A vine bred by crossing two vines of the same species, usually both **Vitis vinifera**. See also **hybrid**.

Crozes-Hermitage   An **AC** wine of the northern **Rhône**. The red wine is produced from the **Syrah** grape variety. Although not approaching the depth and complexity of **Hermitage**, it can be

excellent, with rich, spicy fruit flavours, and the capacity for moderate ageing. Delicately scented white Crozes, made from **Marsanne** and **Roussanne**, is at its best when drunk fresh and young.
PRICE BAND: A–C.

cru A French term, meaning literally 'growth', but usually referring to the quality and status of a particular vineyard site. See **cru bourgeois**; **cru classé**; **grand cru**.

cru bourgeois A classification of the **châteaux** of the **Médoc**, **Bordeaux**, at a level immediately below **cru classé**. The classification of the *crus classés* took place in 1855, and has scarcely altered since, so some of the best *crus bourgeois* now out-perform lesser classed growths.

cru classé The top classification of the **châteaux** of **Bordeaux**. There are five subdivisions: *premier grand cru classé* down to *cinquième cru classé*, referred to in English as 'first growth', 'second growth', and so on. See also **grand cru**.

Cruet See **Vin de Savoie**.

Crusted Port A blended **Port**, usually from two or three vintages. It is bottled at around four or six years old, without filtration, so that it develops a crust, or deposit, and therefore requires decanting. The only convincing approximation to the true Vintage Port style at a more moderate price.

cuvaison The French term for the period,

during the production of red wine, when grape skins are in contact with the fermenting **must**.

cuve The French term for a vat.

cuve close See **Charmat method**.

cuvée The French term, usually used rather loosely to indicate a particular lot of wine, or to refer to a blend. Thus, a producer might refer to his *prestige cuvée*, prepared from selected lots of especially good wine.

Cyprus An island wine-producing country with a long tradition of making table wines, **Commandaria** and so-called 'sherry'.

Dão An **RD** wine of northern **Portugal**, which may be red or white and is made from a large number of grape varieties. The reds must contain at least 20% of the **Touriga Nacional** grape and be aged for at least 18 months in cask and 2 months in bottle. They are firm, full-bodied, fruity and tannic in their youth. The Portuguese taste has traditionally been for more mature, sometimes over-mature, red wines. **Garrafeira** Dão must be aged at least two years in vat and one in bottle, although this period is often exceeded.

The whites must contain at least 20% of the Encruzado grape, and must be aged six months before bottling. They have good acidity and an attractive lemony aroma in their youth. *Garrafeira* whites must be aged for at least six months in vat and six in bottle, developing a rich, honeyed character. Overall quality is improving steadily, and the potential is very good. PRICE BAND: A.

Debina A white grape variety native to **Greece**, which produces the light, crisp, sparkling or semi-sparkling wines of **Zitsa**.

débourbage The process of clearing a white **must** of solid matter before **fermentation**. This can be done by cooling the must and adding **sulphur dioxide**, or by using a centrifuge.

decanting The process of transferring a wine from its bottle to another vessel, usually a glass decanter. The main purpose is to separate the wine from its sediment, particularly important with mature **Vintage Port** and old red wines, including red **Bordeaux**. Younger red wines may also be decanted, in order to aerate them and so help to bring out the aroma and taste.

deep A tasting term which describes the intensity of a wine's colour, aroma and taste.

dégorgement The removal of the sediment that develops during secondary fermentation in bottle, as in the case of **Champagne** and other **méthode champenoise** sparkling wines. After **remuage**, the sediment is concentrated near the mouth of the bottle. The top of the bottle is plunged into chilled brine so that the wine and sediment in the neck freeze. The crown cork is then removed, and the plug of frozen wine and sediment flies out.

dégustation The French term for wine tasting.

Deidesheim A small town in the **Rheinpfalz** region of Germany, which produces high-quality, full-bodied white wines from the **Riesling** grape. There are three **Grosslagen**: Hofstück, Mariengarten and Schnepfenflug an der Weinstrasse. The top **Einzellagen** include Grainhübel, Leinhöhle, Herrgottsacker, Kieselberg and Langenmorgen, and all these are in Mariengarten.

demi-sec The French term for a medium-dry wine.

denominación de origen See **DO**.

denominazione di origine controllata (e garantita) See **DOC** and **DOCG**.

dessert wine A term loosely used to describe sweet, usually white wines, such as **Sauternes**, late-harvest wines from **Germany**, **Austria**, **California** and **Australia**, and **vins doux naturels**. In fact the term is misleading. Sauternes, for instance, is better enjoyed as an apéritif, with foie gras, salty blue cheese, or drunk on its own after a meal, but is rarely at its best with a sweet dessert.

Deutscher Sekt See **Sekt**.

Deutscher Tafelwein A table wine from **Germany**, in a quality category below **QbA**. The wine must be made entirely from grapes grown in Germany, with a minimum **alcohol content** of 8.5%. The wine may be labelled with one of four district names: Rhein-Mosel (subdistricts Rhein, Mosel and Saar); Bayern (subdistricts Main, Donau, and Lindau), Neckar and Oberrhein (subdistricts Römertor and Burgengau). **Tafelwein** (without the Deutscher) can include wine from other countries (often Italy). See also **Landwein**.

developed A tasting term that describes the state of maturity of a wine. A young wine could be described as 'underdeveloped', a mature wine as 'well-developed' and an over-mature wine as 'overdeveloped'.

disgorging See **dégorgement**.

Dizy A village in the **Valleé de la Marne** region of **Champagne**, France. Its vineyards, mainly planted with the **Pinot Noir** grape, are rated 95%.

DO The guarantee of origin used for Spanish wines, roughly equivalent to the French **AC** system. For each DO region the laws specify the delimited area from which the wines may come, permitted grape varieties, permitted vineyard practices, and ageing requirements. The laws are enforced by the DO region's **consejo regulador**, which monitors production and movement of wines within the region. Wines are analysed and tasted before qualifying for the DO.

DOC (denominazione di origine controllata) The guarantee of origin used for Italian wines, roughly equivalent to the French **AC** system. For each DOC region, of which there are more than 200, the laws specify the delimited area from which the wines may come, permitted grape varieties, permitted vineyard practices, and ageing requirements. Although the DOC laws encourage quality they do not guarantee it; many top wines fall outside its specifications, qualifying only as **vini da tavola**.

DOCG (denominazione di origine controllata e garantita) The highest category used for the wines of **Italy**, so far only awarded to **Albana di Romagna**, **Barolo**, **Barbaresco**, **Brunello di Montalcino**, **Carmignano**, **Chianti**, **Gattinara**, **Torgiano** Rosso Riserva and **Vino Nobile di Montepulciano**. The wines are analysed and assessed by a tasting panel before qualifying for the DOCG. In the case of Chianti, for instance, elevation from **DOC** to DOCG involved a change in the permitted mix of grape varieties and lower yields.

dolce A term found on Italian labels meaning sweet. Sweeter than **amabile** or **abboccato**.

Dolcetto A red grape variety of the **Piedmont** region of Italy. It produces deep-coloured, easy-drinking, dry wines, usually of good quality.

There are seven **DOC** zones. The best are Dolcetto d'Alba and Dolcetto di Diano d'Alba, deep, balanced and smooth. Dolcetto di Dogliani and di Ovada are also firm and structured, while Dolcetto d'Asti, delle Langhe Monregalesi and d'Acqui are more lightweight. PRICE BAND: B.

Dôle A red wine of good quality made in the Valais region of **Switzerland**, from the **Pinot Noir** and **Gamay** grapes. PRICE BAND: B.

domaine The French term for a wine estate, used particularly in **Burgundy**.

Donnaz A dry, red **DOC** wine from the **Valle d'Aosta** region of northwest Italy, made from the **Nebbiolo** grape. It is usually lighter than Nebbiolo from **Piedmont**, but is still capable of moderate ageing. Above average quality, but rarely exported.

Donnici A dry, red **DOC** wine from the hills around Cosenza in the **Calabria** region of southern Italy, made from the **Gaglioppo** and Greco Nero grapes. It is usually light red, fruity and flavoursome, and is best drunk while young and fresh.

Dornfelder A red grape variety produced from a crossing of Helfensteiner and Heroldrebe (each of which is also a crossing), grown mainly in the **Rheinpfalz** and **Rheinhessen** regions of Germany. It produces deep-coloured (for Germany) red wines, with good fruit and acidity, with some ageing potential. One of Germany's most promising new red varieties.

Dorsheim   A village near **Bingen** in the **Nahe** region of Germany, in the **Bereich** of **Kreuznach**, and the **Grosslage** of Schlosskapelle. It produces excellent, full-bodied white wines of high quality from the **Riesling** grape. The steep Goldloch vineyard is probably the best **Einzellage**.

dosage   The French term for the sweetness added to **Champagne** and other **méthode champenoise** wines after the second, fizz-producing fermentation, in the form of the **liqueur d'expedition**. Without *dosage* the wine is bone dry and labelled *ultra brut* or *zero brut*. Depending on how much sweetness is added, the wine is labelled **brut**, extra dry, **sec** or **demi-sec**. Most Champagne is sold as *brut*.

double magnum   A large format bottle with a capacity of 3 litres (equivalent to four standard bottles of 75 cl). Known as a **jeroboam** in Champagne.

Douro   A river in northern **Portugal**, which rises in Spain as the Duero and enters the sea at Vila Nova de Gaia. The grapes for **Port** are grown in the steep valleys of the river and its tributaries. The river also gives its name to dry red (and some white) **RD** table wines. The reds tend to be rich and tannic, needing relatively long ageing and can be of a very good quality.
PRICE BAND: A–E.

dry A tasting term, also found on labels, to describe a wine in which no sweetness is detectable on the palate. See also **residual sugar**.

Dry Creek Valley An **AVA** in **Sonoma** county, California.

dulce 1. A term used in Spain to describe a wine that is sweeter than **semi-seco**. 2. A wine used to give sweetness in the blended **Pale Cream** and **Cream** styles of **Sherry**.

Duras A red grape grown mainly in the Tarn region of southwest France. It is used, together with **Fer** and **Négrette**, to make **Gaillac Rouge**, a fruity red wine of moderately good quality. The grape has no connection with the **Côtes de Duras**.

Echézeaux A **grand cru** vineyard of the commune of **Flagey-Echézeaux** in the **Côte de Nuits** region of **Burgundy**. It produces among the finest and most elegant of the region's red wines from the **Pinot Noir** grape. Although technically attached to Flagey-Echézeaux, the vineyard is nearer to **Vosne-Romanée**, and the wines can be declassified to Vosne-Romanée **premier cru**. Quality is good, but generally not as good as the smaller, neighbouring **Grands-Echézeaux**, or the other *grand cru* vineyards of the Côte de Nuits. PRICE BAND: E.

Edelfäule The German term for **botrytis**.

Edelzwicker A blended wine from the **AC**

region **Alsace**. The best grape varieties in Alsace are nearly always bottled and labelled as **varietals**. Edelzwicker tends to be a blend of the less-renowned varieties such as **Chasselas**, **Pinot Blanc** and **Silvaner**. A supermarket wine labelled simply 'AC Alsace' will generally be a similar sort of blend, but it might not bear the word Edelzwicker on the label. Quality and value for money are usually good. PRICE BAND: A.

Eden Valley A region in the north of the **Adelaide Hills** area of **Australia**, where fine **varietal** wines are made from the **Riesling**, **Gewürztraminer**, **Shiraz** and **Cabernet Sauvignon** grapes. Eden Valley Rhine Rieslings are probably Australia's finest wines from that variety.

Edna Valley An **AVA** of **San Luis Obispo** county, **California**, with a growing reputation for its cool-climate white wines, particularly **Chardonnay**.

égrappoir A French term for a machine that separates grapes from their stems. Red wines can be fermented with or without their stems. The stems can add **tannin** to the wine, but also toughness and bitterness, and many quality red wines are today vinified without them. See also **fouloir**.

Ehrenfelser A white grape variety, which is a **cross** between **Riesling** and **Silvaner**, planted mainly in northern Germany. It ripens earlier than Riesling, and produces higher **must weights**

and yields. One of the most promising Riesling-Silvaner crosses.

Einzellage A term used in **German** wine law to indicate an individual vineyard site. The boundaries and names are officially defined, and the names of *Einzellagen* can be used only on quality wines. *Einzellagen* are often large and divided among numerous growers. See also **QbA**; **QmP**.

Eisacktaler The German name for **Valle Iscaro**.

Eiswein A German and Austrian quality white wine category meaning 'ice wine'. The minimum **must weight** is the same as for **Beerenauslese** wines, but the grapes are not affected by **botrytis**. The grapes are left on the vine after the normal harvesting date, sometimes as late as Christmas or even January, in the hope that the temperature will fall so low that the water in the grapes freezes, leaving the sugar and acid unfrozen. The grapes are then quickly pressed, leaving their water content as ice, and yielding juice that will produce sweet, luscious, long-lived wines with high acidity. See **QmP**.

Elba A **DOC** wine from the island of Elba, just off the coast of **Tuscany**, Italy. The red is made from the same grapes as **Chianti**, and is usually a light wine for early drinking. The whites, made mainly from the **Trebbiano** grape, are dry and full-bodied with a crisp finish. A sparkling,

spumante white is also made. The sweet, red dessert wine **Aleatico** is also made on Elba.

Elbling An ancient white grape variety planted in the **Mosel** region of Germany. It is used to make still **varietal** wines and is occasionally used in the production of **sekt**. Elbling is also found in **Luxembourg**, where it is the second most-planted variety, producing thin, tart wine, sometimes sparkling.

Emilia-Romagna A wine region just north of **Tuscany**, in central Italy. The most famous **DOC** wine from this region is the sparkling **Lambrusco**, which can be red, white, or pink, dry or sweet, sparkling or semi-sparkling. White wines include **Albana di Romagna**, Italy's first white **DOCG** wine, and the DOC wine **Trebbiano di Romagna**. Reds include the DOC Sangiovese di Romagna. See also **Bianco di Scandiano**; **Colli Bolognesi**; **Colli di Parma**; **Colli Piacentini**.

Enfer d'Arvier A dry, red **DOC** wine of the **Valle d'Aosta** region in northwest Italy, made from the Petit Rouge grape. The wine, produced in tiny quantities, is dark red with a rich, grapey smell and taste. It improves with moderate bottle age.

England A modern wine-producing country since the 1950s. Most of the vineyards are planted in the south of the country, in the counties of Kent, Sussex, Hampshire, Surrey, Somerset, Norfolk and Suffolk, and on the Isle of

Wight. Viticulture and winemaking follows the German model.

The majority of wines produced are white, from grape varieties such as **Müller-Thurgau**, **Seyval Blanc**, **Huxelrebe**, **Schönburger**, **Reichensteiner** and **Bacchus**. As in Germany, **süssreserve** is often added to the wines to round them out before bottling, but even so they are often hard and acidic. Red and rosé wines are less common, because of the difficulties of ripening in England's relatively short, cool summer. Some encouraging results have been achieved with **Pinot Noir**, as well as Triomphe d'Alsace and Leon Millot.

A handful of producers make sparkling **méthode champenoise** wines, and these can be among the best wines that England produces.

English wine A wine made from grapes grown out-of-doors in England. Not to be confused with **British wine**, which is made in Britain from imported grape concentrates or powders.

Enkirch A village of the **Mittelmosel** in the **Mosel-Saar-Ruwer** region of Germany. It comes within the **Grosslage** of Schwarzlay and the best **Einzellagen** are Steffensberg and Herrenberg.

Entre-Deux-Mers A white **AC** wine of **Bordeaux**, produced in the region between the rivers Dordogne and Garonne. It is made from the **Sauvignon Blanc** grape, either alone or blended with **Sémillon**, and is usually bone dry, crisp and flavoursome. Quality is increasingly good, and the wines are usually good value for money. Generally the wines should be drunk as young as possible, although new, oak-aged versions may have some ageing potential. Many Entre-Deux-Mers properties also make red wine, which is sold as AC Bordeaux. PRICE BAND: A–B.

Epineuil A red **AC** wine made near **Chablis** in the north of **Burgundy**, from the **Pinot Noir** grape. It is a light, fragrant red, but produced in very small quantities.

Erbach A village in the **Rheingau** region of Germany, in the **Grosslage** of Deutelsberg. It produces powerful, firm, scented white wines of excellent quality from the **Riesling** grape. The most famous **Einzellage** vineyard is Marcobrunn, and others of repute include Schlossberg, Siegelsberg, Honigberg, Michelmark, Steinmorgen and Hohenrain.

Erbaluce di Caluso A **DOC** wine made around Caluso in the **Piedmont** region of Italy. The dry white, made from the Erbaluce grape, is light and creamy with good acidity, and should be drunk young. It is a good quality wine and good value for money.

Caluso Passito is a sweet, golden-coloured wine also made from Erbaluce grapes, which have been dried before pressing (see **passito**); it can also be **fortified**.

Erden A village of the **Mittelmosel**, in the

Mosel-Saar-Ruwer region of Germany, in the **Grosslage** of Schwarzlay. It produces spicy, vigorous white wines, mainly from the **Riesling** grape. The best **Einzellage** vineyards include Treppchen, Prälat and Herrenberg.

erzeugerabfüllung   A German term that literally means 'bottled by the producer' (**estate bottled**), but it may also be used by co-operative cellars.

espumoso   The Spanish for sparkling wine. See also **Cava**.

Est! Est!! Est!!! di Montefiascone   A white **DOC** wine from around Lake Bolsena in the **Latium** region of Italy, made from the **Trebbiano** and **Malvasia** grapes. It is usually dry, but can be medium dry. Quality is variable, but the best examples have an attractive crisp, fruity, almond taste. PRICE BAND: A.

Estaing   A **VDQS** wine from the Lot valley in southwest **France**, just east of **Cahors**. Red and white wines are made in extremely small quantities, the reds from **Gamay**, **Cabernet Franc** and **Fer Servadou** grapes, the whites from **Chenin Blanc** and **Mauzac Blanc**.

estate bottled   A term used to indicate that a wine has been bottled on the estate where the grapes were grown. In theory it should guarantee authenticity.

estufa   The oven in which **Madeira** wine is

'cooked' at about 45°C. The cooking process is called *estufagem*.

ethanol See **alcohol**.

Etna A **DOC** wine from the slopes of Mount Etna in **Sicily**. Most of the production is of deep, fruity, full-bodied reds, made from the **Nerello** Mascalese grape, which is also used to make **rosato** wines. The **bianco**, made from the Carricante and **Catarratto** grapes, is dry, light and delicate; *bianco superiore* is distinctly better.

L'Etoile An **AC** wine of the **Jura** region of France. Most of the production is of light, fruity white wine, which may be made sparkling by the **méthode champenoise**, from the **Savagnin** and **Chardonnay** grapes, sometimes with the addition of the dark **Poulsard** grape. **Vin jaune** is also produced within the *appellation* from the Savagnin grape alone.

extract 1. The soluble solids (other than sugar) found in wine, which contribute to its **body** and structure. 2. In tasting, a wine with good body and structure might be described as having good or high extract.

extra sec A term found on **Champagne** labels, indicating a wine drier than **sec** but not as dry as **brut**.

Extremadura A region of western Spain, along the border with Portugal, which produces a large quantity of wine of very low quality. Little is bottled as wine and much of it is distilled into brandy.

Faber A white grape variety, a **cross** of **Pinot Blanc** and **Müller-Thurgau**, planted mainly in the **Rheinhessen** and **Nahe** regions of Germany. It is an early ripener, earlier even than Müller-Thurgau, and with more fruit and a higher **must weight** and **acidity**. It can grow well on nearly any soil and will ripen on sites where **Riesling** will not. Faber produces good, fruity wines with Riesling-like character, although it is often used for blending.

Falerio dei Colli Asolani A dry, white **DOC** wine grown in the hills between Ascoli Piceno and the coast in the **Marches** region of Italy. The wine is produced from the **Trebbiano** grape and is light and fairly neutral with good **acidity**. It is best drunk young.

Falerno A dry table wine from the **Latium** and **Campania** regions of Italy. The red is made from the **Aglianico** grape variety, grown around Mondragone in Campania, and Formia, Gaeta and Fondi in Latium (where it may also contain **Barbera**). The red is fruity and full-bodied. The white, in both regions, is produced from the Falanghina grape, but is rarely very good. The name Falerno derives from Falernum, the celebrated wine of ancient Rome.

Fara A dry, red **DOC** wine grown in the Novarra hills in the **Piedmont** region of Italy, made from the **Nebbiolo**, **Bonarda** and Vespolina grape varieties. It is a full-bodied and perfumed wine which can age well for 5 to 10 years.

Fargues One of the villages entitled to the **AC** of **Sauternes**.

Faro A dry, red **DOC** wine produced around Messina, **Sicily**, from the **Nerello** Mascalese grape. It is capable of very good quality, with fine aromas, but sadly very little is made.

fattoria The Italian for a farm or estate, commonly used in **Tuscany**.

Faugères A dry, red wine grown just north of Béziers in the **Languedoc-Roussillon** region of France. It is made from the **Carignan**, **Grenache**, **Cinsault** and **Syrah** grape varieties. The wine is a deep, beefy, plummy red, and should generally be drunk young. Quality is good, and improving. Formerly it was an **AC** wine in its own right, but now it is a **cru** of the **Coteaux du Languedoc** AC. There is a small amount of white made from the **Clairette**, **Bourboulenc**, **Grenache** Blanc and **Marsanne** grapes. PRICE BAND: A.

Favorita A dry white wine grown in the Roeri and Langhe hills in **Piedmont**, Italy, made from the grape variety of the same name. Light, crisp and high in **acidity**, the best examples have some complexity. PRICE BAND: B.

Fendant See **Chasselas**.

Fer (also called **Fer-Servadou**) A red grape variety of good quality and colour, which is used in the wines of **Béarn**, Entraygues, **Estaing**, **Gaillac**, **Madiran**, **Marcillac**.

fermentation The process whereby grape sugar is converted into **alcohol** and **carbon dioxide** by the action of enzymes produced by yeast. This is accompanied by many other chemical transformations. Heat is a by-product. For dry wines, the process is allowed to continue until all the sugar has been turned into alcohol. If the initial level of grape sugar is very high, fermentation may stop naturally before all the sugar has been converted, and a sweet wine is the result. The fermentation of **fortified** wines, such as **Port**, is stopped prematurely by the addition of alcohol in the form of grape spirit. See also **malolactic fermentation**.

Fernão Pires (also called **Maria Gomez**) A white grape variety grown throughout **Portugal** producing aromatic, peppery white wines. It is grown in Arruda dos Vinhos, Alenquer, Torres Vedras, the **Douro**, **Alentejo** and **Bairrada** (where it is known as Maria Gomez).

Fiano di Avellino A dry white **DOC** wine grown around the Avellino hills near Naples in the **Campania** region of Italy, made from the Fiano grape. At its best the wine is light coloured, with an aroma of nuts and pears, a smooth taste and a lingering finish, but quality varies enormously. The subdenomination of Fiano di Lapiano is considered superior. PRICE BAND: E.

fiasco The Italian term for flask, used to refer to the traditional wicker-covered bottle, which was once commonly used for **Chianti**. There is still a demand for *fiaschi*, mainly from restaurants, but most serious Chianti is now sold in conventional bottles.

Fiddletown An **AVA** within **Amador County**, California, which produces mainly rich, red **varietal** wines from the **Zinfandel** grape.

Fiefs Vendéens A **VDQS** wine grown in four locations, Mareuil, Brem, Vix and Pissotte, in the Vendée *département* of the **Loire** region of France. The name of the location must appear on the label. The fresh, light red and rosé wines are made from at least 50% of **Gamay** and/or **Pinot Noir** grape varieties, and **Cabernet Sauvignon**, **Cabernet Franc** and **Négrette** are also permitted.

The less-common white wine must be at least 50% from the **Chenin Blanc** grape, plus **Sauvignon Blanc** and **Chardonnay**. In Vix and Pissotte, up to 20% of **Melon de Bourgogne** grape is allowed, and Groslot (**Grolleau**) can be included in the white and rosé wines of Brem.

Figari See **Vin de Corse**.

Finger Lakes The main wine-producing region

of **New York State**. Originally the area was planted with native varieties, but recently more **Vitis vinifera** grape varieties have been planted, including **Chardonnay**, **Riesling** and **Gewürztraminer**, which produce mainly sparkling wines.

fining A clarification process whereby any solids in a wine are removed. A substance, such as isinglass, geltine, casein, dried blood, egg whites or clay (bentonite), is added to the wine, in cask or vat, causing suspended solids to fall to the bottom. The clear wine can then be removed, leaving the solids behind. See also **racking**.

finish A tasting term used to describe the intensity and nature of the final taste sensation once a wine is swallowed (or spat out). A 'long finish', where the taste persists for some moments, is a hallmark of a well-balanced wine. See also **aftertaste**.

fino A pale, bone dry, pungent **Sherry**, made mainly from the **Palomino** grape variety. Its distinctive, tangy aroma and flavour are the result of ageing the wine in the **solera** system under a layer of yeast cells called **flor**. The flor protects the wine from oxygen, and feeds on **alcohol** and **acidity**, producing **acetaldehyde**, which is partly responsible for a *fino*'s distinctive taste. A *fino* from Jerez or Puerto de Santa Maria must spend at least three years in the *solera* system before bottling. *Fino* from Sanlúcar de Barrameda is called **manzanilla**.

Once opened, a bottle of *fino* should be consumed as quickly as any other white wine. *Fino*, served correctly chilled, is one of the best apéritifs of all, and excellent with seafood or tapas. Quality is usually at least very good, and the wine is underpriced. PRICE BAND: B.

firm A tasting term that describes a wine which is structured, with a positive taste in the mouth. See also **flabby**.

first growth See **premier cru**.

Fitou A dry, red **AC** wine of the **Languedoc-Roussillon** region of France (neighbouring **Corbières**), made from at least 70% of the **Carignan** grape, plus **Grenache** and **Cinsault**. The wine is dark red, sturdy and fruity, and good value for money. However, the quality has dropped because producers have struggled to keep up with the demand. PRICE BAND: A.

Fixin A village and **AC** wine at the northern end of the **Côte de Nuits** in **Burgundy**. It produces almost entirely red wine from the **Pinot Noir** grape. The best wines, sturdy, deep, strong reds, are from the **premiers crus**, especially La Perrière and Clos du Chapitre, but they do not reach the heights of the great wines from farther south in the Côte de Nuits.

The wine from the of the village Fixin, which can be very light bodied, may also be sold as **Côte de Nuits-Villages**. The best white Fixin, which is lively and vivacious, is made from the **Pinot Blanc** grape. PRICE BAND: C–D.

flabby A tasting term used to describe a poor wine, which lacks structure and definition and has little **acidity**. See also **firm**.

Flagey-Echézeaux A village in the **Côte de Nuits**, **Burgundy**, whose red wines, made from the **Pinot Noir** grape, are sold under the **AC** of **Vosne-Romanée**. Technically, Flagey contains the **grand cru** *appellations* Echézeaux and Grands-Echézeaux, although in fact they are nearer to Vosne-Romanée.

Fleurie A red **AC** wine, one of the 10 **crus** of the **Beaujolais** region of **Burgundy**, made from the **Gamay** grape. The wine is perfumed, with juicy, ripe sweetness, and cherry and chocolate flavours. The quality is usually very good and it is among the best of all Beaujolais. PRICE BAND: B.

flinty A tasting term usually used to describe the aroma of a white wine. Whites made from the **Sauvignon Blanc** grape are sometimes described as having a gunflint aroma.

Floc de Gascogne An apéritif, technically a **mistelle** rather than a wine, made from unfermented grape juice and Armagnac. It is sweet, grapey and aromatic, and best served chilled. See also **Pineau des Charentes**; **ratafia**.

flor The thick layer of yeast cells that develops

on the **fino** and **manzanilla** styles of **Sherry** while they are maturing. The *flor* protects the wine from oxygen, reduces the **alcohol** and **acidity**, and gives the Sherry its distinctive tangy aroma and taste.

Folle Blanche (also called **Gros Plant**) A white grape variety, once important for the production of brandy in Cognac and Armagnac (where it is known as **Picpoule**), but today it has been largely replaced by **Ugni Blanc**. Most Folle Blanche in France is now found at the western end of the **Loire** valley, near Nantes, where it is called Gros Plant. It produces a dry, thin, tart, very acidic wine. There is also a small amount planted in **California**, particularly in San Benito county, where it is used mainly as a blending wine, to add **acidity**, and also in sparkling wine production.

Forst An important wine-producing village in the **Rheinpfalz** region of Germany, incorporating the **Grosslagen** of Schnepfenflug and Mariengarten. It produces some of the region's finest white wines from the **Riesling** grape. The wines are full-bodied and richly fragrant, but with great elegance, which is said to derive from the black basalt in the soil. The most important **Einzellage** vineyards are Bischofsgarten, Jesuitengarten, Kirchenstück and Ungeheuer.

fortified wine A wine to which brandy, or neutral grape spirit, has been added. In the case of **Port**, spirit is added to stop **fermentation** prematurely, before all the grape sugar has been turned into alcohol. In the case of **Sherry**, the wine is fortified after fermentation. See also **Madeira**; **Marsala**; **vin doux naturel**.

foudre The French term for a wooden barrel of unspecified size, but invariably larger than a **barrique** of 225 litres.

fouloir A French term for a machine, used in making red wines, that gently breaks the skins of the grapes, before they go into the **fermentation** vat. The same machine sometimes incorporates an **égrappoir**, which removes the stems from the grapes.

Fourchaume A **premier cru** vineyard of **Chablis**.

Fourneaux A **premier cru** vineyard of **Chablis**.

foxy A tasting term that describes the earthy flavour of wine made from native American grapes (i.e. not **Vitis vinifera**). It does not imply the smell or taste of the animal, but refers to wild, or 'fox' grapes.

France Probably the most important wine-producing country of the world, producing a huge range of styles and qualities. There are fine reds based on **Cabernet Sauvignon** from **Bordeaux**, and this region also produces **Sauternes**, perhaps the world's greatest sweet white wine.

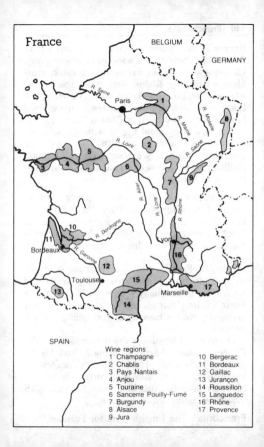

France

BELGIUM

GERMANY

R Seine

Paris

R Marne

R Moselle

R Loire

R Seine

R Allier

R Loire

R Rhône

R Dordogne

R Garonne

Bordeaux

yor

Toulouse

Marseille

SPAIN

Wine regions

1 Champagne
2 Chablis
3 Pays Nantais
4 Anjou
5 Touraine
6 Sancerre Pouilly-Fumé
7 Burgundy
8 Alsace
9 Jura

10 Bergerac
11 Bordeaux
12 Gaillac
13 Jurançon
14 Roussillon
15 Languedoc
16 Rhône
17 Provence

Burgundy is capable of great reds and whites from **Pinot Noir** and **Chardonnay** respectively. **Champagne** produces the world's greatest sparkling wines; the **Rhône** distinctive, spicy reds; **Alsace**, fragrant, superlative white **varietals**; the **Loire**, dry whites from **Sauvignon Blanc**, and luscious sweet wines from **Chenin Blanc**.

The quality pyramid begins with **vin de table**, followed by **vin de pays**, **VDQS** and **AC** (see individual entries). See also **Bergerac**; **Cahors**; **Gaillac**; **Jura**; **Jurançon**; **Languedoc-Roussillon**; **Provence**; **Savoie**.

Franciacorta A **DOC** wine grown around Cortefranca in **Lombardy**, Italy. Pinot Bianco di Franciacorta is a still white wine made from the **Pinot Bianco** grape. It is smooth, fruity and well-balanced, and is best drunk within two to three years. PRICE BAND: B.

Pinot di Franciacorta is a sparkling white or rosé, made from **Pinot Nero**, **Pinot Grigio** and sometimes **Chardonnay** grapes. It is one of the finest of Italy's sparkling wines, and the best examples rival **Champagne** for quality. PRICE BAND: E.

Franciacorta Rosso is a dry red, made from the **Cabernet Franc**, **Barbera**, **Nebbiolo** and **Merlot** grapes. It is also of good quality; somewhat tough in its youth, with blackcurrant aromas, it becomes smooth, rounded, and fragrant with moderate ageing. PRICE BAND: B.

Franconia The English term for **Franken**.

Franken An important wine-producing region of **Germany**, one of the 11 **Anbaugebiet** areas, centred on Würzburg in northern Bavaria. The wines are almost all dry, full-bodied whites, mainly from the **Silvaner** and **Müller-Thurgau** grapes. Even the **Spätlese** and **Auslese** styles, while broader and more robust, are still essentially dry. There are three **Bereich** subregions, **Mainviereck**, **Maindreieck** and Steigerwald.

The wines of Franken have traditionally been sold in the **bocksbeutel**, a squat, flagon-shaped bottle of green glass. PRICE BAND: B–C.

Frascati A white **DOC** wine grown around the towns of Frascati, Grottaferrata and Monteporizio Catone in the hills above Rome, in the Latium region of Italy. It is made largely from the **Trebbiano** and **Malvasia** grapes, and should be crisp, fresh, dry to off-dry, with soft, smooth fruit and a nutty flavour. Sweeter **amabile** Frascati is rare and **spumante** Frascati is rarer still. Quality is variable, but from the best producers it can be very good. PRICE BAND: A–B.

French Colombard See **Colombard**.

fresh A tasting term used to describe a wine with youthful charm, vigour and vibrancy, often marked by **acidity**.

Friuli-Venezia Giulia A region of northeast **Italy**, which has led the Italian white-wine revolution. The combination of an Alpine and Adriatic climate gives rise to a remarkably even growing season. The **DOC** regions are **Aquileia**, **Colli Orientali del Friuli**, **Collio**, **Grave del Friuli**, **Isonzo** and **Latisana**. Each **DOC** produces a wide range of red and white **varietal** wines.

Native white grape varieties include **Tocai Friulano**, **Verduzzo Friulano**, **Ribolla**, **Malvasia** and **Picolit**, but there are extensive plantings of 'foreign' white varieties including **Müller-Thurgau**, **Pinot Bianco**, **Pinot Grigio**, **Riesling Renano**, **Sauvignon** and **Traminer**. Generally most are best drunk young.

Although it is most famous for its whites, Friuli actually produces more red wine, again for drinking young, and mainly from **Merlot**, **Cabernet Franc** and **Refosco** grapes.

frizzante The Italian term for a wine that is lightly effervescent, but not sufficiently sparkling to be labelled **spumante**. See also **pétillant**.

Fronsac An **AC** wine of **Bordeaux**, grown in an attractive hilly area west of **Saint-Emilion**. It produces chunky, deep red-coloured wines, which are well-flavoured, tannic and require some bottle age. The main grape varieties are **Cabernet Franc**, **Cabernet Sauvignon**, **Merlot** and **Malbec**. Quality is improving and the wines deserve to be better known. PRICE BAND: B–C. See also **Canon-Fronsac**.

Frontignan An alternative name for the **Muscat** Blanc à Petits Grains grape. See also **Muscat de Frontignan**.

Fronton See **Côtes du Frontonnais**.

fruity A tasting term used to describe the attractive flavour of a wine made from ripe grapes, which can be reminiscent of a wide range of citrus fruits, red fruits, berries and currants. See also **grapey**.

full A tasting term that describes a wine that is mouth-filling and flavoursome, owing to a high **alcohol** and **extract** content.

Fumé Blanc An alternative term for wines made from the **Sauvignon Blanc** grape, used in Australia and California. It originates from California, where it was used to make wines from this variety seem more fashionable, through association with **Pouilly-Fumé**, and to differentiate them from California's medium-sweet Sauvignon Blanc **varietals**. Today it usually implies an oak-aged Sauvignon Blanc.

Fumé de Pouilly See **Pouilly-Fumé**.

Furmint A white grape variety of **Hungary** used to make the distinctive sweet wines of **Tokaji**, and tart, dry white wines elsewhere in Hungary. It is susceptible to **botrytis**, which is an important factor in making **Tokaji Aszú**.

fût The French term for a small barrel of unspecified size. The claim *elevé en fûts de chêne* (matured in oak barrels) is increasingly found on labels, as a fashionable selling point. See also **barrique**.

Gaglioppo An Italian red grape variety that produces concentrated, deep wines mainly in **Calabria** (where it is used to make **Cirò**), and also in **Abruzzi**, **Campania**, the **Marches** and **Umbria**.

Gaillac An **AC** wine region in the Tarn *département* near Albi, southwest **France**. It produces red, white (still and sparkling) and rosé wines. The still whites, dry or medium-sweet, are somewhat sharp and apple-flavoured, and based on the **Mauzac Blanc** grape, together with l'En de l'El, Ondenc, **Sauvignon Blanc**, **Sémillon** and **Muscadelle**. The reds are sharp and peppery and for drinking young. They are based on the **Duras** grape, together with several other varieties including **Fer**, **Négrette** and **Gamay**. They are rarely very good. Nor is Gaillac Rosé, made mainly from Gamay and **Syrah**.

The star of the region is the sparkling wine, Gaillac Mousseaux, also based on the Mauzac grape, and produced either by the **méthode champenoise**, or by a local method in which the first fermentation is finished off in bottle. At its best it is off-dry, scented, apple-flavoured, and of very good quality. PRICE BAND: B. Gaillac Perlé is a 'barely sparkling' version, which is less good.

Galestro A dry white wine from the **Tuscany** region of Italy, based on the **Trebbiano** grape, together with **Malvasia**, **Pinot Bianco**, **Chardonnay** and Vernaccia. It is a light, fresh, fruity wine, the result of cold fermentation. It was developed by a group of large Tuscan producers, who found themselves with an excess of Trebbiano grapes when the permitted proportion of Trebbiano and Malvasia in **Chianti** Classico was reduced.

Galicia A region in northwest **Spain**, just north of the border with **Portugal**. There are three **DO** regions. The **Ribeiro** DO produces mainly whites: bland wines from the **Palomino** grape, and more characterful ones from **Albariño**. The Valdeorras DO is in decline, it produces bland white and red wines from Palomino and Garnacha Tintorera respectively. The best wines come from **Rias Baixas**, where fresh whites, similar to Portugal's **Vinho Verde**, are made from Albariño, **Loureira**, Godello and Treixadura grapes.

Gamay (Gamay Noir à Jus Blanc) A French red grape variety. It is planted predominantly in the **Beaujolais** region, where it is responsible for every wine from the light, acidic **Beaujolais Nouveau** through to the deliciously vibrant, intensely fruity and sometimes jammy **cru** wines. It is less successful, however, elsewhere in France. In the **Loire**, it produces light red wines in **Anjou-Saumur** and **Touraine** and **Fiefs Vendéens**; in **Savoie** for **Bugey**; and in **Switzerland**, for **Dôle**. Elsewhere in Burgundy, **Passe-Tous-Grains** is made from two-thirds Gamay and one-third **Pinot Noir**, vinified together. **Bourgogne** Grand Ordinaire may be made from 100% Gamay. See also **Napa Gamay**.

Gamay Beaujolais A misleading Californian name for a clone of **Pinot Noir**. The true Gamay is labelled Napa Gamay.

Gambellara A white **DOC** wine grown in the **Veneto** region of Italy, made mainly from the **Garganega** grape. Gambellara Bianco is a dry, fresh, fruity white, similar in style to **Soave**. PRICE BAND: A–B.

Recioto di Gambellara is a sweet, intense, golden-coloured white, occasionally sparkling, made from dried grapes (see **recioto**). A small amount of **Vin Santo** is also produced under the Gambellara label.

Garganega A white grape used notably in Soave in the **Veneto** region of Italy, and also in **Gambellara**, **Bianco di Custoza** and **Colli Euganei**.

Garnacha (also called **Grenache**) A red grape variety of Spanish origin, which produces full-bodied, high alcohol wines. It is widely planted in **Rioja** (where it is usually blended with **Tempranillo**) and **Navarra**. As Grenache, it is found in the **Languedoc-Roussillon**, in southern France, in the southern **Rhône** in **Tavel**, **Châteauneuf-du-Pape** and **Côtes du Rhône**, and in **Provence**. It is also planted in **Corsica**, **Sardinia** (where it is known as **Cannonau**), **Australia** and **California**.

garrafeira A Portuguese term that indicates a vintage red wine, which has been matured for two years before bottling plus one year in bottle, or a vintage white wine matured for six months before bottling plus six months in bottle. In practice these minimum periods are often exceeded, as the Portuguese believe 'the older the better'. A *garrafeira* should also be a wine of good quality and with an **alcohol content** at least 0.5% above the minimum specified for the area. See also **Dão**; **Bairrada**.

Gattinara A dry red **DOCG** wine from **Piedmont**, Italy. It is produced mainly from the **Nebbiolo** grape (known locally as Spanna), with the option of up to 10% **Bonarda**. In theory it should be capable of the same quality as **Barolo** and **Barbaresco**, but it never seems to reach the same depth, complexity and longevity. At its best it is spicy, with tar on the nose and a soft, silky texture. PRICE BAND: B.

Gavi See **Cortese**.

Geelong A wine region in the state of **Victoria**, **Australia**. It has a cool, dry climate and good results have been obtained here with **varietal** wines made from the **Pinot Noir** grape. **Chardonnay**, **Shiraz** and **Cabernet Sauvignon** are also grown.

Geisenheim A village in the **Rheingau** region of Germany that produces top-quality, fruity white wines, almost entirely from the **Riesling** grape variety. There are two **Grosslagen**, Burgweg and Erntebringer, and the best **Einzellage** vineyards include Kläuserweg and Rothenberg. The village is also famous for its wine school and research station.

Germany A wine-producing country important chiefly for its white wines, which range from ordinary to superlative in quality. Some of the best and most distinctive white wines in the world come from the **Riesling** grape, grown on the **Rhine** and **Mosel**.

The quality pyramid begins with **Deutscher Tafelwein**, table wine which can be labelled with one of four broadly based district names. **Landwein**, or 'country' wine, is the next category, with higher natural alcohol than *tafelwein*, and 15 designated regions. **QbA**, or 'quality wine from a designated area' comes from one of the 11 **Anbaugebiet** areas, and can be made only from certain permitted grape varieties. **QmP** is the highest category, with five different **prädikat** ratings, which depend on the natural sugar in the grapes at the time of picking, and the degree of selection at harvest. In ascending order they are **Kabinett**, **Spätlese**, **Auslese**, **Beerenauslese**, and **Trockenbeerenauslese**. **Eiswein** should have the same grape sugar level as Beerenauslese.

The 11 *Anbaugebiet* regions are: **Ahr**, **Baden**, **Franken**, **Hessiche Bergstrasse**, **Nahe**, **Mittelrhein**, **Mosel-Saar-Ruwer**, **Rheingau**, **Rheinhessen**, **Rheinpfalz** and **Württemberg**. There is no doubt that the finest wines are made from the Riesling grape variety, but **Müller-Thurgau** and

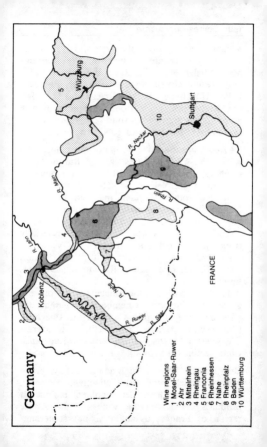

Germany

Wine regions
1 Mosel-Saar-Ruwer
2 Ahr
3 Mittelrhein
4 Rheingau
5 Franconia
6 Rheinhessen
7 Nahe
8 Rheinpfalz
9 Baden
10 Württemburg

FRANCE

Koblenz
Stuttgart
Würzburg

R. Lahn
R. Main
R. Neckar
R. Rhein
R. Nahe
R. Mosel
R. Ruwer
R. Saar

Silvaner are also planted widely, along with **Gewürztraminer**, **Ruländer**, **Weissburgunder**, **Gutedel**, **Morio-Muskat** and **Scheurebe**, plus more recent crossings such as **Kerner**, **Bacchus**, **Faber**, **Huxelrebe**, **Optima**, **Ortega** and **Ehrenfelser**. Red wines, made from the **Spätburgunder** grape, have improved beyond recognition lately, especially in the hands of good producers.

Gevrey-Chambertin An important village and **AC** in the **Côte de Nuits** area of **Burgundy**. It produces some of the world's finest red wines from the **Pinot Noir** grape. The majority of the wine is produced under the village AC of Gevrey-Chambertin, and this can be of good quality, silky, soft and perfumed. PRICE BAND: C.

The **premier cru** wines are better, especially from Clos Saint-Jacques and Clos des Varoilles. They are tannic in their youth, but develop mouth-filling, ripe, **gamey** flavours as they mature. PRICE BAND: D–E.

The best wines of the village come from the **grand cru** vineyards: **Chambertin**, **Chambertin-Clos de Bèze**, **Chapelle-Chambertin**, **Charmes-Chambertin**, **Griotte-Chambertin**, **Latricières-Chambertin**, **Mazis-Chambertin** and **Ruchottes-Chambertin**. PRICE BAND: D–E.

Gewürztraminer A high-quality white grape variety, which produces distinctive, aromatic, floral wines with a deep golden colour. It produces classic **varietal** wines in the **Alsace** region of France, usually dry, but sometimes lusciously sweet **vendange tardive** or **Sélection de Grains Nobles**. It is also planted in **Germany** (particularly in the **Rheinpfalz** and **Baden** regions), **Austria**, the **Alto Adige** in Italy, **California**, **New Zealand** and **Australia**.

Ghemme A dry, red **DOC** wine grown near the town of Ghemme in **Piedmont**, Italy. It is produced from 60–85% **Nebbiolo** grapes plus Vespolina and **Bonarda**. A robust, sturdy red, it is similar to **Gattinara** in quality. PRICE BAND: B.

Gigondas A red (and rosé) **AC** wine produced around the town of Gigondas in the southern **Rhône**, France, from the **Grenache** (up to 65%), **Syrah** (at least 15%), **Mourvèdre** and **Cinsault** grape varieties. The red wine is usually deep coloured, full and supple, with chewy fruit. Quality can be very good, but doesn't usually reach the heights of which **Châteauneuf-du-Pape** is capable. PRICE BAND: B. White wine produced in Gigondas is sold as **Côtes du Rhône**.

girasol The Spanish term for a **gyropalette**.

Girò di Cagliari A red, usually sweet **DOC** wine from **Sardinia**, made from the native Girò grape. It is a bright ruby colour, warm, smooth and similar to **Port** (although unfortified).

Gisborne An important wine region on the north island of **New Zealand**, which produces large quantities of light, but good white wine mainly from the **Müller-Thurgau** grape. Better-quality whites are made in smaller quantities, particularly from **Gewürztraminer**, **Chenin Blanc**, **Sémillon** and **Chardonnay**. Red wines are generally less successful, although there are some good examples of **Cabernet Sauvignon** and **Merlot**.

Givry An **AC** wine from the **Côte Chalonnaise** area of **Burgundy**, which produces mainly dry red wines from the **Pinot Noir** grape, and a small amount of white from **Chardonnay**. The best reds have a delicate, smoky fragrance, and good Pinot flavour, but quality is very variable. PRICE BAND: B–C.

Goldenmuskateller (also called **Moscato Giallo**) A white grape variety of the **Muscat** family, which produces golden yellow, sweet white wines in the **Alto Adige** and **Trentino** regions of Italy.

goût A French term for 'taste'. *Goût de terroir* is used to describe a wine that has an earthy taste, supposedly derived from the soil in which the vines are grown. *Goût anglais* is used in **Champagne** to describe the English taste for dry, more mature wine. *Goût de grelle* indicates an 'off' flavour caused by grapes damaged by hail.

governo A technique formerly widespread among producers of **Chianti**, in which some grapes are reserved and dried, and added to the bulk of the wine after vinification. This causes a second fermentation, which increases the alcohol content and colour and reduces acidity. In the past, this was used to make *normale* Chianti, for early drinking. Today, the extra costs involved mean that the few remaining *governo* practitioners tend to use it for higher-quality, *riserva* Chianti, often with very good results.

Graach A tiny village in the **Bereich** of **Bernkastel** in the **Mosel-Saar-Ruwer** region of Germany. It comes within the **Grosslage** of Münzlay, and the **Einzellage** vineyards are Abtsberg, Domprobst, Himmelreich and Josephshöfer. They produce some of the finest white wines of the Mosel from the **Riesling** grape.

Graciano A red grape variety used as a minor ingredient in the production of **Rioja**, particularly in the Rioja Alta subzone. It produces a wine with a deep colour, highly aromatic and with a good ageing potential. It is also grown in **Navarra**.

grafting The process of joining the fruit-bearing part of a vine to another vine's root. Since the coming of **phylloxera**, in the 19th century, most of the world's vineyards have been planted with the traditional **Vitis vinifera** varieties grafted onto American vine rootstocks, which are resistant to phylloxera. In some countries and regions, notably Colores in Portugal and Chile, the vineyards are free from phylloxera, and ungrafted vines grow unthreatened.

grand cru A French quality designation, meaning literally 'great growth', applied differently in different regions.

In **Bordeaux**, the châteaux were classified in 1855 (the classification was of all Bordeaux, but only one château was from outside the **Médoc**): at the top quality level are the *grands crus classés*, subdivided into *premier*, *deuxième*, down to *cinquième crus*, referred to in English as 'first growth', 'second growth', and so on. In **Saint-Emilion** the top quality level is *premier grand cru classé*, followed by *grand cru classé*, followed by *grand cru*. So *grand cru* in Saint-Emilion is a much lower quality level than *grand cru* in the Médoc.

In **Burgundy**, including **Chablis**, the very top vineyard sites are classified as *grands crus*, and in the **Côte d'Or** each has its own *appellation*. Each *grand cru* vineyard may have several different owners. In Burgundy, **premier cru** comes below *grand cru*. In **Alsace**, certain top vineyard sites are designated *grands crus*, for specified grape varieties only, but the classification process is not yet complete. In **Champagne**, vineyards rated 100% are referred to as *grands crus*.

gran reserva A Spanish term, applied mainly to **Rioja**, which describes a red wine that has been aged for two years in cask and three years in bottle, or a white wine that has been aged for four years, with a minimum of six months in cask. In theory, superior wines are selected for this treatment.

grand vin A French term, not officially regulated, that means 'great wine'. In **Bordeaux**, châteaux producing a **second wine** sometimes refer to their main wine as the *grand vin*.

grande marque A term used to describe **Champagne** made by the 27 producers that belong to the Syndicat de Grandes Marques de Champagne, a club founded in 1964. Most of the great names in Champagne are members, but good quality may also be found outside the *grandes marques*.

Grands-Echézeaux A **grand cru** vineyard of the commune of **Flagey-Echézeaux** in the **Côte de Nuits** region of **Burgundy**. It produces among the finest and most elegant of the region's red wines from the **Pinot Noir** grape. Although technically attached to Flagey-Echézeaux, the vineyard is nearer to **Vosne-Romanée** and the wines can be declassified to Vosne-Romanée **premier cru**. Quality is good and generally better than the larger, neighbouring **Echézeaux**, but not as good as the other *grand cru* vineyards of the Côte de Nuits. PRICE BAND: E.

grape The fruit of the vine, and the only fruit from which real wine can be made. Of the *Vitis* genus of plants, there are many species, although only **Vitis vinifera** is of major importance for wine production. Some American varieties, such as *Vitis labrusca* and *Vitis rupestris*, are used to provide rootstock resistant to **phylloxera** (see **grafting**).

There are several thousand varieties of *Vitis vinifera*, loosely referred to as 'grape varieties'. Of these, some are best suited to producing grapes for eating, some for making raisins and others for making wine. The grape variety used to make a particular wine is one of the most important factors determining its taste and character, along with the soil, climate, cultivation and wine-making technique. Major varieties have their own entries. See also **cross**; **hybrid**.

grapey A tasting term used to describe the smell and taste of fresh grapes. It is often used to describe wines made from the **Muscat** family of grape varieties.

Grauer Burgunder A German name for the **Pinot Gris** grape variety, usually indicating a drier style of wine. See also **Ruländer**.

Grave del Friuli The largest **DOC** zone of the **Friuli-Venezia Giulia** region of Italy. It produces red and white **varietals**, grown on low rolling hills and plains. Most of the red is **Merlot**, dry, supple and fruity, and of generally good quality. Other dry reds are made from **Cabernet** (mainly Franc, but some Sauvignon), **Pinot Nero** and the native **Refosco**. Dry whites are produced from **Chardonnay**, **Pinot Bianco**, **Pinot Grigio**, **Riesling**

Renano, Sauvignon, Tocai Friulano, Traminer Aromatico and Verduzzo Friulano.

Graves An important AC region in the southern part of **Bordeaux**. It includes, at its northern end, the city of Bordeaux itself, and runs along the western (left) bank of the Garonne to just south of **Sauternes**. The name Graves comes from the gravel soil, which is said to give the wines a distinctive *goût de terroir* (see **goût**). Slightly more red than white is produced, mainly from **Cabernet Sauvignon**, plus **Cabernet Franc** and **Merlot** grapes. The whites are dry, made from **Sauvignon Blanc** and **Sémillon** (sometimes 100% Sauvignon). See also **Pessac-Léognan**.

Graves de Vayres A minor, little-known AC wine of **Bordeaux**, located at the north of the **Entre-Deux-Mers** region, but nothing to do with **Graves** itself. Reds and whites of moderate quality are made with the classic Bordeaux grape varieties.

Great Southern The largest wine region in **Australia**, located in the state of **Western Australia**. The overall quality of the wines produced is good, particularly **varietal** wines made from the **Cabernet Sauvignon**, **Shiraz**, **Chardonnay** and **Sauvignon Blanc** grapes, although they are outclassed by the wines of **Margaret River**.

Great Western A region in the state of

Victoria, **Australia**, famous mainly for its spar-kling wines. The relatively cool climate also allows for production of good still wines, par-ticularly **varietal** wines from **Cabernet Sauvignon** and **Shiraz** grapes.

Grechetto A white grape variety grown in the **Umbria** region of Italy, particularly used in making **Orvieto**. It is also grown in eastern **Tuscany** (where it is called Pulcinculo) and in northern **Latium** (as Greghetto).

Greco A white grape variety of Greek origin, grown in the **Campania** region of southern Italy. It is used to make the white **DOC** wines Greco di Tufo, which has a good fruit and crisp flavour, and Greco di Banco, a full-flavoured, sweet dessert wine.

Greece A wine-producing country since an-cient times. Today Greece is famed mainly for **Retsina**, which is usually a white wine made from the Savatiano grape, flavoured with pine resin during fermentation. The country's best wines are gradually improving in quality.

Fine reds are produced from the **Xynomavro** grape grown in Naoussa, Goumenisa and Amin-deo in Macedonia, and from the Agiorgitiko grape from Nemea in the Peloponnese. There are also fine Bordeaux-style reds from the Côtes de Meliton (Domaine Carras), and sweet, port-like reds from the **Mavrodaphne** grape from Patras.

A variety of whites is also produced, including the unusual sparkling **Zitsa** made from the **Debina** grape in Epirus, the crisp, dry **Robola** from the island of Kephalonia and dry whites from the Moscophilero grape in the Peloponnese. There are many sweet whites, especially from the **Muscat** grape, from Patras and the Cyclades, notably Samos. Rhodes produces one of the country's few **méthode champenoise** sparkling wines.

Small 'boutique' wineries are starting to spring up around the country, many producing high-quality, high-price wines from northern European grape varieties, especially **Cabernet Sauvignon**.

green A tasting term used to describe a wine that is youthful, acidic, unripe and raw.

Grenache See **Garnacha**.

Grenouilles One of the seven **grand cru** vineyards of **Chablis**.

grey rot A malignant variety of **botrytis**.

Grignolino A red grape variety that produces pale, delicate wines in the **Piedmont** region of Italy. It makes **DOC** wine in Grignolino del Monferrato Casalese and Grignolino d'Asti which are dry, pale reds, sometimes surprisingly tannic, and fragrant and elegant at their best.

Grillo A white grape variety grown exclusively

in **Sicily**, where it is generally considered the best grape for **Marsala**.

Gringet   See **Savagnin**.

Griotte-Chambertin   A **grand cru** vineyard of **Gevrey-Chambertin**, in the **Côte de Nuits** area of **Burgundy**. It produces red wine of very high quality, if not quite as big and full-bodied as its neighbour **Chambertin**.

Grolleau (also called **Groslot**)   A red grape variety grown mainly in the **Anjou-Saumur** and **Touraine** regions of the **Loire**. It produces high yields of unexciting wine, much of it blended with other varieties, such as **Gamay** and **Cabernet Franc**, in the lesser red and rosé wines of the region, particularly **Rosé d'Anjou**. Grolleau is declining in popularity.

Groppello   A red grape variety grown mainly in the **Lombardy** region of Italy. It is used as part of the blend to make the **DOC** wine **Riviera del Garda Bresciano** and alone to make red **vino da tavola**.

Gros Manseng   A white grape variety that, together with its better-quality sister **Petit Manseng**, is used to make **Jurançon** in southwest France. It is also used to make **Pacherenc du Vic Bilh** and the rare white wines of **Béarn**.

Gros Plant du Pays Nantais   A white **VDQS** wine from the western end of the **Loire** valley, the same region as **Muscadet**. Made from the

Folle Blanche grape (known locally as the Gros Plant) it is a dry, thin, tart, very acidic wine, best drunk with the local seafood. PRICE BAND: A.

Groslot See **Grolleau**.

Grosslage A term used in **German** wine law to indicate a combination of individual vineyard or **Einzellage** sites, which produce wines of similar style. Quality wines in Germany are labelled with the name of their village, followed by either a *Grosslage* or *Einzellage* name. See **QbA**; **QmP**.

Grumello See **Valtellina**.

Grüner Veltliner A white grape variety that accounts for about one-third of total plantings in **Austria**. It produces a pale wine, fruity and spicy with markedly high acidity, providing a good foil for fatty foods. It is also planted in **Hungary**, **Yugoslavia**, Czechoslovakia and **Romania**.

Guenoc Valley An **AVA** of **Lake County**, California, planted mainly with the **Cabernet Sauvignon** grape.

Gutedel See **Chasselas**.

Gutturnio dei Colli Piacentini A dry, red **DOC** wine from the **Emilia-Romagna** region of Italy, made from the **Barbera** and **Bonarda** grape varieties. It tends to be deep, full and generous, and is usually best drunk young. PRICE BAND: A.

gyropalette A mechanical device, often computer-controlled, used in the production of bottle-fermented sparkling wines, such as **Champagne**, to mimic the process of **remuage**. The sediment from the secondary **fermentation** is concentrated in the neck of the inverted bottle, prior to **dégorgement**. The gyropalette is much quicker, and less labour intensive, than manual *remuage*.

halbtrocken A German term meaning medium dry, used to describe wines with not more than 18 g per litre of **residual sugar**. See also **trocken**.

Hallgarten A village in the **Rheingau** region of Germany, which produces fine white wines from the **Riesling** grape. There is one **Grosslage**, Mehrhölzchen, and the individual **Einzellage** sites are Hendelberg, Jungfer, Schönhell and Würzgarten.

hard A tasting term, used to describe an austere wine, high in **tannin** and **acidity**. The severe taste can mellow with time.

Hárslevelü A white grape variety grown mainly in **Hungary**, where it gives a smooth and spicy character to **Tokaji**. It also produces powerfully scented, aromatic **varietal** wines, notably Debroi Hárslevelü from the foothills of the Matra mountains.

Hattenheim A village making some of the finest **Riesling** wines of the **Rheingau** region of

Germany. There is one **Grosslage**, Deutelsberg, and the individual **Einzellage** sites are Engelmannsberg, Hassel, Heiligenberg, Mannberg, Nussbrunnen, Pfaffenberg, Rheingarten, Schützenhaus, Steinberg and Wisselbrunnen.

Haut-Benauge A white **AC** wine produced in small quantities in **Bordeaux**, similar in style to its neighbour, **Entre-Deux-Mers**.

Haut-Médoc The southern half of the **Médoc** area of **Bordeaux**, where most of the best châteaux are found. It includes the communal **ACs** of **Listrac**, **Margaux**, **Moulis**, **Pauillac**, **Saint-Estèphe** and **Saint-Julien**. It is also an AC in its own right, and produces red wines from the classic Bordeaux grape varieties.

Haut Montravel A sweet, white **AC** wine from the west of the **Bergerac** region, and produced from the **Sauvignon Blanc**, **Sémillon** and **Muscadelle** grape varieties. It lacks the richness of the great sweet wines of **Bordeaux**, and is declining in popularity.

Haut-Poitou An **AC** wine of the **Loire** valley, produced around the city of Poitiers southwest of Tours, which can be red, white, or rosé. The whites, mainly **varietal** wines made from **Sauvignon Blanc** and **Chardonnay** grapes, are crisp, clean and good value. The reds, made from **Gamay**, **Cabernet Franc** and **Pinot Noir**, are simple, with good expression of varietal character. PRICE BAND: A.

Hawkes Bay The most important wine region on the North Island of **New Zealand**, which produces fine white wines, particularly from **Chenin Blanc**, **Sauvignon Blanc** and **Chardonnay** grapes. This is also the region where there is the best potential for great New Zealand red wines, and already there are some fine wines made from **Cabernet Sauvignon** and **Merlot**.

hectare (ha) A unit of area, equal to 100 ares, or 10,000 m², or 2.47 acres. Wine yields are normally expressed in terms of **hectolitres** of wine per hectare of vineyard.

hectolitre (hl) A unit of volume equal to 100 litres, or about 22 UK gallons. It is used to measure the bulk quantities of wine, or to express the yields per hectare of a vineyard.

Hermitage An important **AC** wine, mainly red with some white, made near Tain l'Hermitage in the northern **Rhône** valley. The red is probably the greatest of the northern Rhône. It is produced largely from the **Syrah** grape, with occasionally a little **Marsanne** and **Roussanne**. At its best, the wine is rich, concentrated, spicy, leathery, curranty and very long-lived.

The whites are made from the Marsanne and Roussanne grapes. They can be dry, fruity and fragrant wines for early drinking, or extraordinarily long-lived, deep and full-flavoured. PRICE BAND: C–E.

Hessische   Bergstrasse   The   smallest   of

Germany's 11 **Anbaugebiete**. It is situated north of Heidelberg and to the east of the Rhine. About half of the region is planted with **Riesling**, but the **Müller-Thurgau** grape is also important. The wines are similar in style to those of the **Rheingau** and can be of good quality, but they are rarely exported. Most of the production is in the hands of co-operative cellars, and the average vineyard size is very small. There are two **Bereich** subregions, Starkenburg and Umstadt.

Hochheim An important area in the **Rheingau** region of Germany. It produces powerful white wines of good quality from the **Riesling** grape. Hochheim comes within the **Grosslage** of Daubhaus, and includes the individual **Einzellage** sites of Berg, Domdechaney, Herrnberg, Hofmeister, Hölle, Kirchenstück, Königin Victoriaberg, Riechesthal, Sommerheil, Stein and Stielweg.

hock An English term for **Rhine** wines, derived from the town of **Hochheim** in the **Rheingau**.

hogshead A wooden barrel, of variable capacity, between 225 and 273 litres, depending on country and region.

hollow A tasting term used to describe a wine with a satisfactory initial taste and **finish**, but lacking in flavour in the middle palate.

Howell Mountain An **AVA** in **Napa** county,

California, planted mainly with the **Cabernet Sauvignon**, **Zinfandel** and **Chardonnay** grape varieties.

Hudson River Valley A small viticultural area of **New York State**, planted mainly with French-American **hybrid** vines, e.g. **Seyval Blanc**, and, more recently, with European grape varieties.

Hungary A central European country, with a long history of wine production. The most famous wine is the legendary **Tokaji**, produced in the northeast of the country, near the Czechoslovak border. The most famous red table wine is Egri Bikavér, or Bull's Blood, from Eger, a once full-bodied and concentrated wine, it is now a shadow of its former self. In the northwest, around Sopron, light, fresh reds are made from the **Kékfrankos** grape. Around Lake Balaton, dry and sweet whites are made from various grapes including Ezerjó, Kéknyelü and **Olasz Rizling**. The best whites come from the Badascony region.

The Great Plain is Hungary's major wine region. It produces reds, mainly from **Kadarka**, and whites, from Olasz Rizling. Recently, export-oriented producers have started to make **varietal** wines from west European varieties, including **Cabernet Sauvignon**, **Merlot**, **Sauvignon Blanc**, **Chardonnay** and **Muscat**. Initial results are encouraging and Hungary certainly has the potential to imitate the success of **Bulgaria**.

Hunter Valley An important region in the state of **New South Wales**, Australia. It is particularly famous for the very high quality and distinct regional character of its **varietal** wines, produced from **Sémillon**, **Chardonnay** and **Shiraz** grapes. Other varieties grown include **Cabernet Sauvignon**, **Merlot**, **Pinot Noir**, **Riesling**, **Sauvignon Blanc** and **Verdelho**.

Huxelrebe A grape variety that is a cross of **Chasselas** and Courtillier Musqué. It can give very high yields of ordinary, neutral wine, but at low yields it can achieve good **must weight**, acidity and an attractive, **Muscat**-like aroma and flavour. In **Germany** it is planted in the **Rheinhessen** and **Rheinpfalz** regions, and good results have also been achieved in **England**.

hybrid A grape variety made by a combination of two different vine species, usually **Vitis vinifera** and one of the American native vines, such as *Vitis labrusca*, or *Vitis rotundifolia*. Examples include **Baco Noir** and **Seyval Blanc**. The purpose of producing a hybrid is usually to combine the attractive fruit flavour of the *vinifera* variety with the disease resistance, or early ripening ability, of the American vine. A hybrid is distinct from a **cross**, which in viticultural terms is a combination of two *vinifera* varieties. The breeding of hybrids should not be confused with the near-universal practice in Europe of grafting *vinifera* vines on to American, **phylloxera**-resistant rootstock.

Idaho A wine-producing state of the Pacific North-West of the United States, much smaller in wine terms than its neighbours **Washington State** and **Oregon**. Most of the vineyards are planted at high altitudes, mainly with the **Riesling** and **Chardonnay** grape varieties, but also with **Cabernet Sauvignon**, **Chenin Blanc**, **Gewürztraminer** and **Pinot Noir**. The climate seems especially suited to the making of sparkling wines, and this may be where Idaho's best prospects lie.

impériale (also called **imperial**) A large format bottle with a capacity of 6 litres, which is equivalent to eight standard bottles of 75 cl. It is used, but only rarely, in the **Bordeaux** region.

India A country whose wine-producing reputation, in the West, is founded on just one estate, which produces very good quality **méthode champenoise** sparkling wine made from **Ugni Blanc**, **Pinot Noir** and **Chardonnay** grapes, sold under the Omar Khayyam label.

Inferno See **Valtellina**.

Ingelheim am Rhein A town in the **Rheinhessen** region of Germany. It is known mainly for the production of good red wine, one of the country's best, made from the **Spätburgunder** grape variety.

Insolia See **Inzolia**.

Inzolia (also called **Insolia**) A white grape

variety of **Sicily**, where it is used to make good quality white table wines, and as a minor part of the blend in **Marsala**.

Irancy A village southwest of **Chablis** in northern **Burgundy**. It produces the red (and sometimes rosé) **AC** wine Bourgogne Irancy, made from the **Pinot Noir** grape, with the possible addition of César. The wines are delicate, clean reds, with strawberry flavours and capable of moderate ageing. PRICE BAND: B.

Irouléguy A red (and rosé) **AC** wine produced in the Pyrenees from the **Tannat**, **Cabernet Franc** and **Cabernet Sauvignon** grape varieties. The wine is medium-bodied, fairly rough, with peppery fruit flavours and high acidity, and is best drunk young.

Ischia A **DOC** wine made on the island of Ischia, off the coast of the **Campania** region, Italy. The whites are of ordinary quality, produced from the Forastera and Biancolella grape varieties. The small amount of red produced can be better, and is mainly from the Guarnaccia (related to **Garnacha**) grape. Some of the better producers stay outside the DOC system and concentrate on fine **vini da tavola**, particularly white from 100% Biancolella.

Isonzo (also called **Isonzo del Friuli**) A **DOC** wine from the Isonzo river area near Gorizia in the **Friuli-Venezia Giulia** region of

Italy. There are now no fewer than 20 different types of Isonzo. The **bianco** may be dry, **amabile**, or **frizzante**, and is based on the **Tocai Friulano**, **Malvasia**, **Pinot Bianco** and **Chardonnay** grape varieties. The **rosso** can also be dry, *amabile*, or *frizzante*, and is based on **Merlot**, **Cabernet Franc**, **Cabernet Sauvignon**, **Refosco** and **Pinot Nero**. The white **varietal** wines are Chardonnay, Malvasia Istriana, Pinot Bianco, **Pinot Grigio**, **Riesling Italico**, **Riesling Renano**, **Sauvignon**, Tocai Friulano, **Traminer Aromatico** and **Verduzzo Friulano**.

The red varietals, particularly the Cabernets, **Merlot** and **Refosco**, can be among the best quality wines of the region: Cabernet (Franc and/or Sauvignon), Cabernet Franc, Cabernet Sauvignon, Franconia (the local name for **Blaufrankisch**), Merlot, Pinot Nero and Refosco.

Israel   A minor wine-producing country, with relatively new plantings of **Cabernet Sauvignon** and **Sauvignon Blanc**, both varieties producing wines of excellent quality. Other varieties planted include **Chardonnay**, **Chenin Blanc**, **Colombard**, **Merlot**, **Grenache**, **Pinot Noir**, **Riesling** and **Sémillon**. Previously Israel was known mainly for sweet and **fortified** (kosher) **wines**.

Italy   The country producing the largest quantity of wine in the world, with an astonishing variety of qualities and styles. Italy used to be known mainly for inferior examples of wines such as **Valpolicella** and **Chianti**, in wicker-covered

Italy

Milan
Genoa
Rome
Naples
Cagliari
Palermo

1 Valle D'Aosta
2 Piedmont
3 Lombardy
4 Trentino-Alto Adige
5 Veneto
6 Friuli-Venezia Giulia
7 Emilia-Romagna
8 Marches
9 Tuscany
10 Umbria

11 Latium
12 Abruzzi
13 Molise
14 Campania
15 Apulia
16 Basilicata
17 Calabria
18 Sicily
19 Sardinia
20 Liguria

flasks. However, the quality of Italian wines has improved vastly in recent years. The country is now increasingly well-known for its truly great wines. There are still many under-achieving zones, particularly in the south of Italy, and the potential for further improvement is enormous. The greatest red wines, such as **Barolo**, **Barbaresco**, Chianti and **Brunello di Montalcino**, are produced in the central and northwest regions of **Piedmont** and **Tuscany**. The northeast has led the Italian white wine-making revolution in **Friuli-Venezia Giulia**.

Quality levels begin with **vino da tavola**, and range up through **DOC** to **DOCG**. Some producers, however, dissatisfied with the DOC/G wine laws, produce high-quality, high-price wines under *vino da tavola* labels (particularly in Tuscany), which do not have to conform to the sometimes restrictive rules. See **Abruzzi**; **Apulia**; **Calabria**; **Campania**; **Basilicata**; **Emilia-Romagna**; **Latium**; **Liguria**; **Lombardy**; **Marches**; **Molise**; **Sardinia**; **Sicily**; **Trentino**; **Alto Adige**; **Valle d'Aosta**; **Veneto**; **Umbria**.

Jacquère A white grape variety, the most important in the **Savoie** region of France. On its own it produces dry, light, neutral and fairly acidic wines of a moderate quality.

Jasnières A white **AC** wine of the **Loire** valley. It is produced to the north of Tours on the Loir tributary, and made entirely from the **Chenin Blanc** grape variety. The soil is similar to that in **Vouvray**, and the wines are usually dry and elegant, if somewhat austere. At its best, quality can be very good. PRICE BAND: B–C.

Jerez See **Sherry**.

jeroboam A large format bottle of 4.5 litres capacity (six ordinary 75 cl bottles) in Bordeaux, or 3 litres (four ordinary bottles) in Champagne. See also **double magnum**.

Johannisberg 1. The **Bereich** that covers the whole of the **Rheingau** region, or **Anbaugebiet**, of Germany. 2. A famous wine-producing village in the Rheingau region of Germany, which produces fine white wines from the **Riesling** grape. The village lies within the **Grosslage** of Erntebringer. The **Einzellage** sites are Goldatzel, Hansenberg, Hölle, Klaus, Mittelhölle, Schwarzenstein, Schloss Johannisberg and Vogelsang.

Johannisberger An alternative name, used in Switzerland, for the **Sylvaner** grape. It is used particualrly in the Valais region for concentrated, tasty white wine.

Johannisberg Riesling An alternative name for the true **Riesling** grape, used in California.

Juliénas A red **AC** wine produced from the **Gamay** grape, one of the 10 **crus** of the **Beaujolais** region of **Burgundy**. The wine is usually high in **tannin** and **acidity** (for Beaujolais) with attractive, red-fruit flavours and a good ageing potential in better vintages. Quality is usually very good. PRICE BAND: B.

Jumilla A **DO** wine from just south of Valencia and to the west of Alicante, **Spain**. Most of the production is of strong, dark red wines, high in alcohol and made from the **Monastrell** grape. **Rosado** wines are made from the same variety, and white wine from **Airén**, **Merseguera** and **Pedro Ximénez**. Previously, many of the vineyards were planted with ungrafted vines, but most of these have now been replaced with ones resistant to **phylloxera**. PRICE BAND: A.

Jura A region of eastern France that produces red, white, rosé, **vin gris** and **vin jaune**. The whites are based on the **Savagnin** and **Chardonnay** grapes, and the reds on **Trousseau** and **Poulsard**. There are four **ACs**: **Arbois**, **Château-Chalon**, **Côtes du Jura** and **L'Etoile**.

Jurançon 1. A white **AC** wine from southwest France, made in the foothills of the Pyrenees from the **Petit Manseng** and **Gros Manseng** grapes, sometimes with the addition of **Courbu**. The dry version, Jurançon Sec, is of good, average quality. The rarer, sweet, late-harvested Jurançon Moelleux is honeyed and spicy with cinnamon and clove flavours, delicate and sweet but with balancing acidity, and can be of superb quality. PRICE BAND: B. 2. A family of grape varieties, Jurançon Noir, Jurançon Rouge and Jurançon Blanc, which have no connection with

AC Jurançon wine. The white variety is still planted in small quantities in Gascony for producing Armagnac. Jurançon Noir is used in **Cahors** and Jurançon Rouge in **Gaillac**.

Kabinett A German and Austrian quality white wine category, the first in the **prädikat** system, coming before **Spätlese**. In Germany Kabinett (previously spelled Cabinet) wines can only be made from fully-ripened grapes with a minimum **must weight** of 67°–85° *Oechsle* in Germany. No **chapatalization** is permitted. The wines are usually light and low in alcohol, and may be dry or medium dry. See **QmP**.

Kadarka The most important native red grape variety of **Hungary**, grown all over the country. Previously Egri Bikavér (or Bull's Blood) was made almost entirely from this variety, but now, to its detriment, it is usually a blend.

Kaiserstuhl-Tuniberg A **Bereich** of the **Baden** region of Germany, facing the vineyards of **Alsace** across the Rhine. Most of the white wine is produced from the **Müller-Thurgau** grape, but fine whites are also made from **Ruländer**. **Spätburgunder** is used to make the rosé Weissherbst. There are two **Grosslagen**, Attilafelsen and Vulkanfelsen.

Kallstadt A village in the Mittelhaardt **Bereich** of the **Rheinpfalz** region of Germany. It produces high-quality, fruity white wines from the **Riesling**, **Silvaner** and **Scheurebe** grapes. The village is situated within the **Grosslagen** of Kobnert and Feuerberg.

Kalterer (also called **Kalterersee**) See **Caldaro**.

Kanzem A village in the Saar-Ruwer **Bereich**, in the **Mosel-Saar-Ruwer** region of Germany. In good years it produces superb white wines from the **Riesling** grape. The village is within the **Grosslage** of Scharzberg, and the **Einzellage** sites are Altenberg, Hörecker, Ritterpfad, Schlossberg and Sonnenberg.

Kasel A village in the Saar-Ruwer **Bereich**, in the **Mosel-Saar-Ruwer** region of Germany. It produces top-quality white wines from the **Riesling** grape. The vineyards come within the **Grosslage** of Römerlay, and the **Einzellage** sites are Dominikanerberg, Herrenberg, Hitzlay, Kehrnagel, Nies'chen, Paulinsberg and Timpert.

Kékfrankos An alternative name, used in Hungary, for the **Blaufränkisch** grape.

Kerner A white grape variety, which is a **cross** of **Trollinger** and **Riesling**. It produces attractive Riesling-style white wines, with good ageing potential. Kerner is planted throughout Germany, (particularly in the **Rheinpfalz** and **Rheinhessen** regions), in **South Africa** and in **England**.

Klevner An alternative name for **Pinot Noir**, used by the Swiss. See also **Clevener**.

Knights Valley An **AVA** of **Sonoma** county neighbouring **Chalk Hill** and **Alexander Valley**, in California. It has a growing reputation for rich and elegant **varietal** wines produced from the **Cabernet Sauvignon** grape. **Sauvignon Blanc** and **Johannisberg Riesling** are also planted.

Kocher-Jagst-Tauber The smallest of the three **Bereich** subregions of the **Württemberg** region of Germany.

Kreuznach See **Bad Kreuznach**.

Kröv A village in the **Mosel-Saar-Ruwer** region of Germany, which produces medium-quality white wine. It is probably most famous for its **Grosslage** name Nacktarsch (meaning 'bare bottom'), which has inevitably led to particularly vulgar labels. The **Einzellage** sites are Burglay, Herrenberg, Kirchlay, Letterlay, Paradies and Steffensberg.

Kumeu A region on the North Island of **New Zealand**, that produces fine **varietal** wines from **Cabernet Sauvignon**, **Chardonnay**, **Merlot**, **Müller-Thurgau**, **Pinot Noir**, **Riesling**, **Sauvignon Blanc** and **Sémillon** grapes.

La Côte The most westerly of the wine regions of the Vaud area in **Switzerland**. It produces mainly light, floral, elegant white wines from the **Chasselas** grape. PRICE BAND: B.

Lacrima A red grape variety of central eastern

Italy. It is blended with up to 15% of the **Montepulciano** and **Verdicchio** grapes, and used to make the red, plummy **DOC** wine Lacrima di Morro d'Alba in the **Marches** region. It can be dry or medium sweet, and still or **frizzante**.

Lacryma Christi del Vesuvio A **DOC** wine made around Vesuvius in the **Campania** region of Italy. It can be a dry red or rosé, made from the Piedirosso, Sciascinoso and **Aglianico** grapes; or a dry white or fortified **liquoroso** from the Verdeca, Coda di Volpe and Falanghina grapes. The white, red and rosé can be still or sparkling.

Ladoix-Serrigny An **AC** wine of **Burgundy**, made around the villages of Ladoix and Serrigny at the northern end of the **Côte de Beaune**. In practice, most of its production can be classified as **premier cru** or **grand cru Aloxe-Corton**, and much of the rest is declassified into **Côte de Beaune-Villages**, so it is rare to see Ladoix-Serrigny on the label. The quality of the wines, nearly all red and made from the **Pinot Noir** grape, is variable. The best are light to medium-bodied, soft reds, which can be good value. PRICE BAND: C.

lagar (pl. **lagares**) A shallow stone trough, traditionally used in the making of **Port**. Lightly crushed grapes are placed in the *lagar* and a team of bare-footed workers treads the mixture of grape juice and skins, to maximize the amount of colour, flavour and **tannin** extracted. When fermentation has given an **alcohol content** of about 7%, the wine is run out of the *lagares* and mixed with brandy (**aguardente**) to arrest fermentation and to fortify the wine. Some houses still use *lagares*, especially for their best wines; others use more modern vinification methods in stainless-steel tanks. See also **autovinificator**.

Lago di Caldaro See **Caldaro**.

Lagrein A red grape variety grown mainly in the **Trentino** and **Alto Adige** regions of Italy. It makes a delicate, fragrant rosé wine in Lagrein Rosato (Lagrein Kretzer) and, around Bolzano, the deep, robust, smooth Lagrein Scuro (Lagrein Dunkel). PRICE BAND: B.

Lake County A county north of the **Napa Valley** in **California**, which was first planted with wines in the 1880s and has recently undergone a revival. It has significant plantings of mainly **Cabernet Sauvignon** and **Sauvignon Blanc** grapes. Lake County is part of the **North Coast** AVA and has two AVAs of its own, Clear Lake and **Guenoc Valley**.

Lalande-de-Pomerol A red AC wine of the **Bordeaux** region, adjacent to **Pomerol**. The wines have a soft, plummy richness, which makes them attractive to drink in their youth (four to five years). There is more **Cabernet Franc** and less **Merlot** in the blend than in Pomerol, and Lalande never reaches the heights of top Pomerol. Recently there have been signs of an improvement and a search for a more distinctive communal character. PRICE BAND: B–C.

La Mancha A **DO** wine of central **Spain**, and the largest quality wine area of Europe. Most of the wine produced is white and made from the widely planted **Airén** grape variety. Traditionally, it was dark yellow, high in alcohol, and of mediocre quality. Recently, cold-temperature vinification in stainless-steel tanks has resulted in pale, fresh and fruity whites, which are very acceptable quaffing wines best drunk young. The **Macabeo**, Pardilla and Verdoncho grapes are also allowed for the white. **Cencibel** (Tempranillo), **Garnacha** and Moravia are used to make usually pale, easy-drinking reds and **rosado** wines. PRICE BAND: A.

Lambrusco A family of red grape varieties grown mainly in the **Emilia-Romagna** region of Italy. It is used to produce mostly red, but also white and rosé **frizzante** wines sold under the same name. There are four **DOC** wines: Lambrusco di Sorbara, which can be red or rosé, dry or **amabile**; the red Lambrusco Salamino di Santa Croce and Lambrusco Grasparossa di Castelvetro, both of which can be dry or amabile; and Lambrusco Reggiano, which ranges from dry red to sweet pink. The best of these are lightly fizzy, with a sharp acidity in the background, good wines to accompany robust food. Sadly, much of what is sold on export markets is non-DOC, sweet red and white Lambrusco, which is little more than alcoholic lemonade. PRICE BAND: A.

Lambrusco Mantovano A DOC, red, **frizzante** wine of the **Lombardy** region of Italy, similar to **Lambrusco** from the **Emilia-Romagna** region.

Landwein A quality category of German wine, above **Deutscher Tafelwein**, but below **QbA**, and similar in concept to the French **vin de pays** category. It cannot be sweeter than **halbtrocken,** and there are 15 Landwein regions within the four main Deutscher Tafelwein areas: Ahrtaler, Altrheingauer, Bayerischer, Fränkischer, Landwein der Mosel, Landwein der Saar, Nahegauer, Pfälzer, Regensburger, Rheinburger, Rheinischer, Schwäbischer, Starkenburger, Sudbadischer Landwein and Unterbadischer.

Languedoc-Roussillon A large region on the Mediterranean coast of France, which produces a vast quantity of mostly red wine. The wine used to be fairly rough and was high in colour and alcohol. It was a major source of France's everyday **vin de table** and was also frequently used for blending to 'beef up' wines of other regions. More recently, there has been a great improvement in quality, with major programmes of replantation. Red AC wines include **Collioure**, **Corbières**, **Costières-du-Gard**, **Coteaux du Languedoc**, **Côtes du Roussillon**, **Fitou** and

Minervois. Whites include Clairette de Bellegarde and Clairette du Languedoc (see **Clairette**), and **fortified** whites, **Banyuls**, **Muscat de Frontignan**, **Muscat de Rivesaltes** and **Maury**.

lanolin A tasting term used to describe a soft, wet-wool aroma, often found in white wines made from the **Sémillon** grape.

La Romanée See **Romanée, La**.

La Romanée-Conti See **Romanée-Conti, La**.

La Romanée-Saint-Vivant See **Romanée-Saint-Vivant, La**.

Laski Rizling (also called **Laskiriesling**) An alternative name, used in Yugoslavia, for the **Welschriesling** grape variety.

La Tâche A **grand cru** wine of **Vosne-Romanée**, in the **Côtes de Nuits** area of **Burgundy**, made from the **Pinot Noir** grape. This is one of the finest, and most expensive, red wines in the world. The taste of La Tâche is difficult to describe – an extraordinary panoply of smoky, fruity sensations on the nose, and intense concentration on the palate, with truffly, rich and spicy flavours – but once tasted it is never forgotten. PRICE BAND: E+.

Late-Bottled Vintage Port See **LBV**.

late harvest A term, equivalent to **Spätlese** or **Vendange Tardive**, found mainly on New World wine labels. It indicates that the grapes were harvested later than usual, and therefore have a higher concentration of sugar. Such wines are usually rich and sweet, but they may be fermented to dryness, becoming powerful and alcoholic.

Latisana (also called **Latisana del Friuli**) A red, white, and rosé **DOC** wine of the **Friuli-Venezia Giulia** region of Italy. There are 13 different types, 12 **varietals** and one **rosato**. The red varietals are Cabernet (made from **Cabernet Franc** and/or **Cabernet Sauvignon**), **Merlot**, Refosco dal Peduncolo Rosso (a clone of **Refosco**). The whites are from **Chardonnay**, **Pinot Bianco**, **Pinot Grigio**, **Sauvignon**, **Tocai Friulano**, **Traminer Aromatico** and **Verduzzo Friulano**. The *rosato* is made from **Merlot**, the Cabernets, Refosco Nostrano and Refosco dal Peduncolo Rosso.

Latium (also called **Lazio**) A region on the west coast of **Italy**, centred on Rome. The white **DOC** wines **Est! Est!! Est!!! di Montefiascone** and **Capena** come from the north of the region, along with the alcoholic, sometimes fortified, sweet red **Aleatico** di Gradoli and the white and red **Cerveteri**. **Montecompatri-Colonna**, **Marino**, **Colli Albani**, **Colli Lanuvini**, Zagarolo and the white **Frascati** are produced in the hills around Rome. **Velletri** can be red or white. **Cesanese** is made in three **DOC**s in the Ciociaria. From the south comes red and white **Cori** and red, white and rosé **Aprilia**.

Latricières-Chambertin A **grand cru** vineyard of **Gevrey-Chambertin** in the **Côte de Nuits** area of **Burgundy**.

Laudun One of the best villages of the Côtes du Rhône-Villages *appellation* (see **Côtes du Rhône**). It produces fresh, fruity red and rosé from the **Grenache**, **Syrah**, **Cinsault** and **Mourvèdre**, and has a good reputation for whites made from **Clairette**, **Roussanne** and **Marsanne**.

Lavaux One of the three main wine regions of the Vaud area of **Switzerland**, which produces white wines mainly from the **Chasselas** grape. Its wines are richer, deeper and more intense than those of **La Côte**. PRICE BAND: B.

Lazio See **Latium**.

LBV (Late-Bottled Vintage Port) A category of **Port**, made from wine from a single year, bottled four to six years after the harvest. Both the vintage year and the year of bottling must appear on the label. Having matured in cask, it is usually made in a 'ready to drink' style, with no need for decanting, although some shippers make a 'traditional' style, which does have a deposit and benefits from bottle ageing. The best LBVs offer good-value Port, which is lighter than **Vintage Port** in style, but superior to **Ruby Port**. PRICE BAND: C.

Lebanon A wine-producing country of the

Middle East, the reputation of which, in the West, is founded almost entirely on one estate, Château Musar in the Bekaa Valley. The vineyards, are planted with **Cabernet Sauvignon** and **Cinsault** grapes, plus **Syrah**, **Merlot** and **Pinot Noir**. The château wine is dominated by Cabernet and is a concentrated, tannic, long-lived, **Bordeaux**-style wine.

lees The deposit, such as dead yeast, that falls to the bottom of a vat of wine after **fermentation** and **ageing**. Normally the wine is transferred to another container (**racked**), leaving the sediment behind. Some wines, notably **Muscadet**, are sometimes aged for a time on the lees (**sur lie**), leading to a distinctive aroma and taste.

legs A tasting term used to describe the pattern formed when drops of wine trickle down the inside of a glass after the wine has been swirled. Persistent legs usually indicate richness in the wine and a high alcohol content.

Leiwen A village in the **Mosel-Saar-Ruwer** region of Germany, which produces racy, fruity white wines from the **Riesling** grape. The village comes under the **Grosslage** of St Michael, and the **Einzellage** sites are Klostergarten and Laurentius-lay.

Le Montrachet See **Montrachet, Le**.

lemony A tasting term used to describe a citrus fruit flavour and acidity, usually in young

dry white wines, or as a balancing component in
sweet wines.

length A tasting term used to describe the
duration of the final taste sensation after a wine
has been swallowed (or spat out). 'Good length',
where the taste persists for some moments, is a
hallmark of a well-balanced wine.

Léognan See **Pessac-Léognan**.

Léon A small region in northern **Spain**. It
produces mainly red wines made mostly from the
Prieto Picudo grape, but also from **Tempranillo**
and Mencia. Its white wines are made from the
Verdejo and **Palomino** varieties.

Les Clos The largest of the seven **grand cru**
vineyards of **Chablis**.

Les Maranges An **AC** wine of the **Côte de
Beaune** area of **Burgundy**, made in the villages of
Cheilly-les-Maranges, Dezize-les-Maranges and
Sampigny-les-Maranges. It produces light red
Burgundy from the **Pinot Noir** grape of a similar
standard to **Côte de Beaune-Villages**.

Lessona An austere, dry red **DOC** wine from
the Vercelli hills in northern **Piedmont**. It is made
mainly from the **Nebbiolo** grape variety, with up
to 25% **Bonarda** and **Vespolina**.

Leverano A **DOC** wine from the Salento
peninsula in the **Apulia** region of Italy. It
produces red, white and **rosato** wines. The red,

which is the best wine, is based on the **Negro-amaro** grape, together with **Malvasia** Nera, **Sangiovese** and **Montepulciano**. The dry rosé, from the same grapes, can also be good. The white, from Malvasia, **Bombino** Bianco and **Trebbiano** Toscano, is rarely good.

lie The French word for **lees**.

Liebfraumilch A sweet, white **QbA** wine, which is produced mainly in the **Rheinhessen**, **Rheinpfalz** and **Nahe** regions of Germany, from the **Riesling**, **Silvaner** or **Müller-Thurgau** grapes. As a QbA it should have the name of the **Anbaugebiet** on the label, and theoretically be typical of its region, but grape names are not allowed. The wine is immensely popular outside Germany, the most widely exported of German wines, although it is little known on the home market. At its best it is pleasantly fruity, sweet, innocuous and inexpensive. PRICE BAND: A.

Lieser A small village near **Bernkastel-Kues** in the **Mosel-Saar-Ruwer** region of Germany, which produces racy, elegant white wines. The vineyards are split between the **Grosslagen** of Beerenlay and Kurfürstlay, and the **Einzellage** sites are Niederberg-Helden, Rosenlay, Süssenberg and Schlossberg.

Liguria A small region of **Italy**, situated on the Italian Riviera. There are two main **DOC** zones in west Liguria: the dry red Rossese di Dolceacqua; and the red, white and rosé **Riviera Ligure**

di Ponente. In the east of the region the white **Cinqueterre** is made, together with red and white **Colli di Luni**.

Limousin A forest in France, the white oak from which is used for making barrels. Its wood, which has a high phenol content, is less dense, with a wider grain and greater porosity than oak from **Allier** and **Nevers**. It has a particular affinity with **Pinot Noir** and **Chardonnay**, particularly in the New World. Limousin oak is the preferred oak for Cognac.

Limoux See **Blanquette de Limoux**.

liqueur de tirage The mixture of wine, sugar and yeast added to bottles of **Champagne** (and other **méthode champenoise** wines) to induce the bubble-forming, secondary **fermentation** in bottle.

liqueur d'expedition The mixture of wine and, usually, sugar that is used to top-up bottles of **Champagne** (and other **méthode champenoise** wines) after **dégorgement**. See also **dosage**.

liquoroso The Italian term for a high alcohol wine, usually sweet, possibly, but not necessarily, **fortified**.

Lirac An **AC** wine of the southern **Rhône** valley, produced in the villages of Lirac, Roquemaure, Saint-Laurent-des-Arbes and Saint-Géniès-de-Comolas. Most of the wine, and the best, is red, with some white and rosé. The red is made mainly from **Grenache** and **Cinsault** grapes, and is light, fruity and plummy. It ages well for three to four years, but is also delicious when drunk young. Light, strawberry-flavoured rosés are made from the same grape varieties. The white is based on the **Clairette** grape. It is fresh and appley, but it is produced in only small quantities and rarely exported. PRICE BAND: A–B.

Lison-Pramaggiore A **DOC** wine of the eastern part of the **Veneto** region of Italy. There are 12 different **varietals**, all of which may be still or sparkling. The reds are generally dry and rich, with some class. **Merlot** is the most important, followed by Cabernet (**Cabernet Franc** and/or **Cabernet Sauvignon**), and **Refosco**. The whites are also good, and usually good value. They are **Chardonnay**, **Pinot Bianco**, **Pinot Grigio**, **Riesling Italico**, **Sauvignon**, Tocai Italico and Verduzzo.

Listrac A communal **AC** wine of the **Haut-Médoc** region of **Bordeaux**. It produces good, long-lived, tannic **cru bourgeois** wines but no **cru classé**.

Livermore Valley An **AVA** of **Alameda** county, **California**. **Chardonnay** and Gray Riesling are the most planted white grape varieties, and **Sauvignon Blanc** and **Sémillon** grow very well here. The main reds are **Cabernet Sauvignon** and Petite Sirah.

Ljutomer The best known wine-producing area

of **Yugoslavia**, famous for its white wine made from **Laski Rizling**.

Locorotondo A dry white **DOC** wine produced around the town of Locorotondo in Apulia, Italy. The wine may be still or **spumante**, with gentle fruit and an almond finish. It is made mainly from the Verdeca and **Bianco d'Alessano** grapes.

lodges The cellars, located in Vila Nova de Gaia, used by **Port** producers for ageing, blending and bottling.

Loir A tributary of the **Loire** river.

Loire The longest river in France, with important and diverse wine regions located along much of its length. The eastern (Upper) Loire is noted mainly for its fine, dry whites, made from the **Sauvignon Blanc** grape in **Sancerre**, **Pouilly-Fumé**, **Menetou-Salon**, **Quincy** and **Reuilly**.

In **Touraine**, the prominent quality white grape is **Chenin Blanc**, which produces a wide variety of styles in **Vouvray** and **Montlouis**. **Cabernet Franc** makes high-quality red wines in **Chinon**, **Bourgueil** and **Saint-Nicolas-de-Bourgueil**. Similar reds are made in **Saumur-Champigny**, but **Saumur** is chiefly known for its **méthode champenoise** sparkling wines. **Anjou-Saumur** produces large quantities of rosé wine, the best from Cabernet, but its finest wines are whites based on Chenin Blanc, which are either steely dry, as from **Savennières**, or lusciously sweet, as from **Coteaux**

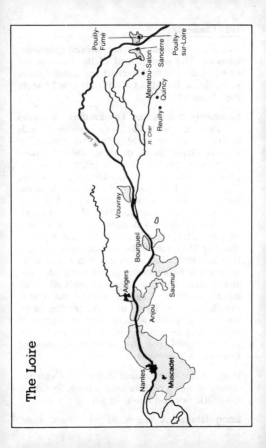

The Loire

du Layon, **Bonnezeaux**, **Montlouis** and **Quarts-de-Chaume**. The western end of the Loire is the home of dry, white **Muscadet** and usually lesser whites made from the Gros Plant (**Gros Plant du Pays Nantais**).

Lombardy (also called **Lombardia**) A region of northern **Italy**. The wine-growing area is centred on the city of Milan and stretches as far as Lake Garda. South of Milan, **Oltrepò Pavese** produces hearty reds and fragrant whites, together with the base for sparkling wines. Nearer Milan, San Colombano al Lambro produces rustic dry reds. In northern Lombardy, **Valtellina** makes sturdy reds based on **Nebbiolo**. To the east, Bergamo produces **Valcalepio**, dry whites based on **Pinot Bianco** and **Pinot Grigio**, and dry reds, based on **Merlot** and **Cabernet Sauvignon**. Around Brescia, world-class sparkling whites and rosés are made in **Franciacorta**, as well as still, dry reds and whites. See also **Capriano del Colle**, **Cellatica**, **Botticino**, **Lugana**, **Riviera del Garda Bresciano**, and **Tocai di San Martino della Battaglia**. In Mantova, Colli Morenici Mantovani del Garda produces simple, dry red, white, and rosé and good, red, dry or **amabile**, sparkling **Lambrusco Mantovano**.

long A tasting term used to describe a wine the flavour of which persists once it is swallowed (or spat out). See also **finish**; **length**.

Long Island A region of **New York State**,

which was planted relatively recently with grape varieties including **Chardonnay**, **Sauvignon Blanc**, **Johannisberg Riesling** and **Gewürztraminer**, among the whites, and **Cabernet Sauvignon**, **Pinot Noir** and **Merlot** among the reds.

Lorch A village in the Rhine Gorge, in the **Rheingau** region of Germany. It produces moderate to good quality white wines, mainly from the **Riesling** grape. The vineyards come within the **Grosslage** of Burgweg. The **Einzellage** sites are Bodenstal-Steinberg, Kapellenberg, Krone, Pfaffenwies and Schlossberg.

Lorchhausen A village in the **Rheingau** region of Germany, which produces light, elegant white wines from the **Riesling** grape. The vineyards come under the **Grosslage** of Burgweg. The **Einzellage** sites are Rosenberg and Seligmacher.

Loupiac A sweet white **AC** wine made on the right bank of the Garonne river in the **Bordeaux** region. The grapes are the same as those used in **Sauternes** and **Barsac** (**Sémillon**, **Sauvignon Blanc** and **Muscadelle**), although higher yields are permitted. The wines are in a similar style to those of Sauternes and Barsac, although never as complex, and they have less ageing potential. PRICE BAND: B.

Loureiro (also called **Loureira**) A white grape variety grown mainly in the **Vinho Verde** region of Portugal and **Galicia** in Spain. It is one of the best of the permitted varieties for Vinho Verde, with good acidity, and an attractive, grapey scent.

Lubéron See **Côtes du Lubéron**.

Lugana A dry white **DOC** wine made near Lake Garda in the **Lombardy** region of Italy. The wine may be still or **spumante** and is made mainly from the Trebbiano di Lugana grape variety. It is elegant, attractive, medium-bodied and one of the region's finest whites, much better than many other Trebbiano-based wines. PRICE BAND: A.

Lussac-Saint-Emilion A red **AC** wine made in a 'satellite' of the main **Saint-Emilion** *appellation* in **Bordeaux**. The wines are produced from the **Merlot**, **Cabernet Franc**, **Cabernet Sauvignon** and **Malbec** grape varieties (the same as Saint-Emilion). Although very pleasant to drink when fairly young, and offering good value, they never reach the heights of the top Saint-Emilions. PRICE BAND: B.

Luxembourg The vineyards of this tiny country are located mainly along the banks of the river Mosel, which forms the border with Germany. The light, fruity, white wines are mainly Germanic in style, and made from **Müller-Thurgau** (known locally as Rivaner), **Riesling**, **Elbling**, **Auxerrois**, **Gewürztraminer** and **Pinot Gris** grapes. Some sparkling wine is made.

MA (marque auxilliere) The letters found on labels of **Champagne**, indicating that the name of the wine does not belong to the producer. For example, the letters are found on a supermarket's own-label Champagne. The numbers following the letters identify the producer.

Macabeo A white grape variety grown in **Spain**, planted chiefly in the **Rioja** region, where it is known as Viura. It makes wines with good acidity and fruity, floral flavour.

maceration The process whereby red wines derive their colour, tannin and some flavour through contact of the fermenting **must** with grape skins. See also **carbonic maceration**; **cuvaison**.

Macharnudo The foremost of the **albariza**-soil areas to the north of the town of Jerez de la Frontera, in the **Sherry** producing region of Spain.

Mâcon The basic **AC** wine of the **Mâconnais** area of the **Burgundy** region. The white, made from the **Chardonnay** grape, is rarely better than a basic, fairly ordinary white wine. The red and rosé, made from **Pinot Noir** and **Gamay**, are rarely exciting. PRICE BAND: A.

Mâcon-Clessé See **Mâcon-Villages**.

Mâcon-Lugny See **Mâcon-Villages**.

Mâcon-Prissé See **Mâcon-Villages**.

Mâcon-Villages An **AC** wine from the **Mâconnais** area of the **Burgundy** region. Most of the wine is white, made from the **Chardonnay** grape, and it is usually a good, medium quality Burgundy. Forty-three villages are entitled to call their wine Mâcon-Villages, or they can add their own name, e.g. Mâcon-Clessé, Mâcon-Lugny, Mâcon-Prissé and Mâcon-Viré (which are among the best). PRICE BAND: B.

Mâcon-Viré See **Mâcon-Villages**.

Mâconnais A large area of **Burgundy**, centred on the town of Mâcon, to the north of **Beaujolais** and south of the **Côte Chalonnaise**. Most of the production is of white wine from the **Chardonnay** grape. The main **ACs** are **Mâcon**, **Mâcon-Villages**, **Pouilly-Fuissé**, Pouilly-Vinzelles, Pouilly-Loché and **Saint-Véran**. The red grapes planted are **Gamay** with a smaller amount of **Pinot Noir**, which produce less interesting reds under the **Bourgogne** and **Passe-Tout-Grains** *appellations*. The wines are seldom great, but they are straightforward, affordable Burgundies.

Madeira A **fortified wine** made on the island of Madeira, which belongs to **Portugal**. The unique method of production involves heating the wine to around 45°C in an oven, called an **estufa**, for about three months. The method originates from the time when sailing ships carried the island's wines through the tropics, and it was found that they were better after their hot voyage.

There are four main types, based on grape

varieties of the same names: **Sercial**, **Verdelho**, **Bual** and **Malmsey**. Sercial and Verdelho, the drier styles, are fully fermented then fortified. Bual and Malmsey are sweeter, and fermentation is stopped by the addition of brandy. Madeira must be aged for a minimum of three years in cask (five years for Reserve, and 10 years for Special Reserve). Dated Madeiras can be **solera** wines, aged in a similar way to **Sherry**, or the rarer, more expensive, true vintage Madeira. It is probably the longest lived of wines, and can survive almost indefinitely, even in an opened, partly-filled bottle.

Madeleine Angevine A white grape variety, a **cross** between Precocé de Malingre and Madeleine Royale. It is planted mainly in **England**, where it can produce a soft white wine with **Muscat**-like aroma.

Madera A county and **AVA** of **California** which produces mainly bulk wine.

maderized A tasting term used to describe an over-mature, oxidized wine.

Madiran A red **AC** wine from the foothills of the Pyrenees, southwest **France**. It produces tannic, rather austere, long-lived wines, mainly from the **Tannat** grape along with **Cabernet Sauvignon**, **Cabernet Franc** and **Fer**. PRICE BAND: B.

maduro Portuguese term for mature. *Vinho*

maduro is an 'aged' wine, as opposed to **Vinho Verde**, which is bottled young.

magnum A large-format bottle, with a capacity of 1.5 litres, equivalent to two standard bottles. It is said to be the ideal size for the bottle maturation of great red **Bordeaux**. In general, wines age slowly in large bottles, developing greater complexity, and quickly in small ones.

Maindreieck The most important of the three **Bereich** subregions of the **Franken** region of Germany, which includes the town of Würzburg. It produces good quality white wines, mainly from the **Silvaner** and **Scheurebe** grape varieties.

Mainviereck One of the three **Bereich** subregions of the **Franken** region of Germany. It produces some good red wines from the **Spätburgunder** and **Portugieser** grape varieties.

Mainz An important wine town in the **Bereich** of **Nierstein** in the **Rheinhessen** region of Germany. Vineyards planted on the outskirts of Mainz come within the **Grosslage** St Alban, and **Einzellage** sites include Edelmann, Hüttberg, Johannisberg, Kirchenstück, Klosterberg, Sand and Weinkeller.

Maipo Valley One of the foremost wine-making areas in the Central Valley region of **Chile**. The majority of the wines are made from classic European grape varieties, including **Cabernet Sauvignon**, **Merlot** and **Cabernet Franc**.

Málaga A fortified **DO** wine produced in southern **Spain**, mainly from the **Pedro Ximénez**, **Airén** and **Moscatel** grapes. A variety of styles is made from *seco* (dry) to *dulce* (sweet), from almost white to dark golden brown. **Arrope** and **vino de color** are sometimes added to give colour and sweetness. The best wines are sometimes aged in **solera**, as with **Sherry**.

Malbec The alternative name, used in **Bordeaux**, for the **Cot** grape variety.

malic acid See **acids**.

Mallorca An island of the Balearics, which are part of **Spain**. There are two main wine-producing regions, Binisalem and Felanitx, both making mediocre, fruity red wines from the Manto Negro and Fogoneu grape varieties.

Malmsey A grape variety, part of the **Malvasia** family, grown on the island of **Madeira**, where it gives its name to a category of wine. Dark, full-bodied and luscious, Malmsey is the sweetest of Madeiras.

malolactic fermentation A second **fermentation**, that wines may undergo, in which the tart malic acid is converted into smoother, softer lactic acid.

Malvasia A white grape variety grown mainly

in central **Italy**, where it is used to make several
wines including **Frascati**, **Chianti** and **Galestro**. It
is also grown in the **Rioja** area of Spain, as well
as in **France**, **Australia**, **Portugal**, **Yugoslavia**,
Austria and **Germany**. It can produce a full-
bodied, scented wine, with good acidity, but in
Italy much of its character is lost in blending with
Trebbiano and in white Rioja by blending with
Viura (**Macabeo**). The **Malmsey** style of **Madeira**
takes its name from the grape, and Malvasia is
also an ingredient in some white **Port**.

Malvoisie An alternative name, used in the
Loire, for the **Pinot Gris** grape variety.

Mammolo A red grape variety which plays a
minor role in **Vino Nobile di Montepulciano** and
Chianti in **Tuscany**.

Mandrolisai A **DOC** wine made in the Bar-
bagia hills of central **Sardinia**. A sturdy red and
light rosé are both made, mainly from the Bovale
Sardo, **Cannonau** and **Monica** grapes.

Manduria See **Primitivo di Manduria**.

Manseng See **Gros Manseng**; **Petit Manseng**.

Mantonico di Bianco A white wine from
around the town of Bianco in the **Calabria** region
of Italy. It is dry to slightly sweet, made from
semidried Mantonico grapes, and can develop a
nutty, heady aroma with age.

manzanilla A style of **Sherry**, very similar to

fino in taste. Essentially, it is a *fino* that has been matured in the Spanish coastal town of Sanlúcar de Barrameda, rather than in Jerez de la Frontera or Puerto de Santa Maria. The sea air is said to give the Sherry a more pungent, aromatic quality. In fact, the difference in character is due to the different sort of **flor** that develops in Sanlúcar. *Manzanilla* is usually of very high quality, as long as it has not been on the shelf for too long, and is very good value for money. It should be drunk chilled, on its own or with seafood. Once opened, as with any white wine, a bottle of *manzanilla* should be finished quickly.
PRICE BAND: B.

Maranges, Les   See **Les Maranges**.

marc   The French term for the solid matter (skins, pips and possibly stalks) left after pressing grapes. It is also the term for the white spirit made from distilling this residue.

Marches (also called **Marche**)   A wine region centred on the town of Ancona on the central eastern coast of **Italy**. The red Sangiovese dei Colli Pesaresi and the dry white **Bianchello del Metauro** are produced in the north of the region. The region's most famous wine, the dry white **Verdicchio** dei Castelli di Jesi, comes from the hills around Ancona, as does the red **Rosso Cònero**. Other wines include the dry white Verdicchio di Matelica, **Bianco dei Colli Maceratesi** and **Falerio dei Colli Asolani**, the bubbly red

Vernaccia di Serrapetrona and the dry red **Rosso Piceno**.

Marcillac A **VDQS** wine produced in very small quantities in Aveyron, southwest **France**. The red, based on the **Fer** grape, plus **Gamay** and **Jurançon** Noir, is strong, dry and assertive. A small amount of rosé is also produced. PRICE BAND: B.

Margaret River An important wine-producing region of **Western Australia**. The climate is temperate, and **varietal** wines made from the **Cabernet Sauvignon** grape variety do particularly well here. **Semillon** and **Chardonnay** have also been successful, and recent experiments with **Pinot Noir** have been encouraging.

Margaux One of the most important communal **ACs** of the **Médoc**, and also the name of its leading château. The *appellation* is based on the village of Margaux, but also takes in the surrounding villages of Soussac, Cantenac, Labarde and Arsac. There are 21 **cru classé** châteaux and a larger number of **crus bourgeois**, many of the latter also making wine of high quality.

Maria Gomez See **Fernão Pires**.

Marignan A **cru** of the **Vin de Savoie** *appellation*.

Marino A white **DOC** wine from the hills around Rome in the **Latium** region of Italy. The wine can be dry or **amabile**, still or **spumante**, and is made mainly from **Malvasia** and **Trebbiano** grape varieties. It is very similar to **Frascati** in style.

Markgräflerland A **Bereich** subregion of the **Baden** region of Germany. It produces mainly white wines, particularly light, spritzy wines from the **Gutedel** grape.

Marlborough The finest wine region of South Island, **New Zealand**. It produces stunning crisp white wines from the **Sauvignon Blanc** grape, and good results have also been obtained with **Cabernet Sauvignon**, **Chardonnay** and **Pinot Noir**.

marque auxilliere See **MA**.

Marsala A fortified **DOC** wine made in the western part of **Sicily**. The production process is complex, involving the use of concentrated and cooked **musts** and long **ageing** in oak barrels. The *oro* (gold) and *ambra* (amber) types are based on white grapes, mainly **Grillo**, **Catarratto** and **Inzolia**. The *rubino* (ruby) style is based on the Perricone, **Calabrese** and **Nerello** Mascalese grapes, plus up to 30% of the white varieties. Fine and Superiore Marsala can be *oro*, *ambra* or *rubino*, and can range from **secco** through to **dolce** in sweetness. Concentrated musts can be used for all types of Fine and Superiore (to give sweetness), but cooked must (to give colour and a burnt caramel flavour) is allowed only for *ambra*. Vergine Marsala can be *oro*, *ambra* or *rubino*, but no cooked or concentrated musts can be used.

Some Marsala is aged in a **solera** system, similar to that used for **Sherry**. Superiore can have a marvellous, deep, caramel sweetness balanced by piercing acidity. Vergine makes a deep, dry, complex apéritif, and Fine is best used for cooking. FINE AND SUPERIORE PRICE BAND: B; VERGINE PRICE BAND: D.

Marsannay An AC wine produced just south of Dijon, in the **Côte de Nuits** area of **Burgundy**. The red is made from the **Pinot Noir** grape and is a reasonable quality Burgundy, best drunk fairly young. The rosé, also from Pinot Noir, is dry, with pleasant cherry fruit. Whites are rarely seen.

Marsanne The predominant white grape variety grown in the northern **Rhône** area of France, where it is used to make white **Saint-Joseph** and **Crozes-Hermitage**, and still and sparkling **Saint-Péray**. It is permitted in red **Hermitage**, but is rarely used. It is also planted, to a limited extent, in **Australia**.

Martina Franca (also called **Martina**) A dry white **DOC** wine produced between Bari and Brindisi in the **Apulia** region of Italy. It can be still or sparkling, and is made mainly from the Verdeca and **Bianco di Alessano** grape varieties. The wine is very similar to **Locorotondo** in style.

Martinborough A small region on the North

Island of **New Zealand**, which produces particularly fine **varietal** wines from **Pinot Noir** and **Chardonnay** grapes, along with **Sauvignon Blanc**, **Gewürztraminer** and **Rhine Riesling**.

Martinsthal A village in the **Rheingau** region of Germany. It produces good quality white wines from the **Riesling** grape variety. The vineyards come within the **Grosslage** of **Steinmächer**, and the **Einzellage** sites are Langenberg, Rödchen and Wildsau.

Marzemino A red grape variety planted mainly in Italy, although probably of Austrian origin. It makes rustic reds for drinking young in the **Trentino** region of Italy, and it is one of the **varietals** authorized for the Trentino **DOC**. Elsewhere in Italy, it is used for blending in **Lombardy** and **Emilia-Romagna**.

Matino A DOC wine produced in the Salento peninsula in the **Apulia** region of Italy. It produces both red and **rosato**, both made from the **Negroamaro** grape, with up to 30% **Malvasia** Nera and **Sangiovese**, and both of mediocre quality.

mature A tasting term, used to describe a wine that is fully aged. How long this takes varies enormously with different wines and regions. It can take from a few months to several decades for a wine to become mature, depending on the initial content of **acid**, **alcohol**, **tannin**, and fruit. Red wine can be seen to be mature when the colour takes on a ruddy brown at the rim, and on the nose and palate all the component parts are harmoniously blended. See also **ageing**.

Maury A sweet, red or rosé **AC** wine made in the **Languedoc-Roussillon** region from the **Grenache** grape variety. It is a **vin doux naturel** (that is, a **fortified wine**), with a strong, Porty taste. It is sometimes aged to make an oxidized, **rancio** style, with a burnt, caramel flavour.

Mauzac Blanc A white grape variety of France, used to make white wines in **Gaillac** and sparkling wines in Limoux, where it goes under the name Blanquette. It is a good, neutral base for sparkling wines, but still wines based on Mauzac tend to be highly acidic, tart and thin.

Mavrodaphne A red grape variety native to **Greece**, where it produces lightly **fortified**, deep, sweet, red wines around Patras in the Peloponnese. Quality can be good, especially with a few years' ageing.

Mazis-Chambertin A **grand cru** vineyard of **Gevrey-Chambertin** in the Côte de Nuits area of **Burgundy**.

McDowell Valley An **AVA** of **Mendocino** county, **California**. It has a short warm season and produces fine **varietal** wines particularly from **Syrah** and **Zinfandel** grapes; also **Cabernet Sauvignon**, **Chardonnay** and **Sauvignon Blanc**.

McLaren Vale A wine-producing area in **South Australia** which produces particularly good white **varietal** wines from the **Chardonnay** grape. Reds from **Cabernet Sauvignon**, **Grenache** and **Shiraz** also do well, as do whites from **Sauvignon Blanc** and **Riesling**.

Médoc 1. The general term for the peninsular area of **Bordeaux** to the west of the Gironde estuary, to distinguish it, for instance, from **Saint-Emilion** and **Pomerol** to the east and the **Graves** region to the south. The area includes the ACs of Médoc, **Haut-Médoc**, **Margaux**, **Listrac**, **Moulis**, **Saint-Estèphe**, **Saint-Julien** and **Pauillac**.
2. A red AC wine of Bordeaux, produced in the northern half of the Médoc peninsula from the classic Bordeaux grape varieties (**Cabernet Sauvignon**, **Cabernet Franc**, **Merlot** and **Petit Verdot**). The wines are usually of good quality, for early drinking, although not approaching the quality of the communal *appellations* of the Haut-Médoc to the south. There are no **crus classés**, but several **crus bourgeois**.

Mélinots A premier cru of **Chablis**.

Melissa A **DOC** wine of the eastern coast of the **Calabria** region of Italy, similar to **Cirò**, but generally of lower quality. The white is made mainly from the **Greco** grape and the red from **Gaglioppo**.

Melon d'Arbois An alternative name, used in the **Jura**, for the **Chardonnay** grape variety.

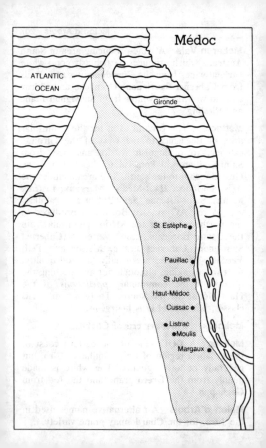

Médoc

ATLANTIC OCEAN

Gironde

St Estèphe

Pauillac

St Julien

Haut-Médoc

Cussac

Listrac

Moulis

Margaux

Melon de Bourgogne (also called **Muscadet**) A white grape variety grown almost exclusively in the Pays Nantais region of the **Loire**, where it is used to make the dry, crisp **AC** wine **Muscadet**.

Mendocino The most northerly of the major wine-producing counties of **California**. It produces premium **varietal** wines from **Chardonnay**, **Sauvignon Blanc**, **Zinfandel**, **Pinot Noir** and **Cabernet Sauvignon** grapes. Important **AVAs** include **McDowell Valley**, and the **Anderson Valley** which is well-suited to Chardonnay and Pinot Noir and is becoming popular as a sparkling wine area. Mendocino producers have spearheaded the move towards **organic** winemaking in California.

Menetou-Salon An **AC** wine made around the village of Menetou-Salon in the eastern **Loire** valley. It is a neighbour of **Sancerre** and the wine is similar to, if not quite as good as, the very best Sancerre and **Pouilly-Fumé**. It is a crisp, refreshing, juicy white made from the **Sauvignon Blanc** grape. Red and rosé Menetou-Salon, made from the **Pinot Noir** grape, can be better than Sancerre. They are fresh, lean, strawberry fruit wines, which are best drunk slightly chilled.

Méntrida A **DO** wine northeast of **La Mancha** in central **Spain**. producing dark, strong, high-alcohol, high-tannin, red and **rosado** wines from the **Garnacha** and **Cencibel** grape varieties.

Meranese di Collina (also called **Meraner Hügel**) A dry red **DOC** wine produced around Merano in the South Tyrol in the **Trentino** and **Alto Adige** regions of Italy. It is made from the Vernatsch (**Schiava**) grape variety. It is light and scented, and best drunk young and slightly chilled.

Mercurey An **AC** wine produced around the village of Mercurey in the **Côte Chalonnaise** region of **Burgundy**. Most of the wines are red, made from the **Pinot Noir** grape, and are among the fullest-flavoured and best-structured of the Côte Chalonnaise. A small amount of white wine is produced from the **Chardonnay** grape, and recent improvements in quality among the better producers are encouraging. PRICE BAND: B–C.

Merlot One of the world's major red grape varieties, traditionally grown in **Bordeaux**, where it is the mainstay of the **Saint-Emilion** and **Pomerol** regions. It also plays an important, but secondary role in the great red wines of the **Médoc**. Merlot is found the world over, and is particularly successful in **California**. It is also grown in northeastern **Italy** especially in **Friuli-Venezia Giulia**, **Trentino** and the **Veneto**.

Merseguera A white grape variety of **Spain**, grown in **Valencia**, **Alicante** and **Tarragona**. It produces dull, bland wine.

méthode champenoise (also called **méthode**

traditionelle) The method by which **Champagne** gets its bubbles, by a second **fermentation** which takes place in bottle. The term is currently found on the labels of bottle-fermented sparkling wines from the rest of France and all over the world, but it is gradually being phased out in EC countries. New terms coined to replace it include *méthode traditionelle* in France and *metodo classico* in Italy.

methuselah A large format bottle of 6 litres capacity (eight ordinary 75 cl bottles) used for **Champagne**.

metodo classico An Italian term for bottle-fermented sparkling wines. See **méthode champenoise**.

Meursault An **AC** wine of the **Côte de Beaune** area of **Burgundy**. The vineyards surrounding Meursault, one of the largest villages of the Côte, produce some of the finest white Burgundies up to **premier cru** level, from the **Chardonnay** grape. There are no **grands crus**. At their best, the whites are pale gold, dry but full, with rich buttery, nutty, creamy aromas and taste. A small amount of red Meursault is produced, from **Pinot Noir**, but much is sold as Volnay-Santenots or **Blagny**. PRICE BAND: D–E.

Mexico A wine-producing country of central America. Many of the vineyards are for table-grape production, and most of the country's wine is distilled into brandy. The quality of table wine production is gradually improving, and some **Vitis vinifera** grape varieties, including **Riesling**, **Pinot Noir** and **Cabernet Sauvignon**, have been grown successfully, especially in the Baja California area. Production also includes some **méthode champenoise** sparkling wines and **fortified** wines similar to **Sherry**.

MIA Abbreviation of **Murrumbigee Irrigation Area**.

Midi The largest wine region of **France**, stretching from the Pyrenees in the west to the Rhône delta in the east. It used to be the source of vast quantities of inferior wine, destined for **vin de table**, or for blending wine to beef up the production of loftier *appellations* farther north. However, with the introduction of new techniques in the vineyard and cellar, the region is coming into its own. It produces good-value, good-quality, modern-style wines from quality grape varieties. Each main **AC** has its own entry. See **Corbières**; **Costières-du-Gard**; **Coteaux du Languedoc**; **Côtes du Roussillon**; **Minervois**. See also **Languedoc-Roussillon**.

millésime The French term for **vintage**.

Minervois An **AC** wine of the **Languedoc-Roussillon** region of France. It produces mainly fruity, easy-drinking red wine, which is best drunk young, from the **Carignan**, **Grenache** and **Cinsault** grapes, with some **Mourvèdre**. **Carbonic maceration** is occasionally used to good effect, in making the wines. Minervois wines are generally lighter and less complex than those from neighbouring **Corbières**. PRICE BAND: A.

mis en bouteille au château A term found on French labels, indicating that the wine was bottled at the château.

Mission A red grape variety, the first **Vitis vinifera** variety to be planted in **California**. It was brought by Jesuit priests in the late 17th century, hence the name Mission. Although now in decline, it is still planted in California, where it produces light, rustic reds. Mission is probably related to the **Pais** grape of **Chile**.

mistelle An alcoholic drink made by the addition of brandy, or grape spirit, to unfermented grape juice. See **Floc de Gascogne**; **Pineau des Charentes**; **Ratafia**.

Mittelhaardt-Deutsche Weinstrasse A **Bereich** subregion of the **Rheinpfalz** region of Germany. It produces some of the country's finest white wines from the **Riesling** grape variety. See **Deidesheim**; **Forst**; **Wachenheim**.

Mittelheim A village in the **Rheingau** region of Germany, which produces good quality white wines mainly from the **Riesling** grape. Part of Mittelheim, with its neighbour **Winkel**, comes within the **Grosslage** of Honigberg; the remainder within Erntebringer. The **Einzellage** sites are Edelmann, Goldberg and St Nikolaus.

Mittelmosel An area of the **Mosel-Saar-Ruwer** region of Germany, approximately corresponding to the **Bereich** subregion of **Bernkastel**.

Mittelrhein A minor **Anbaugebiet** region of Germany, which follows the course of the Rhine from just beyond **Lorch**, in the **Rheingau**, almost as far as Bonn. Most of the vineyards are planted with the **Riesling** grape, and they produce attractive, steely wines, which are seldom exported, and base wine for **Sekt**. There are three **Bereich** subregions: **Bacharach**, Rheinburgengau and Siebengebirge.

moelleux A French term used to describe a rich, luscious wine. It is particularly used in the **Loire** region for sweetish whites made from the **Chenin Blanc** grape, such as **Vouvray** and **Montlouis**.

Molette A white grape variety grown around Seyssel in the **Savoie** region of France. It produces thin, neutral, sometimes bitter wine, which is best used as a base for sparkling wine.

Molinara A red grape variety which produces light, fruity wines. It is chiefly used as a minor part in the blend for **Valpolicella** and **Bardolino** in the **Veneto** region of Italy.

Molise A small wine-producing region just south of **Abruzzi**, on the Adriatic coast of **Italy**. The main wine of the region is **Biferno**, but perhaps the best wines of Molise are made outside the **DOC** system, with good **vini da tavola** made from the **Montepulciano** and **Aglianico** grapes.

Monastrell   One of the most widely planted red grape varieties of **Spain**. It produces deep, full-flavoured, high-alcohol red and rosé wines. The reds can have good ageing potential. It is found mainly in **Alicante** and also in **Almansa**, **Jumilla**, **Penedès**, **Valencia** and **Yecla**.

Monbazillac   A sweet, white **AC** wine of the **Bergerac** region, which is made from the same grape varieties as **Sauternes** (**Sémillon**, **Sauvignon** and **Muscadelle**), but never reaching the same heights of quality. The **botrytis** fungus does not appear as often in Monbazillac, and few growers can risk leaving the grapes on the vines in the hopes that it will develop. At its best, Monbazillac is rich and honeyed, but without the depth of Sauternes. PRICE BAND: B–C.

Mondeuse Noire   A red grape variety grown in the **Savoie** region of France and in the **Friuli-Venezia Giulia** region of Italy, where it is known as Refosco. In Savoie it produces, at best, dense, deep-coloured, austere reds, and at worst, thin, tart wines. In **Bugey** it is successfully blended with other grape varieties, including **Pinot Noir** and **Gamay**. Mondeuse Blanche, a white grape variety, is now rare, even in Savoie.

Monica   A red grape variety, thought to be

native to Spain, but now grown mainly in **Sardinia**, where it makes soft red wines. It is used for **DOC** wines in Monica di Sardegna, producing a soft, light, dry red; and Monica di Cagliari, which is usually a sweet, sometimes **fortified**, light, ruby coloured wine.

Mont de Milieu A **premier cru** of **Chablis**.

Montagne de Reims An important vineyard area of the **Champagne** region, especially good for growing the red **Pinot Noir** grape.

Montagne-Saint-Emilion A red **AC** wine made in a 'satellite' area of the main **Saint-Emilion** *appellation* in **Bordeaux**, and also neighbouring **Pomerol**. The grape varieties are the same as for Saint-Emilion (**Merlot**, **Cabernet Franc**, **Cabernet Sauvignon** and **Malbec**), but the wines, although very pleasant to drink when fairly young and offering good value, never reach the heights of the top Saint-Emilions. Producers in the commune of Saint-Georges have the option of using the AC of either Montagne-Saint-Emilion or **Saint-Georges-Saint-Emilion**. PRICE BAND: B.

Montagny A white **AC** wine from the **Côte Chalonnaise** area of **Burgundy**, made from the **Chardonnay** grape variety. Quality can be good, particularly where the wine has been aged in oak barrels, although the wines never reach the heights of top white Burgundies from the **Côte**

d'Or or Chablis. The term **premier cru** is sometimes seen on Montagny wines, but it does not imply increased quality. PRICE BAND: C.

Montecarlo A **DOC** wine produced around the town of Montecarlo near Lucca in **Tuscany**. The dry white is very good and is based on the **Trebbiano** Toscano grape. It is also permitted to add more exciting varieties, including **Sémillon**, **Sauvignon** and **Pinot Grigio**, which add more interesting flavours and aromas. The dry red, made mainly from the **Sangiovese** and **Canaiolo** grapes, can also be good.

Montecompatri-Colonna A dry or medium-dry white **DOC** wine produced in the hills around Rome, near the towns of Montecompatri and Colonna, in the **Latium** region of Italy. It is made mainly from the **Malvasia** and **Trebbiano** grape varieties, and is similar in style to **Frascati**.

Montée de Tonnerre A **premier cru** vineyard of **Chablis**.

Montefalco A red **DOC** wine produced around the town of Montefalco in Perugia, in the **Umbria** region of Italy. The dry red is based on the **Sangiovese** grape variety, with **Trebbiano** and Sagrantino. PRICE BAND: A.

The best quality red, the full-flavoured, assertive Sagrantino, is made almost entirely from the Sagrantino grape, and is either dry or in the sweet **passito** style, made from dried grapes. PRICE BAND: B.

Montello e Colli Asolani A **DOC** wine produced in the eastern part of the **Veneto** region of Italy. Two **varietal** red wines are produced: Cabernet (made from **Cabernet Franc** and/or **Cabernet Sauvignon**) and **Merlot**. A dry white, usually sparkling **Prosecco** is also produced. None are of better than ordinary quality.

Montepulciano An Italian red grape variety. It is planted widely throughout **Italy** from Apulia to the Marches, and is second only in popularity to **Sangiovese**. Montepulciano d'Abruzzo and **Rosso Cònero** are two of the more notable wines made from it. See also **Cerveterai**; **Cori**; **Leverano**; **Orta Nova**; **San Severo**.

Monterey County A county of **California**, which is particularly suited to the production of white **varietal** wines, especially from the **Chardonnay**, **Chenin Blanc**, **Riesling** and **Sauvignon Blanc** grape varieties. Fine reds have also been produced, from **Cabernet Sauvignonn**.

Monthélie An **AC** wine of the **Côte de Beaune** area of **Burgundy**. The village of Monthélie is a neighbour of **Volnay**, and its red wines, made from the **Pinot Noir** grape variety, are in a similar style, but lighter and generally for earlier drinking. Only a tiny amount of white wine is produced. PRICE BAND: C–D.

Montilla-Moriles A white **DO** wine of southwest **Spain**, similar in style and in its method of production to **Sherry**. Montilla for export is usually not **fortified**, however, and is based on the **Pedro Ximénez** grape. It is usually sold under the labels 'dry', 'medium' and 'cream'. Quality can be very good, but most of what is on sale in export markets is mediocre. PRICE BAND: A.

Montlouis A white **AC** wine of the **Touraine** area of the **Loire**. The wines, all based on the **Chenin Blanc** grape, are produced in similar styles to **Vouvray**: dry, **demi-sec**, **moelleux** and sparkling wines. The quality is usually very good. The dry wines are often high in **acidity**, and can be quite **austere** in their youth, with a characteristic wet-wool aroma. PRICE BAND: A–C.

Montmains A **premier cru** of **Chablis**.

Montmélian A **cru** of the **Vin de Savoie** *appellation*. The wines are mainly dry, biting whites, made from the **Jacquère** grape.

Montrachet, Le A **grand cru** shared by the villages of **Chassagne-Montrachet** and **Puligny-Montrachet** in the **Côte de Beaune** region of **Burgundy**. Le Montrachet is made from the **Chardonnay** grape variety. Its colour begins as a greenish yellow, deepening to gold with age, as the dry but honeyed taste and aromas develop. The wine is rich and mouth-filling, and is best drunk when it is at least 10 years old. It is one of world's finest white wines. PRICE BAND: E.

Montravel A white **AC** wine from the **Bergerac** region of France, made from the **Sémillon**,

Sauvignon Blanc and **Muscadelle** grape varieties. Most of the wine is dry to medium-dry, but many producers sell the wine as Bergerac Sec rather than Montravel. PRICE BAND: A.

Morellino di Scansano A dry red **DOC** wine produced around the town of Scansano in the southern part of **Tuscany**. It is a dry, cherry-flavoured, rustic red, of moderate quality, made mainly from the **Sangiovese** grape.

Morey-St-Denis An **AC** wine from the **Côte de Nuits** area of **Burgundy**. The red wine is made from the **Pinot Noir** grape, and is similar in style to neighbouring **Gevrey-Chambertin**, but in much smaller quantity. Quality can be very good, especially from the **grand cru** vineyards.

Morgon A red **AC** wine that is one of the 10 **crus** of the **Beaujolais** region of **Burgundy** and is made from the **Gamay** grape. The wine is perfumed, with juicy, ripe sweetness, and cherry and chocolate flavours. Its quality is usually very good. It is relatively long-lived and is among the best of all Beaujolais. PRICE BAND: B.

Morio-Muskat A white grape variety made by crossing **Silvaner** and **Pinot Blanc** (Weissburgunder). It is planted in Germany, mainly in the Rheinhessen and Rheinpfalz. It makes blowzy, floral, grapey wine of dubious quality, and its use is in decline.

Moscadello di Montalcino A sweet white

DOC wine, based on the **Moscato** grape, produced around Montalcino in **Tuscany**. It can be still or **frizzante**, and is of very ordinary quality. A better wine is the fortified **liquoroso** version, made from dried grapes.

Moscatel The name used for grapes of the **Muscat** family in **Spain** and **Portugal**. In Spain, the Moscatel de Málaga variety is used to make sweet white wines in **Málaga** and **Valencia**. Moscatel de Setúbal is a **fortified** white **RD** wine of Portugal, which is deep, sweet, luscious and capable of long ageing, in cask or bottle.

Moscato The Italian name for the **Muscat** Blanc à Petits Grains grape variety.

Moscato d'Asti A sweet, aromatic white **DOC** wine made in the same area as **Asti Spumante** in **Piedmont**, Italy. It can be still or **frizzante**. Quality is very consistent and it can be a delicious, refreshing wine to drink chilled, on its own, on a summer day. PRICE BAND: B.

Moscato Giallo See **Goldenmuskateller**.

Mosel-Saar-Ruwer One of the most important of the 11 **Anbaugebiet** regions of **Germany**, named after the Mosel river and two of its tributaries. The region produces mainly white wines, the finest of them made from the **Riesling** grape, on steep, slate vineyard sites. Other

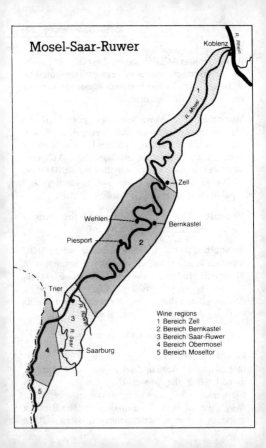

Mosel-Saar-Ruwer

Koblenz

R. Rhein

R. Mosel

1

Zell

Wehlen —•— Bernkastel

Piesport —

2

Trier

R. Ruwer

3

R. Saar

Saarburg

4

5

Wine regions
1 Bereich Zell
2 Bereich Bernkastel
3 Bereich Saar-Ruwer
4 Bereich Obermosel
5 Bereich Moseltor

varieties planted include **Müller-Thurgau** and **Elbling**. There are five **Bereich** subregions: **Zell**, **Saar-Ruwer**, **Obermosel**, **Moseltor** and **Bernkastel**, which contains the finest vineyards.

Moseltaler A sort of 'Mosel Liebfraumilch', a QbA wine of the **Mosel-Saar-Ruwer** region which can be made from **Riesling**, **Müller-Thurgau**, **Elbling** or **Kerner** grapes.

Moseltor The smallest **Bereich** subregion of the **Mosel-Saar-Ruwer** region of **Germany**. Its main production is of the base wine for **Sekt** from the **Elbling** grape variety.

mosto The Italian word for **must**.

Moulin-à-Vent A red **AC** wine that is one of the 10 **crus** of the **Beaujolais** region of **Burgundy** and is made from the **Gamay** grape. The wine is full-bodied, even tough in youth, rich and chocolaty and its quality is usually very good. It is among the best, if perhaps the least characteristic, of all Beaujolais. PRICE BAND: B.

Moulis A communal **AC** wine of the **Haut-Médoc** region of **Bordeaux**. It produces good, long-lived, tough, tannic **cru bourgeois** wines but no **cru classé**. In recent years, with the greater use of new oak, many of the wines have greatly improved in quality.

Mourvèdre A red grape variety which produces well-structured wines, low in acid and relatively light in colour. It is part of the blend for **Bandol** in **Provence** and for **Châteauneuf-du-Pape** in the **Rhône**, and is widely planted throughout southern France. In **Australia** it is called Mataro, and is usually blended with other varieties. It is also found, but in diminishing quantities, in **California**.

mousseux The French term for sparkling. It is normally used on sparkling wines that are made by the **cuve close** method rather than the **méthode champenoise**.

Mudgee A wine-producing region of **New South Wales** in **Australia**. It produces good-quality red wines from the **Cabernet Sauvignon** and **Shiraz** grape varieties, and whites from **Chardonnay** and **Sémillon**. Much of the wine is sold to producers in the **Hunter Valley** region for blending.

muffa nobile The Italian term for **botrytis**.

Mülheim A village in the **Bereich** of **Bernkastel** in the **Mosel-Saar-Ruwer** region of Germany. It produces some very good, elegant white wines mainly from the **Riesling** grape, which rival Bernkastel and **Brauneberg**. It comes within the **Grosslage** of Kurfürstlay, and the **Einzellage** sites are Amtsgarten, Elisenberg, Helenenkloster and Sonnenlay.

Müller-Thurgau A white grape variety, made by crossing **Riesling** and **Silvaner**, or possibly two different varities of Riesling. It is planted extensively throughout **Germany**, where it produces large quantities of good, light quaffing wines; capable of distinction in **Baden**. It is also grown in the **Alto Adige** in **Italy**, in **Austria**, **Hungary**, **Yugoslavia**, **New Zealand** and **England**.

Münster-Sarmsheim A village in the **Nahe** region of Germany. It produces top-quality white wines from the **Riesling** grape variety, and it comes within the **Grosslage** Schlosskapelle. The best **Einzellage** site is Dautenpflänzer, followed by Kapellenberg, Königsschloss, Liebehöll, Pittersberg, Röerberg, Steinkopf and Trollberg. The 'Sarmsheim' part of the name does not appear on the label.

Murray River Valley A wine-producing area of **Victoria** in **Australia**, which is planted mainly with the white **Sémillon** and red **Shiraz** grape varieties.

Murrumbidgee Irrigation Area (MIA) A wine-producing area of **New South Wales** in **Australia**. It produces large quantites of wine, mainly whites from the **Sémillon** and **Trebbiano** grape varieties, and some reds from **Shiraz**. Much of the production ends up in wine boxes, with a handful of quality-conscious producers making fine table wines.

Muscadelle A white grape variety that plays a minor role in the sweet wines of **Bordeaux**, e.g. **Sauternes** and **Barsac**, where it is sometimes included in the blend of **Sémillon** and **Sauvignon Blanc**, to contribute aroma. It has some of the grapey quality of **Muscat**, but is a distinct variety in its own right.

In **Australia** it is used to make rich, dark, dessert wines, known as Liqueur Tokays. The South African Muscadel or Muskadel is Muscat Blanc à Petits Grains rather than Muscadelle.

Muscadet A white **AC** wine of the western part of the **Loire**, made from the grape of the same name, also known as **Melon de Bourgogne**. Muscadet is a crisp, dry white, usually fairly simple, and is ideal for drinking as a refreshing apéritif or with the oysters and other seafood of the region.

Most Muscadet is sold as Muscadet de Sèvre et Maine. It is produced on the gently hilly banks of the Sèvre and Maine rivers, two tributaries of the Loire. Some Muscadet is sold as **sur lie**, meaning that the wine is matured on the **lees**, and, in theory, bottled straight from the barrel. The wine can develop a delicious yeasty complexity, sometimes with a slightly **pétillant** prickle on the tongue.

Muscadet is normally drunk very young, but from exceptional years it can age surprisingly well, developing great complexity, even beginning to resemble white **Burgundy**. PRICE BAND: A (B FOR SUR LIE).

Muscat A family of white grape varieties. The best in quality is the Muscat Blanc à Petits

Grains, which is planted throughout the world. It is mainly found in **France**, especially around Frontignan, where it makes luscious **vin doux naturel** fortified wines. In **Italy** (where it is known as Moscato) it is used, particularly in **Piedmont**, for the light, refreshing **Moscato d'Asti** and **Asti Spumante**. It is also occasionally found in **California** and **Australia**, where it is sometimes called Frontignan. Most of the sweet Australian Liqueur Muscats are made from another member of the family, the Muscat of Alexandria. The majority of the Muscat planted in **Spain** and **Portugal** is also Muscat of Alexandria, and is mainly found around **Alicante** and **Valencia** and **Setúbal**.

The third member of the family is Muscat Ottonel, which is grown chiefly in **Alsace**, where it is usually used to make light, dry **varietal** wine, good as an apéritif.

Muscat de Beaumes-de-Venise A sweet white **AC** wine of the southern **Rhône**, made from the **Muscat** Blanc à Petits Grains grape variety. It is a **vin doux naturel**, or **fortified** wine, produced by adding grape spirit to the partly fermented **must**. It is probably the best sweet Muscat of France, with a rich, grapey aroma and taste, with a balancing, fruity **acidity**. PRICE BAND: B–C.

Muscat de Frontignan A sweet white **AC** wine from the **Languedoc-Roussillon** area of France This is a **fortified** wine, a **vin doux naturel**, made from the **Muscat** Blanc à Petits Grains grape variety. It is rich and raisiny, but lacks the balancing fruity **acidity** found in **Muscat de Beaumes-de-Venise**. PRICE BAND: B.

Muscat de Lunel A sweet white **AC** wine from the **Languedoc-Roussillon** area of France, rarely seen outside its own region. This is a **fortified** wine, a **vin doux naturel**, similar in style to **Muscat de Frontignan**. It is rich and raisiny and sometimes with decent **acidity,** but rarely very inspiring.

Muscat de Mireval A sweet white **AC** wine from the **Languedoc-Roussillon** area of France, rarely seen outside its own region. This is a **fortified** wine, a **vin doux naturel**, similar in style to **Muscat de Frontignan**, rich and raisiny, sometimes with decent acidity, but rarely very inspiring.

Muscat de Rivesaltes A sweet white **AC** wine from the **Languedoc-Roussillon** area of France. This is a **fortified wine**, a **vin doux naturel**, made mainly from the **Muscat** of Alexandria grape, together with some Muscat Blanc à Petits Grains. It is heady and fat, with the aroma of boiling marmalade, and sometimes rather coarse. PRICE BAND: B.

Muscat de Saint-Jean-de-Minervois A sweet white **AC** wine from the **Minervois** region of **Languedoc-Roussillon**. This is a **fortified** wine, a **vin doux naturel**, similar in style to **Muscat de**

Frontignan. It is rich and raisiny and sometimes with decent **acidity**, but rarely very inspiring.

Muscatel An alternative name, used in Australia, for the **Muscat** of Alexandria grape variety.

Musigny A **grand cru** of the **Chambolle-Musigny** *appellation* in the **Côte de Nuits** area of **Burgundy**. It produces almost entirely red wines from the **Pinot Noir** grape. The wines can be of very high quality, but in recent years many have failed to live up to *grand cru* standards. PRICE BAND: E.

musky A tasting term, not uncomplimentary, used to describe a dusty, spicy smell in wine.

must Unfermented grape juice.

must weight The natural sugar content of grape juice before **fermentation** begins. The sugar level is an important factor in deciding when to harvest grapes. It can be measured using a spectrometer or an hydrometer. Scales used to express must weight include **Baumé**, Brix (the American system) and Oechsle (the German system) and specific gravity. Since wine fermentation is the conversion of grape sugar into alcohol, the maximum potential **alcohol content** of a wine is determined by the must weight.

musty A tasting term used to describe a stale smell and taste, which may mean that the wine is slightly **corked**, or which may wear off if the wine is allowed to stand for a while or decanted.

Nackenheim A small town of the **Rheinhessen** region of Germany, producing excellent white wine, mainly from the **Riesling** grape variety. The vineyards are split between the **Grosslagen** of Spiegelberg and Gutes Domtal, and **Einzellage** sites include Engelsberg, Rothenberg (named after its red sandstone soil) and Schmittskapellchen.

Nahe One of the 11 major quality wine regions, or **Anbaugebiete**, of **Germany**. It produces some of the finest of the country's white wines from the **Riesling** grape variety, which dominates the best vineyard sites, particularly at **Spätlese** and **Kabinett** level. The region is split into the two **Bereich** subregions of Kreuznach and Schlossböckelheim.

Napa Gamay The misleading Californian name for the true **Gamay** of **Beaujolais**. See also **Gamay Beaujolais**.

Napa Valley The leading wine area of **California**. An **AVA** in its own right, it also takes in all, or part, of the following: **Howell Mountain**, **Carneros**, Mount Veeder, **North Coast** and **Stag's Leap** AVAs. Wine has been produced here from as early as the 1840s, but the number of wineries has risen from fewer than 30 in 1965 to close to 200 today.

The majority of the quality wines of the Napa

are **varietals**, although some **Bordeaux**-style blends
are appearing. The principal wine of the region is
the red **Cabernet Sauvignon**, which achieves
greater distinction than almost anywhere else in
California, the best examples coming from the
central part of the valley. Reds from **Pinot Noir**
and whites from **Chardonnay** grow best in the
Carneros region in the cooler southern part of
the Napa. Fine Cabernet and excellent **Zinfandel**
are also produced in the north, around Calistoga.
Other important varieties include **Sauvignon
Blanc**, **Chenin Blanc** and **Merlot**; also **Sémillion**
and **Cabernet Franc** are being increasingly
planted.

Nasco di Cagliari A white **DOC** wine from
Sardinia, made from the native Nasco grape. The
wine can be **dolce** *naturale*, medium-sweet and
delicately flavoured, or the drier, slightly bitter
secco. Both versions can also be **fortified**.

Navarra A **DO** wine of **Spain**, produced to the
north and east of the **Rioja** region. Although
similar in style to Riojan wines, they do not
reach the quality of the best Riojan wines. Red
Navarra suffers from being made mainly from the
Garnacha grape (which it is now forbidden to
plant in the region), but there is an increasingly
important contribution from **Tempranillo** and
Cabernet Sauvignon. There are already signs of
improvement in quality.

White wines are also produced, also inferior to
the best of Rioja. Quality is gradually improving

with the introduction of more **Chardonnay** and modern vinification techniques. PRICE BAND: A–B.

Nebbiolo A red grape variety of **Italy**. It is used particularly in **Piedmont**, where it is the sole ingredient in the great reds **Barolo** and **Barbaresco**, as well as **Nebbiolo d'Alba**. Its name derives from *nebbia* (fog), after the mists that are often present when the grape is harvested in late October. Nebbiolo produces **big** wines, tough and tannic in their youth, but capable of ageing into wines of rich complexity, with overtones of tar, roses, leather and game.

Nebbiolo d'Alba A red **DOC** wine made around Roero and the commune of Alba in **Piedmont**, Italy. It is made entirely from the **Nebbiolo** grape, and the wine is usually dry, although there are sweet and **spumante** versions. The dry wine can be very good, offering an early drinking style of Nebbiolo, unlike **Barolo** and **Barbaresco**, which require long ageing in bottle. PRICE BAND: B.

nebuchadnezzar A large format Champagne bottle, of 15 litres capacity (equivalent to 20 ordinary bottles).

négociant The French term for a company or individual who deals in buying and selling (and sometimes making and maturing) wine. This function is particularly important in **Burgundy**, where there are many very small growers without the facilities to make, bottle, mature and market their own wines. In **Bordeaux** many producers sell their château-produced and bottled wines to *négociants*, who in turn sell them to wholesalers. Wines sold under a *négociant's* label can vary from more or less good generic blends up to high-class wines from individual estates, sometimes owned by the *négociant*.

négociant-manipulant See **NM**.

Negrara A red grape variety sometimes used in making **Valpolicella** and **Bardolino**, but of diminishing importance.

Négrette A red grape variety planted almost exclusively around Toulouse in southwest France, where it figures in the blend for **Côtes du Frontonnais**, **Gaillac** and Lavilledieu. It produces soft wine of good quality, ideal for drinking young, but the vine is highly susceptible to disease and plantings of Négrette are shrinking. Négrette is called Pinot Saint George in **California**, where it produces ordinary quality wine.

Negroamaro A red grape variety planted mainly in the Salento peninsula in **Apulia**, Italy, where it produces **big**, austere wines. Negroamaro is usually blended with other grape varieties, as in **Alezio**, **Brindisi**, **Copertino**, **Leverano**, Lizzano, **Matino**, Nardò, **Salice Salentino** and **Squinzano**.

Nelson A minor wine-producing area on the South Island of **New Zealand**, planted with the ubiquitous (for New Zealand) **Müller-Thurgau** grape variety, and also producing **varietal** wines from **Cabernet Sauvignon**, **Gewürztraminer**, **Pinot Noir**, **Riesling** and **Sémillon**.

Nerello   A pair of red grape varieties native to **Sicily**. Nerello Cappuccio is used mainly for blending, to add alcohol and colour to lighter wines. Nerello Mascalese is of a higher quality, and can produce good-quality **varietal** wines, as well as the **DOC** wine **Etna**.

Nero d'Avola   See **Calabrese**.

Neuburger   A white grape variety of **Austria**, a **cross** of **Weissburgunder** and **Silvaner**. It is an early ripener and produces a high **must weight**, yielding a full-bodied wine, sometimes with a distinctive nutty taste.

Neuchâtel   A wine-growing region of **Switzerland** which produces white wine from the **Chasselas** grape variety and reds from **Pinot Noir**.

Neustadt   A town of the **Rheinpfalz** region of Germany, producing mainly white and some red wines of decent average quality. The vineyards come within the **Grosslage** of Meerspinne.

Nevers   A forest in France where some of the best oak is grown for making **barrels** for **ageing** wine. Its wood is dense with a narrow grain and a high phenol content. It imparts a 'green' aroma and flavour; commonly used in Burgundy and the

New World particularly with **Cabernet Sauvignon**. See also **Allier**; **Limousin**.

New South Wales A state of **Australia** which has five main, warm-climate vineyard areas: the Upper and Lower **Hunter Valley**, **Mudgee**, **Murrumbidgee Irrigation Area** and Canberra District. The Lower Hunter is the best known, producing excellent **varietal** wines, mainly whites from **Sémillon** and **Chardonnay** and reds from **Shiraz** and **Cabernet Sauvignon**.

New York State A state of the eastern United States which has traditionally produced wines from non-**Vitis vinifera** grape varieties such as **Catawba**, **Concord** and Delaware. The wines have a curiously earthy (**foxy**) taste, which has limited their appeal outside the region. More recently, many of the vineyards have been replanted with European grape varieties, including **Chardonnay**, **Riesling**, **Cabernet Sauvignon**, **Gewürztraminer**, **Merlot** and **Sauvignon Blanc**. All appear as **varietals**, although a large amount of sparkling wine is also made, particularly in the **Finger Lakes** region, from blends of white varieties.

New Zealand A country which produces increasingly fine red and white **varietal** wines. New Zealand's position on the international wine stage is based firmly on its newly won reputation for producing fine **Sauvignon Blanc**. The vibrant, juicy fruit aromas and flavours, with steely fresh acidity, have provided new and strong competition with the traditional home of Sauvignon, **Sancerre** and **Pouilly-Fumé** in the **Loire**.

However, Sauvignon is a relative newcomer to New Zealand vineyards. In the 1970s, large areas of vineyard were planted with **Müller-Thurgau**, which is still the country's most widely planted variety. By the mid-1980s, the light table wines produced from Müller-Thurgau had fallen in favour. Consumers wanted varietal wines from Sauvignon Blanc and, of course, **Chardonnay**. The pioneering plantings of Sauvignon Blanc were made in the early 1970s. Later the variety was planted in the South Island region of **Marlborough**, which has since emerged as the country's best area for Sauvignon. Other regions include Auckland, **Gisborne**, **Hawkes Bay** on North Island, and **Nelson** on South Island. Among the red wines produced, **Cabernet Sauvignon** is getting better each vintage.

Niederhausen A small area of the **Nahe** region of Germany. It produces very high-quality white wines, mainly from the **Riesling** grape variety and some from the **Traminer**. The vineyards come within the **Grosslage** of Burgweg, and the **Einzellage** sites include Felsensteyer, Hermannshöhle, Kertz, Klamm, Pfaffenstein, Pfingstweide, Rosenberg, Rosenheck, Steinberg, Steinwingert, Stollenberg and Hermannsberg.

Niederösterreich The largest wine region of **Austria**, planted mainly with the **Grüner Veltliner**

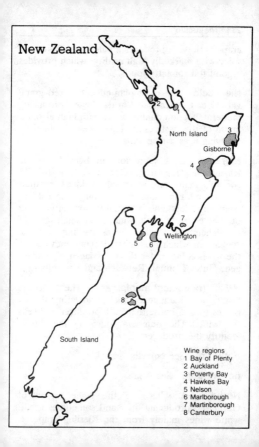

New Zealand

North Island

Gisborne

Wellington

South Island

Wine regions
1 Bay of Plenty
2 Auckland
3 Poverty Bay
4 Hawkes Bay
5 Nelson
6 Marlborough
7 Martinborough
8 Canterbury

grape variety. It produces a pale wine, fruity and spicy with markedly high **acidity**, which provides a good foil for fatty foods.

Nielluccio The most planted native red grape variety of Corsica (see **Vin de Corse**), producing moderately good quality wines with high alcohol. Some of the best results have been obtained by vinifying it as a rosé wine.

Nierstein 1. A subregion, or **Bereich**, of the **Rheinhessen** region of Germany. The *Bereich* contains many fine vineyards, sold under their village and **Einzellage** names, but wine sold as 'Bereich Nierstein' is usually no better than quaffable, fruity white wine. 2. A small town of the Rheinhessen which gives its name to the *Bereich* in which it is located. The vineyards of the town come under the **Grosslagen** of Auflangen, Gutes Domtal, Rehbach and Spiegelberg.

NM (négociant-manipulant) The letters found on **Champagne** labels, indicating that it comes from a house that both produces and sells the wine. The numbers following the letters identify the producer.

noble rot See **botrytis**.

non-vintage See **NV**.

Norheim A village of the **Nahe** region of Germany, producing fine, and sometimes great, white wines mainly from the **Riesling** grape. It comes under the **Grosslage** of Burgweg, and the individual **Einzellage** sites are Dellchen (probably the best), Götzenfels, Kafels, Kirschbeck, Klosterberg, Oberberg, Onkelchen and Sonnenberg.

North Coast An extensive **AVA** of **California**, which includes the counties of **Lake**, **Napa**, **Solano**, Marin and **Mendocino**.

nose A tasting term which covers all the smell characteristics of a wine, including the **aroma** and **bouquet**.

nouveau A term used to indicate a wine produced for drinking immediately after the harvest, e.g. **Beaujolais Nouveau**, often made by **carbonic maceration**. The result is good for the cash flow of the producer, but rarely for the quality of the wine. The Italian equivalent is *novello*.

Nuits-Saint-Georges An **AC** wine and town which gives its name to the northern **Côte de Nuits** region of **Burgundy**'s **Côte d'Or**. Almost all of the production is of plummy, prune-flavoured, chewy, complex red wine, from the **Pinot Noir** grape. The best wines come from the 38 (small) **premier cru** vineyards. There are no **grands crus**. PRICE BAND: D–E.

Nuragus di Cagliari A white **DOC** wine of **Sardinia**, made mainly from the Nuragus grape variety. The wine is usually **neutral**, even taste-less, but the **frizzante** version can be refreshing when served very cold.

NV (non-vintage) A term used to describe a wine for which no year of harvest is specified. Many ordinary table wines and branded wines are NV, so that the blender is able to produce a consistent product by blending wines of different vintages. For most **Champagne** producers, NV **Brut** is their best-selling wine, and many of the top houses believe that the finest Champagne can be made by blending across vintages.

oak A family of trees, whose wood is generally agreed to be the best material for the construction of **barrels** for the storage and **ageing** of fine wines. When a high-quality young wine, with a good concentration of fruit, spends some months or years in oak barrels, this treatment can add an extra dimension of flavours to the wine, rather like the use of seasoning in cooking. The fruit flavours are complemented by the **vanilla** flavour derived from the oak, and the wood can also give extra **tannin** to the wine, which may increase its ageing potential. Small, new barrels will have a more dramatic effect than large, old ones. Ageing in dirty barrels, whatever the size or wood, can render a wine undrinkable.

There are many varieties of oak, and wine-makers will often insist on barrels made from oak of specific forests in France (such as **Allier**, **Tronçais**, **Nevers** and **Limousin**), or from **American** (white) **oak**. Oak and barrel-making are both very expensive, and ageing in oak barrels adds significantly to the cost of producing a wine.

oaky A tasting term that describes a range of sensations, from the smell of freshly sawn wood, the taste and smell of vanilla, to a spicy, cinnamon flavour. The flavours result from **ageing** in **oak** casks, and are attractive in moderation, but undesirable in excess.

Obermosel A **Bereich**, or subregion, of the **Mosel-Saar-Ruwer** region of Germany. It produces mainly basic-quality wine from the **Elbling** grape variety, much of which is made into sparkling wine, or **Sekt**.

Ockfen A village on the Saar river in the **Mosel-Saar-Ruwer** region of Germany. It produces high-quality, floral-scented white wines, mainly from the **Riesling** grape variety. The vineyards come under the **Grosslage** of Scharzberg, and the **Einzellage** sites are Bockstein and Herrenberg (the best two), plus Geisberg, Heppenstein, Kupp, Neuwies and Zickelgarten.

Oestrich A town of the **Rheingau** region of Germany. It produces full-bodied white wines from the **Riesling** grape variety, capable of very good quality. The vineyards are split between the **Grosslagen** of Gottesthal – where the **Einzellage** sites are Lenchen (the best), Doosberg, Klosterberg and Schloss Reichhartshausen – and Mehrhölzchen, which includes parts of Klosterberg.

Olasz Rizling   An alternative name, used in Hungary, for the **Welschriesling** grape variety.

oloroso   A rich, nutty, dark style of **Sherry** which takes its flavour from long ageing in cask, rather than from **flor**. True *oloroso* is dry, but often it is sweetened to make a commercial blend, sold as 'cream', by adding some **Pedro Ximénez** wine, and sometimes it is darkened with **vino de color**.

Oltrepò Pavese   An area of the **Lombardy** region of northern Italy, and a **DOC** wine that comes in 15 different varieties. The **rosso** and **rosato** are based on the **Barbera**, **Uva Rara** and **Croatina** grape varieties. The red can be of good quality, full bodied and lightly tannic. Buttafuoco is a dry red, usually **frizzante**, and the fizzy Sangue di Giuda can be dry, **amabile**, or **dolce**; both are based on the same varieties as the *rosso*.

The red **varietal** versions are **Barbera** (which can be a very high quality, robust wine), **Bonarda** (grapey and rustic) and **Pinot Nero** (which can be good as a still red wine, but is rarely seen). The white varietals are **Cortese** (light and crisp, if somewhat neutral), **Moscato** (produced in a similar style to **Moscato d'Asti**), **Pinot Grigio**, **Riesling Italico** and **Riesling Renano** (both Rieslings produce delicately perfumed wines of real character).

Oltrepò is also an important source of sparkling wines made by the **méthode champenoise**, most importantly from the Pinot Nero and

Chardonnay grapes, but they are often sold anonymously to bottlers in other regions for the production of commercial blends.

Oppenheim A small town of the **Rheinhessen** region of Germany, producing good-quality white wines, mainly from the **Riesling** grape variety. The vineyards come under the **Grosslagen** of Güldenmorgen (**Einzellage** sites are Daubhaus, Gutleuthaus, Herrenberg, Kreuz, Sackträger, Schützenhütte, and Zuckerberg) and Krötenbrunnen (Herrengarten, Paterhof, and Schlossberg).

Optima A white grape variety, a **cross** of **Müller-Thurgau** with another cross of **Silvaner** and **Riesling**. It is planted mainly in the **Mosel-Saar-Ruwer**, **Rheinhessen** and **Rheingau** regions of Germany, and also in **England**. It yields a wine of low **acidity** and high **must weight**, and can produce wines of up to **Auslese** quality in a good year.

Orange Muscat A white grape variety of the **Muscat** family, mainly planted in **California** and Australia, where it can produce lusciously sweet dessert wines.

Oregon A state of the northwestern United States, with a fairly recent reputation for producing **varietal** red wines from the **Pinot Noir** grape variety, especially in the Willamette Valley, and sparkling wines made by the **méthode champenoise**. Producers from **Burgundy** and

Champagne have shown their confidence in the region by investing in Oregon vineyards and wineries in recent years.

organic   According to makers of organic wines, they are made without use of herbicides, chemical fertilizers, or any additives in the winery. In fact there are many exceptions allowed by the various unofficial bodies controlling organic viti-culture and winemaking. For instance, almost all organic wine is made with the use of the chemical sulphur dioxide. All good winemakers, whether or not they describe their wines as 'organic', try to keep the use of chemicals in the vineyard and winery to the absolute minimum.

Orta Nova   A **DOC** wine made around Foggia in the north of the **Apulia** region of southern Italy. It is produced from **Sangiovese**, **Uva di Troia** and **Montepulciano** grape varieties. The wine can be a medium-weight red of everyday quality, or a dry **rosato**.

Ortega   A white grape variety, a **cross** of **Müller-Thurgau** and **Siegerrebe**, grown mainly in the **Mosel-Saar-Ruwer**, **Rheinhessen** and **Rhein-pfalz** regions of Germany, and to a limited extent in the vineyards of **England**. It ripens early, and has a relatively high **must weight**, but its low **acidity** makes it unsuitable for making late-picked wines of **Spätlese** or wines of higher quality.

Ortenau   A **Bereich**, or subregion, of the **Baden**

region of Germany. It produces good quality white wines from the **Riesling** grape variety (called Klingelberger locally), and also some reds from the **Spätburgunder** (including **Affental**). The *Bereich* is split into two **Grosslagen**, Fürsteneck and Schloss Rodeck.

Orvieto A white **DOC** wine of the **Umbria** region of Italy, produced in the hills around the town of Orvieto from a blend of the **Trebbiano**, Verdello, **Grechetto**, and **Malvasia** grape varieties. The *classico* area lies at the centre of the region. The wine is usually a crisp, smooth, dry wine for early drinking, but it may also be **abboccato**, **amabile** or **dolce**. PRICE BAND: A.

Ostuni A **DOC** wine of the **Apulia** region of Italy. It can be a light, delicate, dry **Bianco** made from the Impigno, Francavilla, and Bianco d'Alessano grape varieties, or a light, cherry-coloured, early drinking red called Ottavianello, made mainly from the grape variety of the same name.

oxidation A class of chemical reactions that can result when wine is exposed to an oxidizing agent, most commonly oxygen in the atmosphere. This can occur slowly, if the wine is in a full **barrel** (a slow, controlled oxidation is part of the maturation process), or rapidly, once a bottle of wine is opened and exposed to the air. Eventually a wine is spoiled by oxidation, and the alcohol is oxidized to **acetic acid**.

oxidized A tasting term used to describe a stale, 'off' taste, caused by exposure to oxygen in the air. In extreme cases, the wine may smell and taste of vinegar.

Pacherenc du Vic Bilh A white **AC** wine of southwest France, produced in the same area as the red **Madiran**, from the **Gros Manseng**, **Petit Manseng** and Ruffiac grape varieties. The wine is usually dry and pear-flavoured, although it can be rich and slightly sweet. PRICE BAND: B.

Pais A red grape variety, the most widely planted in **Chile** and probably brought by Spanish missionaries. It is high yielding and produces thin, poor wines, both red and white, which are only for domestic consumption. Pais is gradually being replaced with European grapes, including **Cabernet Sauvignon**, **Chardonnay**, **Sauvignon Blanc** and **Merlot**.

palate A tasting term used to describe the flavour and sensation of the wine in the mouth (as opposed to the **nose** and appearance). More generally, a taster can be said to have a 'good palate'.

Palatinate See **Rheinpfalz**.

Pale Cream A style of **Sherry**, which combines the sweetness of **cream** Sherry with the colour of a **fino**. The style is made by sweetening young *fino* with pale grape juice concentrate. It never has the complex flavour of the traditional Sherry styles. PRICE BAND: A.

Palette An **AC** wine of **Provence**, made in a tiny region just east of Aix-en-Provence. Most of the production is of elegant, herby reds and rosés, made from the **Cinsault**, **Grenache**, **Mourvèdre** and **Syrah** grape varieties. Small quantities of fresh, spicy white wine are made from **Clairette**, Grenache Blanc, **Ugni Blanc** and sometimes **Muscat** and **Sémillon**. PRICE BAND: C.

palo cortado A **Sherry** that falls in style somewhere between an **amontillado** and an **oloroso**. It should combine the elegance of an *amontillado* with the rich, nutty character of an *oloroso*. PRICE BAND: C.

Palomino A white grape variety of **Spain**, used to make nearly all **Sherry**. Although it excels as a base wine for **fortified wines**, such as Sherry, it is rather thin and neutral when vinified as a table wine. It is also planted in Spain outside the Sherry region, and in **South Africa**, **California** and **Australia**, where it is often fortified to make 'sherry-style' wines.

Parellada A white grape variety planted in the **Penedès** region of **Spain**. It is used to make still and sparkling white wines. It is particularly important as an ingredient in the sparkling **Cava**, and is also found in **Tarragona** and Conca de Barbera. Wine made from Parellada has high acidity (important for sparkling wine) and good fruit when young, but lacks **ageing** potential when it is bottled unblended.

Parrina A **DOC** wine of **Tuscany**, produced above the Agrentario peninsula near Grosseto. The dry white **bianco** is made mainly from the **Trebbiano** Toscano grape, and the pleasant red and **rosato** versions are based on **Sangiovese**.

Paso Robles An **AVA** of **San Luis Obispo** county, **California**. It has a growing reputation for rich and well-structured **Zinfandel** and **Cabernet Sauvignon**, and is pioneering the development of **Nebbiolo** in the US.

Passe-Tout-Grains A red **AC** wine of **Burgundy** made, unusually, from a mixture of **Gamay** and a minimum of one-third **Pinot Noir** grapes. Bourgogne Passe-Tout-Grains, with its light, fresh, fruity flavour, is best drunk relatively young, within three or four years of the vintage. The best examples offer good value for money. PRICE BAND: B.

passito An Italian term for strong, often sweet, wines made from the concentrated juice of semi-dried (or *passito*) grapes.

Patrimonio See **Vin de Corse**.

Pauillac A communal **AC** wine of the **Haut-Médoc** area of **Bordeaux**, produced around the small town of the same name. This is the source of some of the greatest Claret, including three of Bordeaux's five **premiers crus** and 15 other **crus classés**. It also boasts a number of good **cru bourgeois** properties.

The wines of Pauillac are the archetype of Bordeaux and the blackcurrant taste of the **Cabernet Sauvignon** grape. The wines are full-bodied, concentrated, and high in **tannin**. In their youth, they are **austere**; at their peak, which may come 20 or (many) more years after the vintage, they are rich, smooth, and sophisticated. The top wines come from individual châteaux, but 'generic' Pauillac from a **négociant** can offer good value for money. PRICE BAND: D–E.

Pécharmant A red **AC** wine from within the **Bergerac** region of southwest France, produced from the **Merlot**, **Cabernet Sauvignon**, **Cabernet Franc** and **Malbec** grape varieties. The wines are among the finest produced in Bergerac. They are light but well-balanced, with a good concentration of blackcurrant fruit, and capable of moderate **ageing**. PRICE BAND: B.

Pedro Ximénez (also called **PX**) A white grape variety planted throughout **Spain**, but particularly used to make sweet, dark, thick wines in **Montilla-Moriles** and **Málaga**. PX is a dark **mistelle** made by adding brandy to the unfermented juice of concentrated **must** from Pedro Ximénez grapes. It is added to **Sherry** to make the sweeter styles. A small amount of Sherry is made from unblended Pedro Ximénez.

It is intensely sweet, with a dark, almost black colour, and makes an absolutely delicious dessert when poured over ice-cream.

pelure d'oignon A French tasting term, meaning 'onion skin', which is used to describe the tawny-pink colour of some rosés and **vins gris**, or faded old reds. It may be characteristic, e.g. in Provence rosé, or indicate tiredness or **oxidation**.

Penedès A DO wine of northeast **Spain**, produced in a coastal region just west of Barcelona, and the home of **Cava** production. Most of the wine produced is white, from the native grape varieties of **Parellada**, **Xarel-lo** and **Macabeo**, usually blended together, and generally not very good as a still wine -- there are a few notable exceptions. **Chardonnay** is now permitted under the DO regulations, and is a very welcome addition to the blend.

However, many of the best wines are produced outside the DO system, from imported white varieties such as **Chenin Blanc**, **Gewürztraminer**, **Sauvignon Blanc** and **Riesling**. Reds are also produced from both native grapes, e.g. **Garnacha**, **Tempranillo** and **Cariñena**, and imported varieties (mainly **Cabernet Sauvignon**), or blends of the two. PRICE BAND: A–E.

perfumed A tasting term, used to describe an attractive, delicate **bouquet**.

Periquita (also called **João de Santarém**) A

red grape variety planted widely in southern **Portugal**, particularly in the **Setúbal** peninsula, **Alentejo** and **Ribatejo** regions. It produces a full, robust wine, harsh in its youth, but capable of mellowing with bottle age.

perlant See **pétillant**.

perlé See **pétillant**.

perlwein A German term for cheap semi-sparkling wine, made by pumping carbon dioxide into the wine, or by fermentation in pressurised tanks. Quality is almost always poor.

Pernand-Vergelesses An **AC** wine of the **Côte de Beaune** area of **Burgundy**. Mainly red wine is produced, from the **Pinot Noir** grape variety, plus some white from **Chardonnay** (and **Aligoté**). The reds, especially the **premiers crus**, are soft, attractive, raspberry flavoured wines for relatively early drinking. Part of the **grand cru** of **Corton** also comes within the *appellation*, producing much finer, longer-lived reds.

The whites sold as Pernand-Vergelesses are good-quality, soft wines, best drunk three to four years after the vintage. Part of the white *grand cru* of **Corton-Charlemagne** also comes within the *appellation*, and here the wines are among the longest-lived of all Chardonnays. They need 10 years or more to develop their nutty, spicy flavour. PRICE BAND: C–D.

Pessac-Léognan An **AC** wine produced in

the northern part of the **Graves** region of **Bordeaux**. All the classed growths of the Graves come under this *appellation*, and the soil here is at its most gravelly; an important factor in determining the Graves style. Reds are made from the classic Bordeaux grape varieties, **Cabernet Sauvignon**, **Cabernet Franc** and **Merlot**, and there is a wide variety of styles (and prices). The top wines rank alongside the best that Bordeaux has to offer, and Pessac-Léognan is also probably the source of Bordeaux's most exciting dry whites, made from the **Sauvignon Blanc** and **Sémillon** grapes. They are fruity and concentrated in their youth, and can develop glorious nutty complexity as they mature. PRICE BAND: C–E.

pétillant (also called **perlant**; **perlé**) A French term used to describe a semi-sparkling wine, and sometimes found on labels. It is also a tasting term used to describe a wine with any hint of a bubble.

Petit Manseng A white grape variety planted in southwest France. Along with **Gros Manseng** it is used to make **Jurançon**, **Pacherenc du Vic Bihl** and some of the rare white wines from **Béarn**.

Petit Verdot A red grape variety planted mainly in **Bordeaux**, where it forms a minor part of the blend at some châteaux. It produces deep, tannic, spicy, dark-coloured wine, which can make an important contribution to the longevity of a blend. However, it is a late ripening variety (indeed it will not ripen at all in poor years) and so many châteaux no longer grow it.

petrolly A tasting term, used, generally with approval, to describe the oily, kerosene smell that can develop in fine mature wine made from the **Riesling** grape, especially when affected by **botrytis**.

phylloxera A disease of the vine caused by the aphid *Phylloxera vastatrix*, which attacks the root system. It wiped out most of Europe's vineyards in the late 19th century. The cure was to **graft** the European **Vitis vinifera** grape varieties on American-vine **rootstock** (which is resistant to phylloxera) and most of the world's vineyards are now planted in this way. An important exception is **Chile**, where ungrafted *vinifera* vines grow successfully. Ungrafted vines also survive in **Colares**, Portugal, yielding dark, strong, tannic wines.

Piave A **DOC** wine of the **Veneto** region of Italy, produced on the plains on both sides of the Piave river. There are eight types, labelled according to their grape variety. The reds include the native **Raboso** (warm, earthy, and high in tannin in its youth) plus the French varieties **Cabernet** (a mixture of Franc and Sauvignon), **Merlot** and **Pinot Nero**. The whites include **Verduzzo Friulano** and Tocai Italico (fresh and fruity when young, with good acidity), plus **Pinot Bianco** and **Pinot Grigio**.

Picardan A white grape variety, one of 13 permitted in the production of **Châteauneuf-du-Pape**.

Picolit A white grape variety native to the **Friuli-Venezia Giulia** region of Italy, used to make expensive, good-quality dessert wine.

Picpoul See **Piquepoul Gris**.

pièce The name used in parts of France for a **barrel** with a capacity of between 205 and 225 litres. See also **barrique**.

Piedmont (also called **Piemonte**) An important wine-producing region in northwest **Italy**. This is the home, particularly around Alba, of the **Nebbiolo** grape, which is used to make the great, long-lived **DOCG** wines **Barolo** and **Barbaresco**. Nebbiolo also thrives in the north of the region, in the Alpine foothills.

The other main red grapes are **Barbera** and **Dolcetto**, which are used to make varietally labelled wines in Alba and neighbouring Asti. Asti's chief claim to fame for many wine lovers is the sweet, white, sparkling **Asti Spumante**, made from the **Moscato** grape.

Piemonte See **Piedmont**.

Piesport An important wine-producing village

of the **Mosel-Saar-Ruwer** region of Germany. It produces high-quality white wines from the **Riesling** grape variety. The vineyards come within the **Grosslage** of Michelsberg and the **Einzellage** sites are Goldtröpfchen (the best), Domherr, Falkenberg, Gärtchen, Grafenberg, Günterslay, Hofberger, Kreuzwingert, Schubertslay and Treppchen. Wine sold under the *Grosslage* name, as Piesporter Michelsberg, is rarely distinguished and often mediocre, especially when made from grapes other than Riesling.

Pigato A new **DOC**, and a white grape variety planted in the **Liguria** region of Italy. The grape produces full-bodied, dry white wines, often surpassing **Vermentino** in finesse.

Pineau d'Aunis A red grape variety grown in the **Loire** valley, especially in **Touraine**, where it is sometimes part of the blend in Touraine Rouge.

Pineau des Charentes A **mistelle** made in the Cognac region by the addition of brandy to unfermented (or very slightly fermented) grape juice. It can be white or red, with an appley, grapey, sweet flavour, and is generally drunk chilled as an apéritif.

Pinot Bianco See **Pinot Blanc**.

Pinot Blanc (also called **Pinot Bianco**; **Weissburgunder**) A white grape variety of the

Chardonnay family, grown in **Alsace** where it is used to make **varietal** Pinot Blanc, as part of the blend for **Edelzwicker**, and as an ingredient in the sparkling **Crémant d'Alsace**. In **Germany** it is called Weissburgunder, and it is probably at its best in **trocken** and **halbtrocken** wines.

In Italy it is called Pinot Bianco (although in some regions there is still much confusion between what is Chardonnay and what is Pinot Blanc), and it is widely planted all over the country, particularly in **Friuli-Venezia Giulia**, **Lombardy**, **Trentino**, **Alto Adige** and the **Veneto**. It is **DOC** in many regions, and is also an important part of the blend in Italian **méthode champenoise** sparkling wines.

It is also planted in **Austria**, **Yugoslavia**, **Hungary** and **California**. Almost all 'Pinot Blanc' in **Australia** is, in fact, Chardonnay.

Pinot Grigio See **Pinot Gris**.

Pinot Gris (also called **Pinot Grigio**; **Ruländer**; **Tokay-Pinot Gris**) A grape variety that produces wine which is usually a relatively deep-coloured white, but is occasionally slightly tinged with pink. It is most widely planted in **Germany**, where it is called Ruländer (or Grauburgunder when vinified in the modern, drier style), and in **Alsace**, where it is called Tokay-Pinot Gris, producing a spicy, subtly aromatic wine.

In Italy, it is widely planted as Pinot Grigio, especially in **Friuli-Venezia Giulia**, **Trentino**, **Alto Adige** and **Oltrepò Pavese**. It mainly produces popular, but fairly neutral, low-acid, easy drinking white wine, with only a few examples showing any complexity.

It is also planted in **Austria**, **Luxembourg**, **Romania**, **Switzerland** and **Yugoslavia**.

Pinot Meunier A red grape variety which, along with **Chardonnay** and **Pinot Noir**, is used to produce **Champagne**. Although it is the least well-known of the Champagne grapes, it is in fact the most extensively planted variety in the region. It has a reputation for not ageing well, but if properly vinified it can make an important contribution to the Champagne blend. Experience has shown that the longest-lived Champagnes tend to be those based on the two Pinots.

Pinot Nero See **Pinot Noir**.

Pinot Noir (also called **Pinot Nero**; **Spätburgunder**) An important red grape variety, the main red grape of the **Côte d'Or** area of **Burgundy** and also important in **Champagne**. Although capable of greatness in these areas, it is very difficult to cultivate and produces only indifferent light wines elsewhere in Europe and the New World, although there have been encouraging successes in **Oregon** and **California**.

Pinotage A red grape variety of **South Africa**, a **cross** of **Pinot Noir** and **Cinsault**. (Cinsault is known as 'Hermitage' in South Africa.)

pipe A barrel used for storing, maturing and

selling **Port**. 'Shipping pipes' have a capacity of 534 litres; 'Douro pipes', 550 litres; and 'lodge pipes', between 580 and 620 litres. One *pipe* is equivalent to 21 **almudes**, and there are about 12 **canadas** (of 2.1 litres) in one *almude*.

Piquepoul Gris (also called **Picpoul**) A white grape variety, one of the 13 varieties allowed in the production of **Châteauneuf-du-Pape**. It is also part of the blend for the rather dull white Picpoul de Pinet in the **Coteaux du Languedoc** region.

piss See **cat's pee**.

Pollino A pale red **DOC** wine of the **Calabria** region of Italy, made in the high-altitude vineyards of the Pollino mountains. The wine is based on the **Gaglioppo** and **Greco** Nero grape varieties, with the possibility of the addition of up to 20% of white varieties, including **Malvasia**. This, and the short period of **maceration**, accounts for the wines' pale colour. At their best, the wines are light, fresh, and fruity.

Pomerol A red **AC** wine produced near Libourne in the **Bordeaux** region. It is made from the classic Bordeaux grape varieties, **Cabernet Sauvignon**, **Cabernet Franc** and **Merlot**. Merlot is the most important because it thrives on Pomerol's clay soil. The resulting wines are velvety, smooth and seductive, relatively low in **tannin**, and with great concentration of fruit. The top wines, always in short supply, rank alongside the best of

Bordeaux, and the prices reflect this. PRICE BAND: C–E.

Pomino A **DOC** wine produced in high-altitude (700 m) vineyards around the village of Pomino, **Tuscany**, overlapping in part with a corner of the **Chianti** area. The white **bianco** version is made from **Pinot Bianco** and **Chardonnay**, plus **Trebbiano**. The rich, soft **rosso** is based on **Sangiovese**, blended with **Cabernet** (Franc and/or Sauvignon), **Merlot** and **Pinot Nero**. Both are usually very good, especially when aged in oak. White and red **Vin Santo** is also made, from the same grapes used for the dry wines. PRICE BAND: B–D.

Pommard A red **AC** wine of the **Côte de Beaune** area of **Burgundy**, made from the **Pinot Noir** grape variety. At its best, Pommard can be a good, sturdy, beefy red Burgundy, with power and richness. Sadly the popularity of the easily pronounceable name in English-speaking countries has resulted in many thin, over-priced, over-alcoholic examples appearing on the market. Taste before you buy. PRICE BAND: C–D.

Port A **fortified wine** of **Portugal**, produced in the Douro valley and matured and bottled in Vila Nova de Gaia. Port is usually red and sweet, although there are white Ports, which range from off-dry to sweet. The main grape varieties for red Port are **Roriz** (the same as **Tempranillo**), **Touriga Nacional**, **Touriga Francesa**, **Tinta Cão**,

Tinta Barroca, Mourisco Tinto, Tinta Amarella and **Tinta Francisca**.

Despite the wide variety of styles of Port available, all red Port starts off life in the same way. At vintage time the grapes are harvested on the steep slopes of the **Douro** valley and brought to the winery. They are lightly crushed and then fermented, either in the traditional stone **lagar** (with foot treading), or in an **autovinificator**. Once the alcohol level has reached about 7%, **aguardente**, or grape spirit, is added in the ratio of 1:4, to stop fermentation. The result is a sweet red fortified wine with an alcohol level of about 20%, which is later removed to the Port shippers' lodges in Vila Nova de Gaia.

After about two years, the Port shipper will decide on the wine's fate. It might be blended with Ports from different vintages to make an ordinary young **Ruby**. Vintage Character denotes a superior Ruby. It may be kept unblended with other years, and bottled after four to six years, as a **Late Bottled Vintage**. Exceptionally good lots, from a fine year, will be bottled after two years, and these will become Vintage Port – a 'bottle-matured' Port, demanding lengthy maturing and capable of great longevity – the finest and most expensive style.

The alternative route is to make 'wood-matured' or **Tawny Port**. Except for the most basic and commercial Tawnies, which may be blended from red and white Ports, the Port is aged in wooden barrels for at least eight years, and sometimes for many decades. It may be sold as a blend of vintages of indicated age (10-year-old Tawny, 20-year-old Tawny, etc.), or as a dated Tawny from a single year, or **Colheita Port**.

Porto Vecchio See **Vin de Corse**.

Portugal A wine-producing country of the Iberian peninsula, most famous for its superb **fortified** wines **Port** and **Madeira**. There is also a wealth of white wines, ranging from the crisp, acidic **Vinho Verde** to the luscious, golden **Moscatel** de Setúbal, together with good reds from **Dão**, **Douro** and **Bairrada**. See also **Alentejo**; **Algarve**; **Bucelas**; **Colares**; **RD**.

Portugieser An alternative name for the **Blauer Portugieser** grape variety.

Potter Valley An **AVA** of **Mendocino** county, **California**. Its vineyards are at the highest altitude in the county, which means that there is a short growing season, with a wide day to night temperature variation. Good results have been obtained with **Riesling**, some of it affected by **botrytis**, and both **Chardonnay** and **Pinot Noir** show great promise, but its reputation rests on outstanding **Sauvignon Blanc**.

Pouilly-Fuissé A white **AC** wine produced in the **Mâconnais** area of **Burgundy**, from the **Chardonnay** grape variety. The wine is made from the vineyards of five different villages, Pouilly, Fuissé, Chaintré, Solutré and Vergisson.

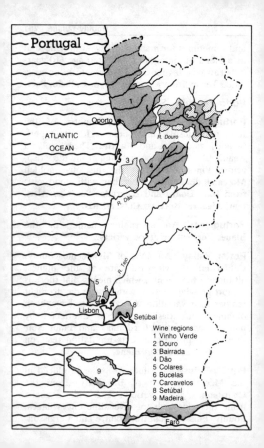

Portugal

ATLANTIC
OCEAN

Oporto

R. Douro

R. Dão

R. Tejo

Lisbon

Setúbal

Wine regions
1 Vinho Verde
2 Douro
3 Bairrada
4 Dão
5 Colares
6 Bucelas
7 Carcavelos
8 Setúbal
9 Madeira

Faro

The best wines, from individual growers, are rich, full, buttery Chardonnays. However, there are also many inferior examples on the market, although quality does seem to be improving.

The nearby *appellations* of Pouilly-Loché and Pouilly-Vinzelles make wines in a similar style, but in much smaller quantities. PRICE BAND: B–E.

Pouilly-Fumé A white **AC** wine produced in the eastern part of the **Loire** from the **Sauvignon Blanc** grape. The wines can be superb: bursting with juicy fruit, with gooseberry and blackcurrant flavours, sometimes even asparagus, all balanced with racy acidity. The wines are in a similar style to the nearby **Sancerre**; although Pouilly-Fumé can have more weight and last longer, it is generally best drunk young. The *fumé* in the name refers to the grey (smoky) appearance of the Sauvignon grapes as they ripen. PRICE BAND: B–E.

Pouilly-Loché An *appellation* of **Burgundy**, France. See **Pouilly-Fuissé**.

Pouilly-sur-Loire A white **AC** wine produced in the same vineyard area as **Pouilly-Fumé**, but made from the **Chasselas** grape rather than **Sauvignon Blanc**. The wines are thin and neutral and may soon disappear because producers are replacing the Chasselas vines with Sauvignon Blanc.

Pouilly-Vinzelles An **appellation** of **Burgundy**, France. See **Pouilly-Fuissé**.

Poulsard A red grape variety of the **Jura** region of **France**. It produces highly perfumed wine, that is delicate yet well-structured, with red fruit flavours.

pourriture noble The French term for **botrytis**.

prädikat See **QmP**.

predicato An unofficial designation used by some large producers in **Tuscany**, for wines that do not qualify for one of the **DOCGs** or **DOCs** because of the use of unauthorized grape varieties. There are four categories: Predicato del Muschio, for whites from **Chardonnay** or **Pinot Bianco**, with up to 20% **Müller-Thurgau**, **Pinot Grigio**, or **Riesling**; Predicato del Selvante, for whites from **Sauvignon Blanc**, with up to 20% Müller-Thurgau, Pinot Grigio, or Riesling; Predicato di Biturica, for red from **Cabernet Sauvignon** with up to 30% **Sangiovese** and 10% other red grapes; and Predicato di Cardisco, for red from Sangiovese with up to 10% other red grapes. Although the *predicato* system was designed to help consumers, it has probably only added to the confusion.

premier cru A French quality designation which literally means 'first growth'. Its application varies in different regions.

In **Bordeaux**, the châteaux were classified in 1855 (the classification was of all Bordeaux, but only one château was from outside the **Médoc**):

at the top quality level are the **grands crus classés**, subdivided into *premier cru*, *deuxième cru*, down to *cinquième cru*, referred to in English as 'first growth', 'second growth', and so on.

In **Burgundy**, including **Chablis**, the very top vineyard sites are classified as *grand cru*, and *premier cru* is the next level down. Each *grand cru* of **Côte d'Or** has its own **AC**, whereas wines from *premier cru* vineyards are labelled with the village *appellation* plus the name of the *premier cru*. In Chablis, *grand cru* and *premier cru* wines are labelled 'AC Chablis' plus the name of the *cru*: if a wine is a blend from more than one *premier cru* vineyard, it can be labelled 'Chablis Premier Cru'.

Premières Côtes de Blaye An **AC** wine of **Bordeaux**, produced on the east side of the Gironde estuary, facing the Haut-Médoc. Nearly all the wine produced is red, made from the **Cabernet Sauvignon**, **Cabernet Franc**, **Merlot** and **Malbec** grape varieties. These are fresh, fruity, easy-to-drink wines, which are best drunk relatively early. PRICE BAND: B.

Premières Côtes de Bordeaux An **AC** wine of **Bordeaux**, produced on a long strip of land on the east side of the Garonne river, facing the **Graves** region. Traditionally a sweet white wine area, most of the production is now solid, good-value red and clean, dry white, made from the classic Bordeaux grape varieties.

There are still some sweet whites produced, under the Premières Côtes AC and as AC **Cadillac**. They can be good-value, light, sweet wines, but they do not have the richness, elegance and concentration of **Sauternes** or **Barsac**. PRICE BAND: B.

Pressac The name used for the **Malbec** grape variety in the **Saint-Emilion** and **Pomerol** areas of **Bordeaux**. Also known as **Cot** in **Cahors**.

Preuses One of the seven **grand cru** vineyards of **Chablis**.

Primitivo A red grape variety grown in **Apulia**, Italy, and possibly related to **Zinfandel**, which is grown in **California**. Apulian Primitivo was much used as a blending wine, to beef up reds from the north of Italy, but it makes **DOC** wines in **Primitivo di Manduria** and Gioia del Colle.

Primitivo di Manduria A red **DOC** wine produced in the Salento peninsula of the **Apulia** region of Italy from the **Primitivo** grape. The wine is strong and full, but lacking in elegance and complexity. It can be dry, **amabile**, or fully sweet, and there are also **fortified** versions.

Prosecco A white grape variety, possibly native to **Friuli-Venezia Giulia**, but now grown mainly in the **Veneto** region of Italy, where it is used to make **Prosecco di Conegliano-Valdobbiadene**.

Prosecco di Conegliano-Valdobbiadene A

usually sparkling **DOC** wine of the eastern **Veneto** region of Italy, produced in the hills northwest of Treviso, around the towns of Conegliano and Valdobbiadene. The wine is based on the Prosecco grape, with the possible addition of Verdiso, **Chardonnay**, **Pinot Bianco** and **Pinot Grigio** up to 15%. The best wines, usually designated Superiore di Cartizze, are almost dry and fully **spumante**, fresh and fruity, with gentle bitter-almond flavours in the background. Ideal for drinking outdoors on a hot day, and good value for money. Sweet Prosecco, which may include **Sauvignon** and **Malavasia**, is a fruity, scented wine with some class. PRICE BAND: B.

Provence   A region of southeast **France** which produces some fine red and white wines, along with large quantities of often mediocre rosé. The largest **AC** is **Côtes de Provence**, source of much of the rosé, but also of increasingly good reds made from **Mourvèdre**, **Grenache**, **Syrah** and, more recently, **Cabernet Sauvignon**. The small amount of white produced, from **Ugni Blanc** and **Clairette** among other grape varieties, is rarely any good.

Cabernet assumes a more important role in the AC **Coteaux d'Aix-en-Provence**, where again red and rosé wine predominate. Within this AC, the enclave of Coteaux des Baux-en-Provence produces better reds, based mainly on Syrah and Grenache.

The smaller ACs of Provence are **Bandol** (fine, long-lived reds based on the **Mourvèdre** grape variety), **Bellet**, **Cassis** (mainly white), and **Palette** (elegant whites and herby reds).

Prugnolo Gentile A red grape variety, a clone of **Sangiovese**, used to make **Vino Nobile de Montepulciano**.

Puglia See **Apulia**.

Puisseguin-Saint-Emilion A red **AC** wine made in a 'satellite' of the main **Saint-Emilion** *appellation* in **Bordeaux**, to the northeast of the town of Saint-Emilion. The grape varieties are the same as for Saint-Emilion, **Merlot**, **Cabernet Franc**, **Cabernet Sauvignon** and **Malbec**, and the wines, although very pleasant to drink young (three to five years), and offering good value, never reach the heights of the top Saint-Emilions. PRICE BAND: B.

Puligny-Montrachet An **AC** wine of the Côte de Beaune area of **Burgundy**. Nearly all the wine produced is white, made from the **Chardonnay** grape. The straight village wines are highly variable in quality. The best are pale gold, dry but full, with rich buttery, creamy aromas and taste. PRICE BAND: D.

The **premiers crus** are nearly always better, and the **grand crus**, Bâtard-Montrachet, Beinvenues Bâtard-Montrachet, Chevalier-Montrachet and Le Montrachet (especially the last two) are among the most intensely flavoured and comlex

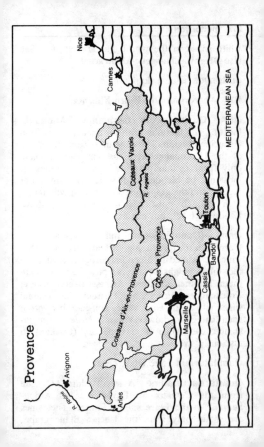

white wines in the world. PRICE BAND: E+. See also **Blagny**; **Chassagne-Montrachet**.

puttonyos See **Tokaji**.

PX Abbreviation of **Pedro Ximénez**.

QbA (Qualitätswein bestimmter Anbaugebiete) The German term for quality wines from a specified region. The wine must come from one of the 11 **Anbaugebiet** areas, and can be made only from certain permitted grape varieties. It must not be blended with wine from any other region, and the grapes used to make it will have a high enough **must weight** to raise it above **Landwein** level, but not as high as for **QmP**.

QmP (Qualitätswein mit Prädikat) The German term for the highest category of quality wines, classified in ascending order according to the **must weight** of the grapes used to make them: **Kabinett**, **Spätlese**, **Auslese**, **Beerenauslese**, **Trockenbeerenauslese**, and **Eiswein**. The **residual sugar** left in the wine varies considerably within each category, however, and *Auslese*, for instance, can range from bone dry (**trocken**) to lusciously sweet.

Qualitätswein See **QbA**; **QmP**.

Quarts de Chaume A sweet white **AC** wine from the **Coteaux du Layon** area of **Anjou-Saumur** in the **Loire** valley, France. The wines are made only from the **Chenin Blanc** grape,

which in good years is affected by **botrytis**. They are wines of the very highest quality, rich and luscious, with acidity balancing the honeyed fruit.
PRICE BAND: C–D.

Queensland A hot-climate, wine-producing state of **Australia**. It produces good-quality **fortified** wine (in the style of **Madeira**) and **varietal** wines (in the cooler, high-altitude Granite Belt region) made from the **Cabernet Sauvignon**, **Chardonnay**, **Sauvignon Blanc**, **Sémillon** and **Shiraz** grape varieties.

Quincy An **AC** wine made between Bourges and Vierzon in the eastern **Loire** valley. The vineyards are to the west of **Sancerre**, and the wine is similar, although not as good as the very best Sancerre and **Pouilly-Fumé**: crisp, pungent, juicy white from the **Sauvignon Blanc** grape.
PRICE BAND: A–B.

quinta The Portuguese term for a wine estate producing its own grapes.

quintal A unit of weight equivalent to 100 kg. The *quintal* is used in **Italy** to express yields in terms of *quintals* per hectare.

QWPSR The EC term meaning quality wine produced in a specified region, a general term covering *appellations* such as the French **AC**, the Italian **DOC** and the Spanish **DO**.

Raboso An Italian red grape variety, found particularly in the **Veneto** region, where it makes the lively, deep-coloured and high-tannin **DOC** wine **Piave**.

racking The process of transferring a maturing wine from one vessel to another, to aerate it and separate it from any sediment.

Ramandolo See **Colli Orientali del Friuli**.

Ramisco A red grape variety that makes tough, tannic wine in the **Colares** region of **Portugal**.

rancio A tasting term used to describe the pungent, intentionally oxidized smell of some wood-aged **fortified** wine and **vin doux naturel**.

Rasteau An **AC** wine of the southern **Rhône**. It is a **fortified** (**vin doux naturel**) wine based on the red **Grenache** grape variety. The traditional style is a sweet, heavy, tannic red. However, most Rasteau is fermented without the grape skins, resulting in the *dorée* style, a deep, golden colour, honeyed and sweet. The third style receives long ageing in oak barrels, and the wine develops a **rancio** character. PRICE BAND: B–C. See also **Côtes du Rhône**.

ratafia A **mistelle** of the **Champagne** region, made by adding brandy to unfermented grape juice. White, rosé, or red, it is similar to **Pineau des Charentes**.

RD 1. The abbreviation of **récemment dégorgé**.

2. The abbreviation of the Portugeuse term **Região Demarcada**.

récemment dégorgé (RD) A term found on Champagne labels, literally meaning 'recently disgorged' (see **dégorgement**), indicating that the wine has been matured in bottle on its lees, and disgorged only when required for shipment. The letters RD are a trademark of one Champagne house, Bollinger.

recioto A term used in **Italy**, particularly in **Valpolicella** and **Soave** in the **Veneto** region, for wine made from grapes that have been concentrated by drying. The name *recioto* comes from the dialect word *recie*, meaning the 'little ears' of grapes at the top of the bunch. These are the smallest, sweetest berries, which are harvested separately and left to dry on wooden trays until they are ready to be pressed in January.

Recioto della Valpolicella An unusual sweet, heady red wine from **Valpolicella**, in the **Veneto** region of Italy. About 10 days before the normal vintage, carefully selected grapes (of the usual Valpolicella varieties), are laid out on straw mats, in a dry, airy room. They are allowed to dry until January, when the shrivelled grapes are crushed and fermented slowly. Some barrels stop fermenting at around 13% alcohol, and become Recioto della Valpolicella. Others continue to ferment to dryness, reaching about 16% alcohol, and produce the strong, bitter-sweet Recioto della Valpolicella Amarone. The wines are produced in very limited quantities, and quality can be stunningly good with long ageing potential. PRICE BAND: C–E. See also **Amarone**.

Recioto di Gambellara A sweet, intense, golden-coloured **DOC** wine, sometimes semi-sparkling, grown in the **Veneto** region of Italy. It is made from dried grapes of the **Garganega** and **Trebbiano** di Soave varieties. See also **Gambellara**; **recioto**.

Recioto di Soave A sweet, intense, golden-coloured **DOC** wine, occasionally sparkling, made from dried grapes of the **Garganega** and **Trebbiano** di Soave varieties. See also **recioto**; **Soave**.

récoltant-manipulant See **RM**.

récolte The French term for harvest. On a label it indicates vintage.

Refosco See **Mondeuse Noire**.

Região Demarcada (RD) The Portuguese term for a demarcated wine region. It is equivalent to the French **AC** or Spanish **DO**.

Régnié A red **AC** wine, the newest (since 1988) of the 10 **crus** of the **Beaujolais** region of **Burgundy**, made from the **Gamay** grape. The wines are fruity, supple, and full of flavour.

However, their elevation above Beaujolais-Villages AC has been a matter of debate. PRICE BAND: B.

rehoboam A large format Champagne bottle, of 4.5 litres capacity (equivalent to six ordinary bottles).

Reichensteiner A white grape variety, a **cross** derived from **Müller-Thurgau** and another crossing (**Madeleine Angevine** and **Calabrese**), planted in the northern wine regions of **Germany** and in **England**. It has a relatively high **must weight** and good **acidity**, but makes rather neutral wine. In England it has been used to produce successful **méthode champenoise** sparkling wine.

Reims The capital city of the **Champagne** region, where many of the producers have their cellars.

remontage The French term for the process of pumping **must** from the bottom of a **fermentation** vessel to the top, in order to extract colour and tannin from the floating cap of grape skins.

remuage The French term for the process of shaking and turning bottles of **Champagne** and other **méthode champenoise** wines. It moves the sediment produced during the second, bubble-forming fermentation to the neck of the bottle, ready for **dégorgement**. This can be done by hand or by machine, using a **gyropalette**.

rendement The French term for yield.

reserva A term used to describe Spanish wines that have been aged for a certain minimum period, part of it in oak barrels. The term refers especially to the red and white wines of **Rioja**.

residual sugar The amount of sugar left in a wine once it has been fermented and is ready for bottling. The quantity of sugar is usually measured in grams per litre. This level determines whether the wine can be described as dry, **sec**, medium dry, **demi-sec**, and so on.

Retsina A wine of **Greece**, made mainly in the Attica region, usually from the **Savatiano** grape. The unique part of the wine-making process is that pine resin is added to the wine, which gives it a distinctive resinous taste. Retsina is nearly always white and it should be drunk as cold and as young as possible. Retsina for export always seems to be less resinated than that found in Greece. PRICE BAND: A.

Reuilly An **AC** wine of the eastern part of the **Loire** valley. The white version is made from the **Sauvignon Blanc** grape variety, and is rarely better than a pale imitation of good **Sancerre**. Uninteresting red wines are also made, from **Pinot Noir**, but Reuilly Rosé, made from Pinot Noir or, occasionally, from **Pinot Gris**, can be very good, with a light, pinkish hue, and soft, fresh, grapy fruit. PRICE BAND: B-C.

Rhein The German name for the Rhine, the river which, together with its tributaries, dominates the fine wine-producing regions of **Germany**. The Rhein rises in the Swiss alps, and flows through the heart of Germany's wine country, fed by the Neckar, Main, Nahe, Mosel and Ahr.

Rheingau One of the 11 major quality wine regions, **Anbaugebiete** of **Germany**. It produces mainly high-quality white wines from the **Riesling** grape variety, including some of the greatest and most well-known names. The region follows the north bank of the **Rhein**, from Lorch in the west to Hochheim in the east, and includes such famous names as **Assmannshausen**, **Rüdesheim**, **Johannisberg**, **Geisenheim** and **Hattenheim**.

The Rheingau is a relatively small *Anbaugebiet*, and there is only one **Bereich**, Johannisberg. This is divided into 10 **Grosslagen**: Burgweg, Daubhaus, Deutelsberg, Erntebringer, Gottesthal, Heiligenstock, Honigberg, Mehrhölzchen, Steil and Steinmächer.

Rheinhessen The largest of the 11 major quality wine regions, **Anbaugebiete**, of **Germany**. It is planted with **Riesling**, together with many new cross-bred varieties, especially **Scheurebe**. It is not surprising that such a large region produces a wide variety of qualities, from some of Germany's best (especially along the banks of the **Rhein**, in the east of the region from Dienheim to Nackenheim), to bland bulk wine, including much **Liebfraumilch**. The region is divided into

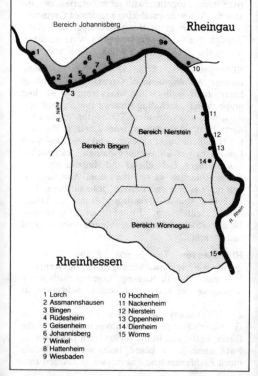

Rheingau & Rheinhessen

Bereich Johannisberg

Rheingau

R. Nahe

Bereich Nierstein

Bereich Bingen

Bereich Wonnegau

R. Rhein

Rheinhessen

1 Lorch
2 Assmannshausen
3 Bingen
4 Rüdesheim
5 Geisenheim
6 Johannisberg
7 Winkel
8 Hattenheim
9 Wiesbaden

10 Hochheim
11 Nackenheim
12 Nierstein
13 Oppenheim
14 Dienheim
15 Worms

three **Bereich** subregions, **Bingen** in the west, **Nierstein** in the east, and **Wonnegau** in the south.

Rheinpfalz (also called **Palatinate**) One of the 11 major quality wine regions, **Anbaugebiete**, of **Germany**. It produces high-quality white wines, particularly in the northern of the two **Bereich** subregions, **Mittelhaardt-Deutsche Weinstrasse** (top villages include **Bad Dürckheim**, **Wachenheim**, **Forst** and **Deidesheim**), and less good wines in the southern *Bereich*, **Südliche Weinstrasse**.

The **Riesling** grape variety dominates on the best sites, but **Müller-Thurgau** is more widely planted in the region as a whole. **Scheurebe** is used as well to make increasingly successful wines. The Rheinpfalz is also an important source of **Liebfraumilch**.

Rhine Riesling The 'true' **Riesling**, as opposed to **Welschriesling** or **Riesling Italico**.

Rhône An important wine-producing region of southeast **France**. The region divides neatly into distinct halves. The northern Rhône is dominated by red wine made from the **Syrah** grape variety. It includes the great, rich, concentrated wines of **Hermitage** and **Côte Rôtie**, along with **Saint-Joseph**, **Crozes-Hermitage** and **Cornas**. White wine is produced in tiny quantities in **Château Grillet** and **Condrieu** from the **Viognier** grape. Sparkling wine comes from **Saint-Péray** and is made mainly from **Marsanne**.

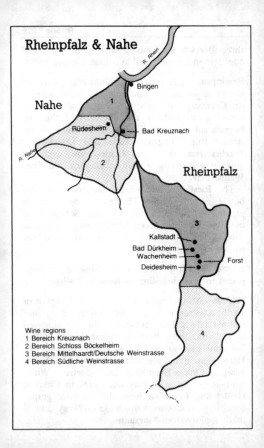

Rheinpfalz & Nahe

Nahe

Bingen

Rüdesheim

Bad Kreuznach

R. Nahe

Rheinpfalz

Kallstadt

Bad Dürkheim

Wachenheim

Forst

Deidesheim

R. Rhein

Wine regions
1 Bereich Kreuznach
2 Bereich Schloss Böckelheim
3 Bereich Mittelhaardt/Deutsche Weinstrasse
4 Bereich Südliche Weinstrasse

In the southern Rhône, Syrah is not dominant. This part of the region is centred on **Châteauneuf-du-Pape** and produces red (and some white) wines from no fewer than 13 authorized grape varieties. Also in the south, **Gigondas** produces red wine based mainly on **Grenache**; **Tavel** is rosé, and **Lirac** can be red or rosé, both based on Grenache and **Cinsault**; and **Muscat de Beaumes-de-Venise** and **Rasteau** are fortified **vin doux naturel** wines. See also **Clairette**; **Coteaux du Tricastin**; **Côtes du Rhône** (Côtes du Rhône-Villages); **Côtes du Ventoux**; **Côtes du Vivarais**.

Rias Baixas A DO wine of **Galicia**, in north-west **Spain**. Fresh whites, similar to Portugal's **Vinho Verde**, are made from **Albariño**, **Loureira**, Godello and Treixadura grapes.

Ribatejo A wine-producing region of **Portugal**, along the banks of the River Tejo (Tagus) north of Lisbon. It produces full-bodied, beefy reds based mainly on the **Periquita** grape variety, and aromatic, peppery whites largely from the **Fernão Pires** grape.

Ribeiro A DO wine of **Galicia**, in northwest **Spain**. Most of the production is of white, bland wines from the **Palomino** grape, and more characterful ones from the **Albariño**.

Ribera del Duero A DO wine of north-central **Spain**, produced along the banks of the Duero river (which becomes the Douro in Portugal).

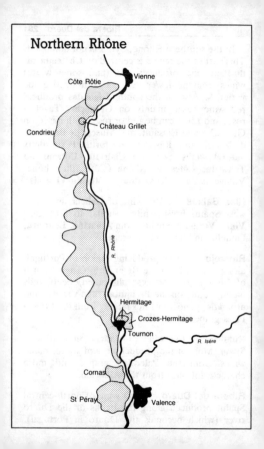

Northern Rhône

Vienne

Côte Rôtie

Condrieu

Château Grillet

R. Rhône

Hermitage

Crozes-Hermitage

Tournon

R. Isère

Cornas

St Péray

Valence

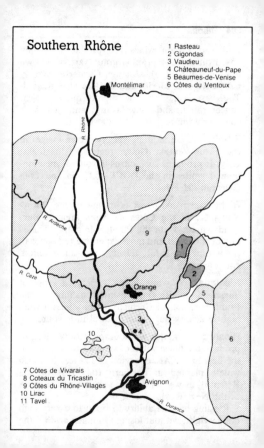

Southern Rhône

1 Rasteau
2 Gigondas
3 Vaudieu
4 Châteauneuf-du-Pape
5 Beaumes-de-Venise
6 Côtes du Ventoux

Montélimar

R. Rhône

R Ardeche

R Ceze

7

8

9

Orange

2

5

3
4

10
11

6

Avignon

R. Durance

7 Côtes de Vivarais
8 Coteaux du Tricastin
9 Côtes du Rhône-Villages
10 Lirac
11 Tavel

Red and **rosado** wines are produced, mainly based on the **Tempranillo** grape variety (known here as Tinto Fino), although **Garnacha, Cabernet Sauvignon, Merlot** and **Cot** are also planted. The best wines are of superb quality: rich, concentrated, and long lasting; and quality is constantly improving. PRICE BAND: A–E.

Ribolla A white grape variety grown mainly in the **Friuli-Venezia Guilia** region of northeast **Italy**. It produces soft, citrus-flavoured, medium-bodied whites in the **DOC**s of **Collio** and **Colli Orientali del Friuli**.

Richebourg A **grand cru** wine of the **Vosne-Romanée**, in the **Côtes de Nuits** area of **Burgundy**, made from the **Pinot Noir** grape. This is one of the finest and most expensive red wines in the world, and is fat, velvety, spicy and scented. PRICE BAND: E+.

Rieslaner A white grape variety, a **cross** of **Silvaner** and **Riesling**, planted mainly in the **Franken** region of **Germany**. It produces a wine high in acidity but rather neutral in flavour.

Riesling A major white grape variety, used to produce the finest wines of **Germany** and some of the best in the **Alsace** region of France. It is also widely planted in northern **Italy** (as Riesling Renano), as well as the wine-producing countries of the New World.

Riesling has the ability to ripen to a very high **must weight**, without losing too much **acidity**, the key to the balance in Germany's fabulous sweet white wines. Because it ripens late, it can take advantage of **botrytis** in good years, leading to the shrivelled, concentrated grapes that go to make **Beerenauslese** and **Trockenbeerenauslese** wines. However, German wine made from Riesling can cover a wide spectrum of flavours, from steely, dry and aromatic wines through to the exotic fruit and honey of the sweetest, which can also develop a **petrolly** aroma and taste with age.

In Alsace, Riesling tends to be made dry, although in exceptional years it can make sweet, rich **vendange tardive** and **Sélection de Grains Nobles** wines. In **California** (where the variety is often called Johannisberg Riesling), botrytis can also play a role, but the 'late-harvest' wines seldom have the elegance of their racy German equivalents.

Lighter, spritzy Rieslings are made in the **Alto Adige** region of Italy. **Australia** and **New Zealand** produce mainly dry, fruity wines from Riesling, the best examples capable of elegant ageing.

Riesling Italico The Italian term for **Welsch-riesling**.

Riesling Renano The Italian term for **Rhine Riesling**.

Rioja A **DO** wine produced along the Ebro valley, from Conchas de Haro in the west, to just east of the town of Alfaro, in northern **Spain**. The valley is crossed by seven tributaries, from one of which, the Rio Oja, the district takes its name.

Red Rioja is made mainly from the **Tempranillo** grape, plus **Garnacha** and sometimes a small proportion of the white Viura (**Macabeo**). The best examples are probably the finest red wines of Spain. They are rich, ripe, concentrated and, above all, oaky.

The back label is the key to the degree of oak ageing: **crianza** is wine in its third year, with one year in cask; **reserva** is aged for at least three years, at least one year in cask; **gran reserva** is wine of a great vintage, aged at least two years in oak cask and three years in bottle. Rioja with none of these descriptions will have received little or no oak ageing.

The majority of Rioja is a blend from at least two of the three subregions, Rioja Alta, Rioja Alavesa and Rioja Baja, although a few examples of single-estate Rioja are available. The two western subregions, Alta and Alavesa, enjoy an Atlantic climate, with snow in the winter, rain in the spring, and short hot summers. To the east, the Rioja Baja has a much more continental climate, with less rain and more sunshine, producing coarser wine for blending.

White Rioja is made from the Viura and **Malvasia** grape varieties. There are two main styles: fresh, fruity, rather neutral whites; and oak-aged whites, with great complexity, depth and ageing potential. For oaked white Rioja, *crianza* is wine in its third year, matured for at least 6 months in cask; *reserva* must be aged 24 months, of which at least 6 months is in cask; and *gran reserva* should be aged 48 months, of which at least 6 months is in cask. PRICE BAND: A–E.

ripasso See **Valpolicella**.

Ripaille A **cru** of the **Vin de Savoie** *appellation*.

riserva A term used in **Italy** to indicate wines of higher than usual quality, which have been aged for a certain minimum period. See **Chianti** (Classico).

Rivaner The name used for the **Müller-Thurgau** grape variety in **Luxembourg** and **Yugoslavia**.

Rivesaltes See **Muscat de Rivesaltes**.

Riviera del Garda Bresciano A **DOC** wine of **Lombardy** in northwest **Italy**, produced southwest of Lake Garda. The red, and refreshing pink **chiaretto**, wine is made from a blend of **Groppello**, **Sangiovese**, **Barbera**, **Marzemino** and other grape varieties.

Riviera Ligure di Ponente A **DOC** wine produced in a zone covering most of western **Liguria**, northwest **Italy**. **Varietal** red and **rosato** wines are produced from the **Dolcetto** (labelled as Ormeasco), and Rossese (reds only) grapes. The full-bodied white wines, which are better, are made from **Vermentino** or **Pigato**, and also labelled by grape variety.

Riverside A county of southern **California**

which produces mainly white **varietal** wines from **Chardonnay** and **Sauvignon Blanc**.

RM (récoltant-manipulant) The letters found on **Champagne** labels which indicate that it comes from a grower who both produces and sells the wine. The numbers following the letters identify the grower.

Robola A white grape variety of **Greece**, producing a full-bodied, citrus-flavoured white wine of the same name on the island of Cephalonia. Quality can be excellent, so long as the wine is fresh. PRICE BAND: A.

Roche-aux-Moines, La See **Savennières**.

Rochegude See **Côtes du Rhône**.

Roero A **DOC** wine made in the **Alba** area of **Piedmont**, northwest **Italy**. Roero is a dry red made from the **Nebbiolo** grape. Roero Arneis (or Arneis di Roero) is a dry white, sometimes sparkling, made from **Arneis**.

Rolle An unusual white grape variety used, along with **Chardonnay**, to make the rare white wine of **Bellet** in **Provence**.

Romanée, La A **grand cru** wine of **Vosne-Romanée**, in the **Côte de Nuits** area of **Burgundy**, made from the **Pinot Noir** grape. Although it produces fine wines, they do not approach the splendour of the neighbouring *grands crus*, e.g. **Romanée-Conti, La, Richebourg** and **La Tâche**. PRICE BAND: E.

Romanée-Conti, La A **grand cru** wine of **Vosne-Romanée**, in the **Côte de Nuits** area of **Burgundy**, made from the **Pinot Noir** grape. This is one of the finest, most expensive and longest-lived red wine in the world. It has an extraordinary panoply of smoky, fruity sensations on the nose, and intense concentration on the palate, with truffly, rich and spicy flavours. PRICE BAND: E+.

Romanée-Saint-Vivant, La A **grand cru** wine of **Vosne-Romanée**, in the **Côte de Nuits** area of **Burgundy**, made from the **Pinot Noir** grape. It produces very fine red wines, spicy and scented, although not in the same class as **Romanée-Conti, La** and **La Tâche**. PRICE BAND: E.

Romania An eastern European country which has a vast and increasing area under vine. Traditionally, production has been of sweet white wine from native grape varieties, most of it exported to the Soviet Union. However, large areas have recently been planted with western grape varieties, including **Cabernet Sauvignon**, **Merlot**, **Pinot Noir**, **Chardonnay** and **Sauvignon Blanc**. So far little has been exported to the west, but quality is increasing rapidly. The handful of wines already available in the West represent good value for money. PRICE BAND: A.

Rondinella A red grape variety of the **Veneto**

region of **Italy**, playing a secondary role to the major variety, **Corvina**, in the production of **Valpolicella** and **Bardolino**. It adds colour, body, and acidity to the wine.

rosado The Spanish for pink or rosé wine.

rosato The Italian for pink or rosé wine.

rosé The French for pink wine.

Rosé d'Anjou A rosé **AC** wine of the **Loire** valley, produced mainly from the **Grolleau** grape variety. The wine is usually quite a vivid pink, fruity at its best, and can vary between medium-dry and sweet. It is produced in vast quantities, and some of the cheaper wines lack freshness and fruit. The best to be hoped for is a good-value, refreshing, medium-dry wine, to be drunk young and well-chilled, without much thought. PRICE BAND: A. See also **Cabernet d'Anjou**; **Rosé de Loire**.

Rosé de Loire A rosé **AC** wine produced in **Anjou** and **Touraine** in the **Loire** valley. It is similar to **Rosé d'Anjou**, but is better because it is usually drier, and the **Grolleau** grape variety is blended with at least 30% **Cabernet Sauvignon**. PRICE BAND: A.

Rosé des Riceys A rare, still, rosé **AC** wine of the **Champagne** region, made from the **Pinot Noir** grape variety in exceptionally good years.

Rosette A medium-sweet white **AC** wine in

the **Bergerac** region of southwest **France**, produced from the **Sémillon**, **Sauvignon Blanc**, and **Muscadelle** grape varieties. The wine is light and of rarely more than adequate quality. There are fewer bottles produced each year, and it may die out completely before long.

Rossese di Dolceacqua A red **DOC** wine produced in **Liguria**, northwest **Italy**, from the Rossese grape variety. At best it is a fragant, medium-bodied, fruity red, but too often it is thin and pale coloured.

rosso The Italian for red wine.

Rosso Barletta A dry red **DOC** wine of central **Apulia** in southern **Italy**, made mainly from **Uva di Troia** (plus, occasionally, **Montepulciano**, **Sangiovese** and **Cot**). Quality can be good and it is usually best drunk young.

Rosso Canosa A dry red **DOC** wine of central **Apulia** in southern **Italy** made mainly from **Uva di Troia** (plus, occasionally, **Montepulciano** and **Sangiovese**). A robust red, for relatively early drinking.

Rosso Cònero A red **DOC** wine produced around the town of Ancona in the **Marches** region of **Italy**. Most of the wine is produced from the **Montepulciano** grape variety, although **Sangiovese** is allowed up to 15%. The wine is full, round, high in tannins, and capable of long ageing. Quality can be exceptionally high and it is very good value for money. PRICE BAND: A–B.

Rosso di Montalcino A red **DOC** wine of **Tuscany**, produced in the same area, and from the same grape variety, as **Brunello di Montalcino**. The idea is that producers will select their best grapes for Brunello, and make the rest into Rosso, in an early-drinking style. In poor years, they can make all their wine as Rosso. This benefits the consumer because Rosso is delicious and lovely to drink when relatively young, costs much less than Brunello and the selection process should lead to an improvement in the quality of Brunello. PRICE BAND: B.

Rosso di Montepulciano A red **DOC** wine of **Tuscany**, produced in the same area, and from the same grape varieties, as **Vino Nobile di Montepulciano**. As with **Rosso di Montalcino**, the idea is for Vino Nobile producers to declassify lighter years to Rosso, which can be sold after six months' ageing rather than two years. PRICE BAND: A–B.

Rosso Piceno A red **DOC** wine of the **Marches** region of **Italy**, made from the **Sangiovese** and **Montepulciano** grape varieties. Quality is moderate compared with the vastly superior **Rosso Cònero**.

Rotgipfler A white grape variety of **Austria**, which along with **Zierfändler** is used to produce the heady, spicy, rich wine Gumpoldskirchner.

rotling A German term for rosé wine, produced by fermenting red and white grapes together (not by blending red and white wine).

rotwein The German for red wine.

rouge The French for red.

Roussanne A white grape variety that, along with **Marsanne**, is used to make white wines in the northern **Rhône**. Its presence in the blend results in a more vivacious and aromatic wine than is available from pure Marsanne. Roussanne is also one of the 13 varieties permitted in red **Châteauneuf-du-Pape** in the southern Rhône.

Roussette See **Altesse**.

Roussillon See **Languedoc-Roussillon**.

Ruby Port The basic style of young **Port**, full-bodied, sweet, vigorous and fruity. The average age of Ruby is usually around three years. It requires no decanting, and can be drunk immediately after purchase. PRICE BAND: B. See also **Vintage Character**.

Ruchottes-Chambertin A **grand cru** vineyard of **Gevrey-Chambertin** in the **Côte de Nuits** area of **Burgundy**.

Rüdesheim 1. A town of the **Rheingau** region of **Germany**, which produces fine-quality, full-flavoured white wines from the **Riesling** grape variety. The vineyards come within the **Grosslage** of Burgweg, and the best **Einzellage** sites are Berg Roseneck, Berg Rottland, Berg Schlossberg, Klosterberg, Klosterlay, Bischofsberg and Rosengarten.

2. A village of the **Nahe** region of **Germany**, which produces modest white wines from the **Müller-Thurgau** and **Silvaner** grape varieties. The vineyards come within the Grosslage of Rosengarten.

Rueda A white **DO** wine of northwest Spain, made mainly from the native Verdejo grape variety, along with Viura (**Macabeo**) and **Sauvignon Blanc**. Traditionally the region made **fortified wines** from **Palomino**, in a similar style to **Sherry**, but today nearly all the production is of young, white table wines. Quality is usually extremely good, and fresh, fruity, nutty Rueda is one of the best white wines of Spain. PRICE BAND: B.

Rufina See **Chianti** (Rufina).

Ruländer The alternative name, used in Germany, for the **Pinot Gris** grape.

Rully An **AC** wine of the **Côte Chalonnaise** region of **Burgundy**, which produces white wines from **Chardonnay** and reds from **Pinot Noir**. The whites are soft, medium-bodied and nutty, sometimes with a touch of oak, and offer good value for money. Reds are lighter bodied, and less successful so far, but there are signs of improvement. PRICE BAND: B–C.

Russia See **Soviet Union**.

Russian River Valley An **AVA** of **Sonoma** county, **California**, in a relatively cool climate. It produces good **varietal** wines from **Chardonnay**, **Pinot Noir**, **Riesling** and **Gewürztraminer**. Successful **méthode champenoise** sparkling wines are also made from Chardonnay and Pinot Noir.

Rutherglen A wine-producing region of the state of **Victoria** in **Australia**, with a great reputation for luscious, intensely sweet and complex **fortified** wines, particularly 'Liqueur Muscat' and 'Liqueur Tokay' (from **Muscadelle** grapes).

Ruwer See **Mosel-Saar-Ruwer**.

Saar-Ruwer A **Bereich** subregion of the **Mosel-Saar-Ruwer** region, or **Anbaugebiet**. The best white wines are made from the **Riesling** grape variety, light but strong-flavoured and steely, with a pronounced slaty character especially in the Saar valley.

Saarburg A town on the Saar river, in the **Mosel-Saar-Ruwer** region of **Germany**, producing fine, aromatic, slaty white wines from the **Riesling** grape variety. The vineyards come under the **Grosslage** of Scharzberg, and the best **Einzellage** sites are Klosterberg, Fuchs and Schlossberg.

Sablet See **Côtes du Rhône**.

Sacramento Valley A county of **California**, which produces mainly ordinary-quality jug wine.

Saint-Amour A red **AC** wine, one of the 10 **crus** of the **Beaujolais** region of **Burgundy**, made from the **Gamay** grape. The wines are among the finest of Beaujolais, juicy, aromatic and full of flavour although light and delicate. PRICE BAND: B.

Saint-Aubin An **AC** wine of the **Côte de Beaune** region of **Burgundy**. Most of the wine produced is full-bodied red, from the **Pinot Noir** grape variety. The whites, from **Chardonnay**, are more interesting: toasty, with good acidity and sometimes a touch of oak, offering good value for money, especially those labelled **premier cru**. PRICE BAND: C.

Saint-Bris-le-Vineux See **Sauvignon de Saint-Bris**.

Sainte-Croix-du-Mont A sweet white **AC** wine made on the right bank of the Garonne river in the **Bordeaux** region. The grapes are the same as those used in **Sauternes** and **Barsac**, **Sémillon**, **Sauvignon Blanc** and **Muscadelle**, although higher yields are permitted. The wines are in a similar style to those of Sauternes and Barsac, but never as rich or fine, and they have less ageing potential. PRICE BAND: B.

Saint-Emilion 1. A red **AC** wine of **Bordeaux**, centred on the the town of Saint-Emilion on the north bank of the Dordogne river. It is made from the classic Bordeaux grape varieties, **Cabernet Sauvignon**, **Cabernet Franc** and **Merlot**. Merlot has more importance here than in the **Médoc**, where Cabernet Sauvignon is king.

The wines are classified into *premier grand* **cru classé**, at the top (11 châteaux); **grand cru** *classé* (more than 60); *grand cru* (around 200); and the rest. The wines are soft, aromatic, fleshy, and slightly spicy, ready to drink sooner than the great red wines of the Médoc. Quality varies, although the top wines are nearly always reliable, and there is good value to be found lower down the classification. PRICE BAND: B-E. See also **Lussac-**, **Montagne-**, **Puisseguin-** and **Saint-Georges-Saint-Emilion**.

2. An alternative name, used in the Charentes region of **France**, for the **Trebbiano** grape variety.

Saint-Estèphe A red AC wine of the **Haut-Médoc** area of **Bordeaux**, and the largest of the four great communal *appellations*. Saint-Estèphe does not enjoy as high a reputation as the others, **Pauillac**, **Margaux** and **Saint-Julien**. There are only five **crus classés**, and the wines can be tannic, tough and unapproachable in their youth, requiring long ageing. However, there are also many good-quality **cru bourgeois** wines available, and these can offer good value for money. PRICE BAND: B-E.

Saint-Georges-Saint-Emilion A red AC wine

made in a satellite area of the main **Saint-Emilion** *appellation*, **Bordeaux**. The grape varieties are the same as for Saint-Emilion, **Merlot**, **Cabernet Franc**, **Cabernet Sauvignon** and **Malbec**, and Saint-Georges wines are probably the best of the satellites, if never reaching the heights of the top Saint-Emilions. Producers in Saint-Georges also have the option of using the AC of **Montagne-Saint-Emilion**. PRICE BAND: B.

Saint-Joseph An **AC** wine of the northern **Rhône**. The red wine is made mainly from the **Syrah** grape variety, sometimes with the addition of the white grapes **Marsanne** and **Roussanne**, which are also used to make white Saint-Joseph. The reds are more important, and more consistently good, with rich, concentrated blackberry and blackcurrant fruit, although less long-lived than **Hermitage**. Good whites exist, but are difficult to find: the best are full-bodied, with pear and apricot flavours. PRICE BAND: B–C.

Saint-Julien An important communal **AC** of the **Médoc**. It produces very high-quality red **Bordeaux**, with great balance, finesse, rounded fruit flavours and depth, and capable of lasting as long as the great wines of **Pauillac**. There are 11 **cru classé** châteaux, nearly all making consistently superb wine.

Saint-Nicolas-de-Bourgueil A red **AC** wine of the **Touraine** region in the **Loire** valley, made mainly from the **Cabernet Franc** grape (called

Breton locally). It is one of the finest-quality red wines of the Loire, with grassy, raspberry fruit flavours, and is capable of long ageing. **Bourgueil** is similar, but has its own AC. PRICE BAND: B–C.

Saint-Péray A white **AC** wine of the northern **Rhône**, made from the **Marsanne** and **Roussanne** grapes. Most of it is turned into a good-quality **méthode champenoise** sparkler, although some is bottled as still wine.

Saint-Romain An AC wine of the **Côte de Beaune** region of **Burgundy**. Production is divided between light, but earthy reds, made from the **Pinot Noir** grape, and dry, flinty whites from **Chardonnay**. PRICE BAND: C.

Saint-Véran A white **AC** wine of the **Mâconnais** region of **Burgundy**, made from the **Chardonnay** grape variety. This soft, fresh white should be drunk young, and offers good value for money. PRICE BAND: B.

Salice Salentino A **DOC** wine produced in the **Apulia** region of southern **Italy**. Good quality, robust, rich reds are made from the **Negroamaro** grape, along with fresh, floral **rosato** wines.

salmanazar A large format Champagne bottle, of 9 litres capacity (equivalent to 12 ordinary bottles).

Sancerre An AC wine produced in the eastern part of the **Loire**. Most of the production is of white wine made from the **Sauvignon Blanc** grape variety. These can be superb; bone-dry, but bursting with juicy fruit, with gooseberry and blackcurrant flavours, sometimes even asparagus, all balanced with racy acidity. Dry red and rosé Sancerre, made from **Pinot Noir**, is less successful. PRICE BAND: B–E.

San Colombano al Lambro A red **DOC** wine produced in the **Lombardy** region of northwest Italy. This dry, rustic red, which has moderate ageing potential, is made from the **Croatina**, **Barbera**, and **Uva Rara** grape varieties.

Sangiovese A red grape variety grown throughout **Italy**, but to best effect in **Tuscany**, where it is responsible for the best part of the blend for **Chianti** and for all of **Brunello di Montalcino**. There are many different **clones** of Sangiovese, of which the best is called Sangioveto (or 'Brunello' in Montalcino). Also in Tuscany, Sangiovese is used to make superb **vini da tavola**, either on its own, or blended with **Cabernet Sauvignon**.

Sangue di Giuda See **Oltrepò Pavese**.

San Joaquin Valley A hot-climate, wine-producing region of **California**, making mostly large quantities of mass-market 'jug' wine.

Sanlucar de Barrameda See **manzanilla**; **Sherry**.

San Luis Obispo A county of **California**, with a growing reputation for good-quality **varietal**

wines, especially reds from the **Zinfandel** and **Cabernet Sauvignon** grape varieties, and white from **Chardonnay**.

San Severo A DOC wine produced in the **Apulia** region of southern **Italy**. Large quantities of good-value, simple red, white and **rosato** wine are made. The whites are based on the **Bombino** and **Trebbiano** grapes, the red and rosé on **Montepulciano** and **Sangiovese**.

Sant'Anna di Isola Capo Rizzuto A DOC wine produced in the **Calabria** region of southern Italy. Neutral, bland red and **rosato** is made, based on the **Gaglioppo** and **Nerello** Mascalese grape varieties

Santa Barbara A county of **California**, which produces mainly white **varietal** wines from the **Chardonnay**, **Chenin Blanc** and **Riesling** grape varieties, together with good-quality red **Pinot Noir**.

Santa Maddalena (also called **St Magdalener**) A DOC wine produced in the **Alto Adige** region of northeast Italy. Dry, red, full, fruity wine is produced from the **Schiava** grape variety.

Santenay An AC wine of the **Côte de Beaune** area of **Burgundy**. Quite good-value, earthy, fruity, ripe, red Burgundy is made from the **Pinot**

Noir grape variety, together with a small quantity of white, made from **Chardonnay**. PRICE BAND: C.

Sardinia An island belonging to **Italy**, making good dry reds from the **Cannonau** grape. It also produces sweet, red **Girò di Cagliari**, sturdy red **Mandrolisai** and soft light reds from the **Monica** grape variety. Dry to sweet white **Nasco di Cagliari**, neutral white **Nuragus di Cagliari** and dry red **Campidano di Terralba** are also made.

Sartène See **Vin de Corse**.

Sassella See **Valtellina**.

Saumur An **AC** wine of the **Loire** valley, produced around the town of Saumur. Good, white **méthode champenoise** sparkling wine (often labelled Saumur d'Origine) is made from the **Chenin Blanc** grape, plus **Cabernet Franc** and, increasingly, **Chardonnay**. PRICE BAND: B–C. Still wines are made, both white and red, based mainly on Chenin Blanc and Cabernet Franc respectively; both are usually rather thin and astringent.

Saumur-Champigny A red **AC** wine produced in vineyards near **Saumur**, in the **Loire** valley. This dry, grassy, usually good-quality red is based mainly on the **Cabernet Franc** grape variety, sometimes with **Cabernet Sauvignon**. PRICE BAND: B.

Sauternes A sweet white **AC** wine of Bordeaux, produced from the **Sémillon**, **Sauvignon**

Blanc and **Muscadelle** varieties. This is one of the world's finest **dessert wines**, with marvellous richness and complexity of exotic fruit flavours. Its distinctive rich balance between fruit and acidity derives from the action of **botrytis** on the grapes. The particular concentration of Sauternes also has a lot to do with low yields, and successive pickings at harvest time, to ensure that every grape is gathered at the optimum degree of ripeness. Consequently, Sauternes can never be 'cheap'. PRICE BAND: C–E++. See also **Barsac**.

Sauvignon Blanc An important white grape variety, planted in many wine-producing countries of the world. Its two main homes, in France, are **Bordeaux** and the **Loire**. In the Loire, **Sancerre** and **Pouilly-Fumé** are the archetypal examples of 100% Sauvignon. In Bordeaux, it is sometimes vinified alone to make a crisp dry wine, but more usually blended with **Sémillon** (and **Muscadelle**) to make dry wines (in **Graves** and **Entre-Deux-Mers**), or lusciously sweet dessert wines (in **Sauternes** and **Barsac**).

In **Italy** it is found in **Alto Adige** and **Friuli-Veneiza Giulia**. Many New World countries have adopted Sauvignon, but none with more success than **New Zealand**, with zesty, juicy fruit wines than can rival the best of the Loire.

Sauvignon de Saint-Bris A crisp, white **VDQS** wine of northern **Burgundy**, produced in Saint-Bris-le-Vineux, not far from Chablis, from the **Sauvignon Blanc** grape variety. At its best, it can rival much Sauvignon from the **Loire**, in terms of quality and value for money. PRICE BAND: A–B.

Savagnin (also called **Gringet**) A white grape variety almost unique to the **Jura** region of **France**, where it contributes to the blend for the white table wines, and is central to the production of **vins jaunes**.

Savennières A white **AC** wine of **Anjou-Saumur**, in the **Loire** valley, probably the finest expression of dry wine produced from the **Chenin Blanc** grape. The wines are highly assertive and acidic in their youth, mellowing, and becoming almost honeyed, as they slowly mature. There are separate ACs for two particularly good sites: Coulée-de-Serrant and La Roche-aux-Moines. PRICE BAND: B–C.

Savigny-lès-Beaune An **AC** wine of the **Côte de Beaune** region of **Burgundy**. Fairly good, if somewhat light, strawberry-flavoured reds are produced from the **Pinot Noir** grape variety, plus a little white from **Chardonnay**. PRICE BAND: B–C.

Savoie See **Vin de Savoie**.

Savuto A red **DOC** wine produced in the **Calabria** region of southern **Italy**. A dry juicy red, it ranges from pale cherry to full ruby in colour, made mainly from the **Gaglioppo**, **Greco** Nero and **Nerello** Cappuccio grape varieties.

schaumwein The German term for basic-quality sparkling wine.

Scheurebe A white grape variety, a **cross** of **Silvaner** and **Riesling**, planted throughout the wine regions of **Germany**. It has been underestimated in the past, but has recently been shown to be capable of producing excellent **QmP** quality wines.

Schiava (also called **Trollinger**; **Vernatsch**) A red grape variety, planted widely in the **Alto Adige** region of northeast **Italy** (where it is often known as Vernatsch), and in **Württemburg** in Germany (alias Trollinger). It is really a table grape, and produces quite light red wine, lacking in character and tannin, and best drunk young and fresh. See also **Caldaro**.

schloss The German term for a castle. Wines that bear the name of a particular *schloss* must have been produced entirely from vines grown in the estate's vineyards. However, the word *schloss* may also feature in an *Einzellage* or district name, so it does not always indicate an estate wine.

Schloss Böckelheim A **Bereich** subregion of the **Nahe** region of **Germany**, producing good-quality white wines, especially from the **Riesling** grape.

Schlossböckelheim A small, but important, village in the **Nahe** region of **Germany**. It produces very high quality white wines from the **Riesling** grape. The vineyards come under the **Grosslage** of Burgweg, and the best **Einzellage** site is Kupfergrube.

Schönburger A white grape variety, a **cross** between **Pinot Noir** and Pirovano (itself a cross of Chasselas Rosé and Muscat of Hamburg), grown in limited quantity in the **Rheinhessen** and **Rheinpfalz** regions of Germany, and also in **England**. The grapes are pink, producing white wine, with an aroma similar to **Gewürztraminer**, but slightly flabby and lacking in acidity.

schoppenwein The German term for 'house wine', sold by the carafe or glass.

sec The French term meaning dry for still wines, but relatively sweet (sweeter than **brut**) for sparkling wines.

secco The Italian term meaning dry for still wines, but quite sweet for sparkling wines.

seco The Spanish and Portuguese term for dry.

second wine A category of wine produced in **Bordeaux**, particularly by the **cru classé** châteaux of the **Médoc**. The production of the very highest quality red Bordeaux involves careful selection of vats of wine, after fermentation. Only the very best vats of wine will be blended to form the **grand vin**, which will bear the château name. Slightly inferior lots of wine, particularly those made from young vines, may be bottled under a different name and sold earlier at a lower price. This improves cash flow for the producer, and provides consumers with excellent wine from top vineyards at an affordable price. Second wines are not to be confused with 'second growths', or *deuxièmes* **crus classés**.

Sekt A German term for sparkling wine. Unless the label says Deutscher Sekt, the wine is probably made from low-quality imported base wine, from Italy or France. A few producers make an effort to produce quality Deutscher Sekt some using **Riesling** and the **méthode champenoise**, but in general quality leaves something to be desired. PRICE BAND: A–B.

Sélection de Grains Nobles A special category of wines from **Alsace**, made from late-picked grapes affected by **botrytis**. Usually made from the **Riesling** or **Gewürztraminer** grapes (sometimes **Muscat** or **Pinot Gris**), they are usually sweet, very concentrated, and of very high quality (and price). PRICE BAND: E. See also **vendange tardive**.

semi-secco The Italian term for medium dry; in practice the taste is medium-sweet.

semi-seco The Spanish term for medium dry; in practice the taste is medium-sweet.

Sémillon A white grape variety, grown in many wine-producing regions throughout the world, but to best effect in **Bordeaux** and **Australia** (especially the **Hunter Valley**). The great white wines of Bordeaux, whether sweet, (e.g **Sauternes** and **Barsac**), or dry, (e.g. **Graves**), are usually a blend of Sémillon with **Sauvignon Blanc**, and possibly also **Muscadelle**.

The variety's particular susceptibility to **botrytis** is of great importance in the sweet wines. The best Australian Sémillon is bottled as a **varietal** wine. It is nearly always dry, and often capable of developing great complexity with bottle age. Large plantings of Sémillon also exist in **Chile** and **Brazil**, but yields here are so high that the wine rarely has any varietal character. See also **Bergerac**; **Buzet**; **Entre-Deux-Mers**; **Gaillac**; **Haut Montravel**; **Loupiac**; **Monbazillac**; **Montecarlo**; **Montravel**; **Pessac-Léognan**.

Sercial A grape variety, grown on the island of **Madeira**, where it gives its name to a category of wine. Light, delicate and perfumed, savoury and high in acid, Sercial is the driest, lightest style of Madeira.

Setúbal See **Moscatel**.

Sèvre et Maine See **Muscadet**.

Seyssel A white **AC** wine of the **Savoie** region of France. The **méthode champenoise** Seyssel Mousseux is a light, refreshing sparkler made from the **Molette** and **Altesse** grape varieties. The still wine is based on Altesse, and is dry, full-bodied, spicy, and aromatic.

Seyval Blanc A white grape variety, a **cross** between two varieties of **Seibel** (themselves both **hybrids**), widely planted in the vineyards of **England**. It produces high yields of medium-quality wine, often with a distinctive grapefruit flavour.

Seyve-Villard 5276 An alternative name for the **Seyval Blanc** grape variety.

Sfursat See **Valtellina**.

sharp A tasting term, used to indicate a wine with too much **acidity**. A sharp young wine may achieve better balance with maturity.

Sherry (also called **Jerez**; **Xérès**) A **fortified wine**, produced in Andalusia in southern **Spain** around the towns of Jerez de la Frontera, Sanlúcar de Barrameda and Puerto de Santa Maria. The most important grape is the **Palomino**, best grown on the chalky white **albariza** soil, and small amounts of **Pedro Ximénez** and **Moscatel** are also grown.

Fino is a pale, bone dry, pungent Sherry. Its distinctive, tangy aroma and flavour are the result of ageing the wine in the **solera** system under a layer of yeast cells called **flor**. A *fino* must spend at least three years in the solera system, in Jerez or Puerto de Santa Maria, before bottling. *Fino* from Sanlúcar de Barrameda is called *manzanilla*. *Fino* and *manzanilla*, served correctly chilled, are among the best apéritifs of all.

Amontillado is a completely dry, nutty Sherry, with an amber colour, which results when a *fino* is allowed to mature without being refreshed with younger wines. Less expensive medium-sweet Sherries are often described as *amontillado*, but in fact these are sweetened blends containing only a small amount of true *amontillado*. The same is true of **oloroso**, which is used to describe any dark, sweet Sherry. A true *oloroso* is a rich, nutty, dark style, which takes up its flavour from long ageing in cask, rather than from flor. True *oloroso* is dry, but often it is sweetened to make a commercial blend by adding some Pedro Ximénez wine, and sometimes it is darkened with **vino do color**.

Cream Sherry is basically a sweetened, darkened *oloroso*. **Pale cream** combines the sweetness of cream sherry with the colour of a *fino*. The style is made by sweetening young *fino* with pale grape juice concentrate. It never has the complex flavour of the traditional Sherry styles. Real Sherry comes only from Spain. The anomalous 'British Sherry' and 'South African Sherry' are best used for cooking. See also **almacenista**; **Palo Cortado**.

Shiraz An alternative name, used in Australia, for **Syrah**.

short A tasting term, used to describe a wine in which the flavour does not persist on the palate, once the wine is swallowed. See **finish**; **length**.

Sicily An island off the coast of southern **Italy**. It was traditionally famed for its **fortified** wine **Marsala**, but now has a growing reputation for table wines, mostly produced outside the **DOC** system. Most of the wines are based on native Italian grape varieties, including the white **Catarratto**, **Inzolia** and **Grillo**, and the red **Calabrese** (or Nero d'Avola) and **Nerello** (both Cappuccio and Mascalese). See also **Ambrato di Comiso**; **Alcamo**; **Etna**; **Faro**.

Siegerrebe A white grape variety, a **cross** of **Madeleine Angevine** and **Gewürztraminer**, grown to a limited extent in **Germany**, mainly in the **Rheinhessen** and **Rheinpfalz** regions, and also in **England**. It produces wines with a relatively high **alcohol content**, low acidity, and powerful aroma. Occasionally it is bottled as a **varietal**, but more usually it is used in tiny quantities to add richness and flavour to commercial blends with other grape varieties.

silky A tasting term, used to describe a wine with a soft, smooth, yet firm texture on the palate.

Silvaner (also called **Sylvaner**) A white grape variety, planted widely in **Germany**, and also in **Alsace** (where it is usually spelled Sylvaner). In

Germany it produces a fairly neutral wine, high in acidity and lacking in aroma, and is usually blended with more characterful varieties, such as **Riesling** and **Scheurebe**. In Alsace, Sylvaner is gradually being replaced by **Pinot Blanc** and **Riesling**; what remains often ends up blended with other Alsatian varieties, and labelled **Edelzwicker** or just AC Alsace. Sylvaner is also important in the **Alto Adige** in northern **Italy**, where it produces crisp, dry, fairly neutral whites.

sin crianza A Spanish term, used to describe a wine with little or no oak **ageing**. See **Rioja**.

Single Quinta Port A category of **Port**, which in theory means a **Vintage Port** made from grapes grown in a single estate, or **quinta**. In fact, there are a number of variations. Some shippers use the Single Quinta category to market Port from an 'off' year, not good enough to declare as their true Vintage Port. Others, confusingly, use a single *quinta* name on Port that is a blend of wines from several *quintas*. The method of production is the same as for Vintage Port, although the required length of maturation in bottle may be shorter, because the wine is usually less concentrated and complex.

Sizzano A dry red **DOC** wine of northern **Piedmont** in **Italy**, produced around the village of the same name. Made from the **Nebbiolo** grape variety (known locally as **Spanna**), plus **Vespolina**

and **Bonarda**, it is light (for Nebbiolo), but full-flavoured and easy to drink in its youth, although capable of up to 10 years ageing.

smoky A tasting term, used to describe a subtle wood-smoke aroma. It is used particularly for some good-quality white wines, made from **Chardonnay**, and many high-quality reds made from **Pinot Noir**, **Syrah** or **Cabernet Sauvignon**, among others.

Soave A dry white **DOC** wine of the **Veneto** region of **Italy**, and one of the best-known of all Italian wines. Soave is made mainly from the **Garganega** grape variety, with some **Trebbiano**. Traditionally, it has been thought of as a rather bland, neutral white, and that reputation remains true for much of what is produced today, although there are exceptions.

The best vineyard sites are on the hills of the Soave Classico subregion, and wines from here are nearly always better. Also, some quality-conscious producers have produced characterful Soave by reducing yields, making single-vineyard wines from particularly good sites and, in some cases, ageing the wines in **barrique**. The best Soave has soft fruit, with a nutty, creamy taste. It is sometimes made **spumante**, by the **Charmat method**. There is also a sweet **recioto** version, made from dried grapes. See **Recioto di Soave**.
PRICE BAND: A–C.

soft A tasting term, used to describe a wine

with a mellow, unaggressive taste and texture. It is also often used to qualify **tannin** (gentle, rather than harsh tannin); and **fruity** (rounded, well-integrated fruit).

Solano County A minor wine-producing county of **California**, located just south of **Napa Valley**, producing generally inferior wines.

solera The system by which **Sherry** (and some other **fortified wines**) are aged. A *solera* can be thought of as a series of rows of **butts** (barrels of 600 litres) piled one on top of the other. When Sherry is required for bottling, it is drawn off from the bottom row of butts (the *solera*). These are then topped up with slightly younger wine from the row above (**a criadera**), and so on. In fact, the *solera* is often more complicated than this, and the different scales are often not one on top of the other – they may even be in different **bodegas**; but the general principle is the same, i.e. the production of a consistently aged and refreshed final blend. See also **amontillado**; **fino**.

solid A tasting term, used to describe a concentrated full-bodied wine, with high levels of **alcohol**, fruit extract, **tannin** and **acidity**.

Somontano A **DO** wine of northeast **Spain**, produced in the foothills of the Pyrenees. Most of the production is of red wine, mainly from the local Moristel grape, plus some new plantings of **Cabernet Sauvignon** and **Tempranillo**, among other varieties. A little **rosado** is produced, also mainly from Moristel, and a very small quantity of white from **Macabeo**. The reds are light, aromatic and easy-drinking, and quality is improving rapidly.

Sonoma An important wine-producing county of **California**, just to the west of **Napa Valley**. The region and microclimates are extremely varied, meaning that almost all the California varieties can be grown successfully somewhere in Sonoma.

The Alexander Valley **AVA**, produces fine **Zinfandel**, **Pinot Noir**, **Cabernet Sauvignon** and **Chardonnay**. **Russian River Valley** has a relatively cool climate, producing good Chardonnay, Pinot Noir, **Riesling** and **Gewürztraminer**. Successful **méthode champenoise** sparkling wines are also made here, from Chardonnay and Pinot Noir.

Dry Creek Valley AVA is probably better for white wines, particularly **Sauvignon Blanc**, **Chenin Blanc** and Chardonnay, than for reds, from Zinfandel and Cabernet Sauvignon. **Knights Valley** has a growing reputation for rich and elegant Cabernets. See also **Carneros**.

Sorni A **DOC** wine of the **Trentino** region of **Italy**. The white version is based on the Nosiola grape variety; the red on **Schiava**. Both are light, fresh and fruity, best drunk young.

South Africa The main wine-producing country

of Africa, traditionally making **fortified wines** in the style of **Port** and **Sherry**. Today **varietal** table wines have become more important. **Chenin Blanc** (or **Steen**) is the most important white, and the best reds are made from **Cabernet Sauvignon**; **Pinotage**, a cross of **Pinot Noir** and **Cinsault**, is declining in importance. The economic sanctions against South Africa have meant that the wines have not had a ready export market, and many winemakers have been isolated from their colleagues in the rest of the wine world.

South Australia The largest wine-producing state of **Australia**, including the regions **Adelaide Hills**, **Barossa Valley**, **Clare Valley**, **Coonawarra**, **McLaren Vale**, Padthaway and **Riverland**. Many of the country's largest wine companies are based here.

Soviet Union A group of republics with a massive area under vine. It produces the third largest quantity of wine after France and Italy, although very little of it has been seen in the west so far. The main wine regions are Crimea, Georgia, Armenia (also produces brandy) and Azerbaijan. Traditionally, the Crimea has produced some superlative **fortified** wines of immense longevity, made in the style of **Port**, **Sherry** and **Madeira**, as well as ordinary-quality red table wine. Sparkling wine is also important for the domestic market, usually made rather sweet by western standards. The potential for producing quality wine is there, but winemakers have, until recently, been isolated from developments in viticulture, and modern equipment has been difficult to obtain.

Spain An important wine-producing country, best known for **Sherry** and for its reds from **Rioja** and **Ribera del Duero**. Rioja's neighbour, **Navarra**, produces wines in a similar style, although not yet reaching the high quality of top Rioja. See also **Léon**. Just west of Ribera, **Rueda** produces some of Spain's best whites. In the northeast of the country, **Penedès** produces good reds and whites, mainly from 'foreign' grape varieties, and is the main centre for **Cava** production; Priorato is rich, high-alcohol red wine. See also **Alella**; **Ampurdán-Costa Brava**; **Somontano**; **Tarragona**; **Terra Alta**.

In central Spain, **La Mancha** is a source of vast quantities of easy-drinking reds and whites, while **Valdepeñas** has some rapidly improving reds; see also **Méntrida**. Eastern central Spain is home of large quantities of mediocre red and white; see **Alicante**, **Almansa**, **Jumilla**, **Utiel-Requena** and **Valencia**. In **Galicia** in the northwest, near the Portuguese border, the best wines are fresh, fruity whites from **Rias Baixas**. Other **fortified wines** apart from Sherry are **Málaga** and **Montilla-Moriles**. See also **Mallorca**.

Spanna An alternative name, used in northern **Piedmont**, for the **Nebbiolo** grape variety; particularly by the makers of **Boca**, **Bramaterra**, **Fara**, **Gattinara**, **Ghemme**, **Lessona** and **Sizzano**.

Spain

1 Rias Baxas
2 Ribeiro
3 Valdeorras
4 El Bierzo
5 Rioja
6 Navarra
7 Toro
8 Rueda
9 Cigales
10 Ribera del Duero
11 Cariñena
12 Tarragona
13 Priorato
14 Costers del Segre
15 Penedés
16 Alella
17 Madrid
18 La Mancha
19 Valdepeñas
20 Utiel-Requena
21 Valencia
22 Jumilla
23 Yecla
24 Alicante
25 Condado de Huelva
26 Jerez
27 Montilla-Moriles
28 Málaga

Spätburgunder An alternative name, used in **Germany**, for the **Pinot Noir** grape variety.

Spätlese A German and Austrian quality white wine category, meaning 'late harvest'. The ripe grapes are picked at least seven days after the official start of the harvest, resulting in a higher **must weight** (the minimum is 76–85° *Oechsle* in Germany) than for **Kabinett** wines. The wines can be relatively sweet and honeyed, although many *Spätlese* wines are produced in the **trocken** (dry) or **halbtrocken** styles. See **QmP**.

Spätrot An alternative name for the **Zierfändler** grape variety.

spicy A tasting term, used to describe a herby, aromatic flavour. It can derive from the grape variety, for example **Syrah** often has a spicy taste, or from **ageing** the wine in oak barrels.

spumante An Italian term for fully sparkling wine. See also **frizzante**.

Squinzano A **DOC** wine of the **Apulia** region of southern **Italy**, produced around the town of Squinzano, mainly from the **Negroamaro** grape variety. Red and **rosato** wines are produced, both dry, and both capable of reasonably good quality.

Stag's Leap An important **AVA** in the **Napa Valley** area of **California**. Red **varietal** wines made from **Cabernet Sauvignon** can be of world class, and are as good here as from any part of the Napa.

stalky A tasting term, used to describe a fresh, sappy, immature aroma and taste, usually used of young, fairly raw red wine.

Steen An alternative name, used in South Africa, for **Chenin Blanc**.

Steigerwald A **Bereich** subregion of **Franken**, Germany.

Südliche Weinstrasse A **Bereich** subregion of the **Rheinpfalz**, Germany. It produces mainly cheap and cheerful wines, inferior to those of the northern Rheinpfalz *Bereich*, the **Mittelhaardt-Deutsche Weinstrasse**.

Südtirol See **Alto Adige**.

sugar A vital ingredient in grapes, sugar is converted into **alcohol** by the action of **yeast** during **fermentation**. In some areas, where grapes do not always have a sufficient level of natural sugar, the addition of sugar (**chaptalization**) is permitted to boost the final alcohol content. The amount of sugar that can be added is controlled by law.

sulphur dioxide An essential additive to nearly all wines, even those described as **organic**, although all good winemakers will keep its use to an absolute minimum. It is used to kill wild **yeast** on grape skins before they are fermented, to sterilize barrels and bottles, and to eliminate any bacterial infection – and prevent **oxidation** – in fermented wine.

supple A tasting term, used to indicate a wine with a soft, easy-drinking combination of fruit, acidity and **tannin**.

sur lie A term found on some French wines, usually **Muscadet**, to indicate that the wine is matured on the **lees**, or dead yeast cells, and, in theory, bottled straight from the barrel. The wine can develop a delicious yeasty complexity, sometimes with a slightly **pétillant** prickle on the tongue.

süssreserve A German term for unfermented grape juice, which is added to fermented wine before bottling to increase the sweetness. The quality and origin of the juice is regulated by law. The same technique is sometimes used for English wine.

Swan Valley A wine-producing region of **Western Australia**. It has a hot climate (one of the hottest wine regions in the world), and produces mainly big white wines, from **Chenin Blanc** and **Verdelho**, some reds from **Shiraz** and **Cabernet Sauvignon**.

sweaty A tasting term, used to indicate a pungent, **leathery** aroma, often associated with wines made from the **Syrah** grape variety.

sweet A tasting term, self-explanatory for

white wines, where it indicates a relatively high level of **residual sugar**. It is also used for red wines, which although technically dry may have rich, ripe fruit flavours, which give an impression of sweetness.

Switzerland A wine-producing country known mainly for its white wines from the cantons of Vaud and Valais. Valais, in the upper Rhône valley, produces light, white wines from the **Chasselas** grape, and a red wine, **Dôle**, from **Gamay** and **Pinot Noir**. Vaud includes the vineyards along the shore of Lake Geneva and the wine area of **La Côte**. Chasselas is again the principal grape variety grown. Among the most notable whites are those from the villages of Aigle and Yvorne in the Chablais region, in the west of Vaud.

Sylvaner See **Silvaner**.

Syrah A red grape variety, grown particularly in the northern **Rhône**, where it makes the great red wines of **Hermitage**, **Cornas** and **Côte Rôtie**, and in **Australia** (where it is known as Shiraz) and may be used for blending, often with **Cabernet Sauvignon**, although it makes characterful varietal wine. When vinified on its own, Syrah can produce top-quality wines, with a peppery, spicy flavour, sometimes smoky, and often very long lived. The top Rhône wines, especially, need time to show their best. Syrah also provides structure and longevity to many other French wines, particularly elsewhere in the Rhône (where it is often blended with **Grenache**), in **Provence** and in the **Midi**.

table wine 1. A general term for any wine that is not **fortified**. 2. A general term for a wine not entitled to any quality designation. Defined by the EC as the category of wine below 'quality wine'. See also **tafelwein**; **vin de table**; **vino da tavola**; **vino de mesa**.

Tâche, La See **La Tâche**.

tafelwein The lowest category of **German** wine. *Tafelwein* can include wines from outside Germany (often from **Italy**), while **Deutscher Tafelwein** must be 100% German.

Tannat A red grape variety of southwest **France**, used as part of the blend to make **Madiran**, **Tursan**, **Irouléguy** and **Béarn**. It produces wines of deep colour, red-fruit flavours, and high alcohol and **tannin** (leading to good ageing potential).

tannin 1. A chemical substance which contributes importantly to the structure and **ageing** potential of red wines. Tannin is found in grape skins, along with the pigments that give red wine its colour. A long **maceration** during **fermentation** leads to a high level of tannin. Grape tannin can be supplemented by **oak**-derived tannins, by ageing the wine in small oak **barrels**.
 2. A tasting term used to describe the level and

quality of tannin in red wine. Tannin is usually identified as a dry sensation on the gums and roof of the mouth, sometimes accompanied by a leathery, or cold tea, smell and taste. In high-quality young red wines, the high tannin content can mask the fruit flavours; as the wine matures, the tannin should integrate with the fruit and **acidity** to yield a harmonious, well-knit flavour.

Tarragona A **DO** wine of northeast **Spain**, produced in a coastal region southwest of **Penedès**. Traditionally this was a source of high-alcohol dessert wines; today most of the production is of average-quality white wine. Production is dominated by co-operatives and much of the wine is sold for blending. There are three subregions. El Campo de Tarragona produces mainly white wine from the Penedès grape varieties, **Macabeo**, **Parellada** and **Xarel-lo**. The red varieties **Cariñena** and **Garnacha** are cultivated in the cooler Conca de Falset area. Whites from Macabeo and Garnacha Blanca are produced farther inland, in the more extreme climate of Ribera de Ebro.

tartaric acid A naturally occuring acid, found in grape juice and, hence, in wine. Tartaric acid is the most important contributor to **acidity** in wine, essential for balance, a refreshing taste, and good ageing potential. White crystals of tartrate salts can be precipitated from wine when chilled; they are harmless and tasteless. Nevertheless, many wine producers chill wines to around −5°C, so that tartrates are precipitated before bottling.

Tasmania An island wine-producing region of **Australia**, the most southern and therefore enjoying the coolest climate. The usual **varietal** wines are produced, from **Cabernet Sauvignon**, **Pinot Noir** and **Chardonnay**, with mixed results. There are some fine Cabernets, with a distinctive cool-climate definition. However, the region shows greater potential for **méthode champenoise** sparkling wine.

tastevin A round, shallow, saucer-shaped cup, usually made of silver or silver plate, used for tasting wine, particularly in **Burgundy**. For serious tasting, especially appreciation of the **nose**, there is no substitute for a proper tasting glass.

Taurasi A red **DOC** wine of the **Campania** region of southern **Italy**, produced in the hills surrounding the village of the same name, mainly from the **Aglianico** grape variety. This can be one of Italy's better reds, with deep colour and good ageing potential, although austere **tannins** can mask the fruit flavours in young Taurasi. PRICE BAND: C–D.

Tavel A rosé **AC** wine of the southern **Rhône**, made chiefly from the **Grenache** and **Cinsault** grape varieties, although others are allowed. It is a deep-coloured pink, always dry and high in alcohol, and the best examples have fresh, young

strawberry fruit. It is best drunk young. PRICE
BAND: B.

Tawny Port The class of **Port** that is matured
in wooden barrels, rather than in bottle (as with
Vintage Port), and hence develops a characteristic tawny colour. Tawny Port of indicated age can
be described as 10-year-old, 20-year-old, 30-year-
old, or over 40 years old. Most producers will
aim for an average age corresponding to these
descriptions, but the regulations simply require a
10-year-old, for instance, to have the characteristics expected of a 10-year-old Tawny Port. Dated
Tawny, or **Colheita Port**, is Port of a single year,
matured in wooden casks. The year of bottling
must appear on the label, along with the year of
harvest, and the label must state 'matured in
wood', to help avoid confusion with Vintage
Port. Cheap Tawny is usually made by blending
Ruby and **White Port**.

teinturier A general term for those few red
grape varieties that have pink juice.

Tempranillo A red grape variety grown widely
in **Spain**, particularly in the **Rioja** region where it
is the most important variety in the blend for red
wines, and **Navarra**. It can produce light, fruity
wine for drinking young, as well as deep, full-
flavoured reds, suitable for long ageing in both
barrel and bottle. It is known as Tinto Fino in
Ribera del Duero, Cencibel in **La Mancha** and
Valdepeñas and Ull de Llebre in Catalonia. In

Portugal it is a highly regarded grape for **Port** production, and goes under the name Tinta Roriz.

tenuta The Italian word for an estate or farm.

Terlano (also called **Terlaner**) A white **DOC** wine of the **Alto Adige** region of northeast **Italy**, produced on both banks of the Adige river, west of Bolzano. Terlano without a **varietal** designation is a fresh, fruity blend with at least 50% **Pinot Bianco**; it can be still or **spumante**. Apart from this there are seven **varietal** wines, made from **Chardonnay**, **Müller-Thurgau**, **Pinot Bianco**, **Riesling Italico**, **Riesling Renano**, **Sauvignon**, or **Silvaner**, Sauvignon is the most promising varietal, although at present it is produced in small quantities. PRICE BAND: A–B.

Teroldego Rotaliano A **DOC** wine of the **Trentino** region of northeast **Italy**, producing deep, well-structured reds capable of long ageing, and light, flavourful **rosato** (or *kretzer*), best drunk young. Both are made from the Teroldego grape variety, unique to this region. PRICE BAND: A–B.

Terra Alta A **DO** wine of northeast **Spain**, produced in a region just to the west of **Tarragona**. Like Tarragona, the traditional wines of Terra Alta were high-alcohol dessert wines. Now average-quality whites are made from **Garancha** Blanca and **Macabeo**, and rather coarse reds from **Cariñena**, Garnacha and

Tempranillo. The region is also an important source of sacramental wine, for use in the Roman Catholic Mass.

Terret A red grape variety, one of the 13 permitted for **Châteauneuf-du-Pape**.

terroir A French term meaning soil, but often extended to embrace all the characteristics of a vineyard site. Although New World winemakers have pursued the **varietal** path, the French maintain that it is *terroir* which determines the distinctive identity of a wine. See also **goût**.

tête de cuvée An unofficial French term designating the best lots of wine from a grower or *appellation*. In exceptional years an estate (e.g. **Sauternes**) may make a separate *tête de cuvée* bottling; or a producer may use the term on the label to distinguish what is considered a superior wine.

Texas A wine-producing state of the United States, where fairly recent plantings of **Vitis vinifera** grapes are producing **varietal** wines, especially **Chardonnay** and **Cabernet Sauvignon**.

Tinta Barroca A red grape variety planted mainly in the **Douro** region of **Portugal**, and used as part of the blend for **Port**. It produces big, full, earthy, tannic wines. Also planted in **South Africa**, where it is used to make Port-style wines and table wines.

Tinta Cão   A red grape variety planted in the **Douro** region of **Portugal**, where it is used as part of the blend for **Port**. It produces fine and complex wine, but at low yields. It is also allowed in **Dão** and red **Vinho Verde**.

Tinta Francisca   A red grape variety planted in the **Douro** region of **Portugal**, where it is sometimes used in making **Port**, although it lacks concentration and is not one of the highest quality Port grapes. It is not related to **Pinot Noir**, as was once thought; nor is it related to **Touriga Francesa**.

Tinta Negra Mole   A red grape variety planted on **Madeira**, where it is the most important ingredient in the island's **fortified** wines. Although the wines of Madeira are described by **varietal** names, most are blends consisting mainly of Tinta Negra Mole. It produces wines of high acid and deep colour, but otherwise fairly neutral, allowing the character of the designated grape variety (**Sercial**, **Verdelho**, **Bual**, or **Malmsey**) to show through.

Tinta Roriz   See **Tempranillo**.

tinto   The Spanish and Portuguese word for red wine.

Tinto Fino   See **Tempranillo**.

Tocai di San Martino della Battaglia   A white **DOC** wine of the **Lombardy** region of **Italy**, produced just to the south of Lake Garda from the **Tocai Friulano** grape variety. It is a light, dry white, sometimes with a hint of lemony acidity, of moderate quality. PRICE BAND: B.

Tocai Friulano A white grape variety found in the **Friuli-Venezia Giulia** region of northeast **Italy**, where it makes fresh, crisp white wines, especially in **Collio** and **Colli Orientali del Friuli**. It is also found in the **Veneto** and **Lombardy** regions. It is unrelated to **Tokay-Pinot Gris** or to the Hungarian **Tokay**.

Tokaji (also called **Tokay**) A white wine of **Hungary**, produced in the Tokaj-Hegyalja region in the northeast of the country, in 28 villages including Tokaj itself, from the **Furmint** and **Hárslevelü** grape varieties.

When less than half of a particular vineyard is affected by **botrytis**, all the grapes are harvested together and used to make Szamorodni, which can be dry or sweet, depending on the natural sugar content of the grapes. The most famous style is Tokaji Aszú. During the harvest, botrytis-affected (**Aszú**) grapes are kept separate, while the others are fermented to make a base wine, which is stored in casks of 136 litres. The *Aszú* grapes are crushed to make a paste, and the base wine is then poured over it.

The style of wine depends on how many hods, or *puttonyos*, of *Aszú* grapes are used for each cask of base wine: typically, Tokaji Aszú will be labelled as 3, 4, or 5 *puttonyos*. One to two days after mixing the base wine and *Aszú* grapes, the mixture is pressed and aged in barrel for four to six years. In the cellar, it is affected by a fungus similar to **flor** in **Sherry**. It is pale to deep amber in colour, with appley raisiny aromas, and rich, sweet, concentrated apple flavour on the palate. Tokaji Aszú Eszencia is an *Aszú* with more than 6 *puttonyos*. Tokaji Eszencia is an exceedingly rare wine made from the free-run juice of *Aszú* grapes; it takes years to ferment, often reaching only a few degrees of alcohol. It has traditionally been reserved for the death beds of kings and emperors, where miraculous efficacy is needed. Tokaji is sold in squat 50 cl bottles.

Tokay An anglicized name for **Tokaji**.

Tokay-Pinot Gris See **Pinot Gris**.

Torgiano A **DOC** (and **DOCG**) wine of the **Umbria** region of **Italy**. The fresh and fruity **bianco** is made mainly from **Trebbiano** and **Grechetto**, and the **rosso** (known as Rubesco), full-flavoured and high quality, from **Sangiovese** and **Canaiolo**. Torgiano Rosso *riserva*, aged for three years, is entitled to the DOCG designation.

Toro A **DO** wine of northwest **Spain**. Most of the production is good-quality, fruity red wine, made mainly from the **Tempranillo** grape variety plus some **Garnacha**. Quality is improving with each vintage. Some whites are also made, mainly from **Malvasia**.

tough A tasting term, used to indicate a full-bodied wine (usually red) with an over-high **tannin** content. A tough young wine should mellow as it matures.

Touraine A wine-producing region of the **Loire** valley, centred on the city of Tours. High quality white wines are made from the **Chenin Blanc** grape variety in the **ACs** of **Vouvray** and **Montlouis**, which can be dry, **demi-sec** or **moelleux**, and still or sparkling. **Jasnières**, produced to the north of Tours, is bone dry Chenin Blanc. The best reds are made from **Cabernet Franc** in **Chinon**, **Bourgueil** and **Saint-Nicolas-de-Bourgueil**. The basic Touraine AC includes the white Sauvignon de Touraine (variable in quality, but much cheaper than **Sancerre**). Red AC Touraine, again of variable quality, is made mainly from the **Gamay** grape variety, occasionally **Pinot Noir**. Touraine Tradition is a blend of Gamay, Cabernet Franc, and **Cot**, which works well.

Three villages can add their names to the Touraine AC. Touraine-Amboise includes good red made from Cot, light fruity red from Gamay, and good dry Chenin Blanc. Touraine-Azay-le-Rideau makes unexciting rosé from **Grolleau** and decent whites, dry or *demi-sec*, from Chenin Blanc. Touraine-Mesland produces excellent red from Gamay, and some decent dry Chenin Blanc.

Touriga Francesa A red grape variety, planted in the **Douro** region of **Portugal**, where it is one of the most important ingredients in the blend for **Port**. It produces good-quality, aromatic wine, slightly lighter in colour and weight than **Touriga Nacional**. It is not related to **Tinta Francisca**.

Touriga Nacional   A red grape variety, planted in the **Douro** region of **Portugal**, where it is probably the finest ingredient in the blend for **Port**. It produces deep, dark, powerful wines, with intense aromas and black-fruit flavours. It is also found in red **Dão**, where it must make up at least 20% of the blend.

Traben-Trarbach   A village of the **Mosel-Saar-Ruwer** region of **Germany**, which produces medium-quality white wines from the **Riesling** grape variety. The vineyards come under the **Grosslage** of Schwarzlay, and the **Einzellage** sites include Burgberg, Gaispfad, Hühnerberg, Königsberg, Kräuterhaus, Kreuzberg, Schlossberg, Taubenhaus, Ungsberg, Würzgarten (the best) and Zollturm.

Traminer   A **clone** of the **Gewürztraminer** grape variety, used in **Alsace** (where it is also called Klevener), and in **Germany** to produce similarly spicy, but less pungent wine.

Traminer Aromatico   An alternative name, used in Italy, for the **Gewürztraminer** grape.

Trebbiano (also called **Ugni Blanc**)   A white grape variety, producing more wine than any other variety in the world. Its home is **Italy**, where it produces more or less characterless white wine throughout the country: it also contributes to the blend for several red wines, including **Chianti**. In **France** it is the most important variety in the Charentes area, where it is known as **Saint-Emilion**: most of it is distilled to make Cognac, the finest brandy. As Ugni Blanc, it is used to make Armagnac brandy. Ugni Blanc also contributes to the blend for many white wines of the **Midi**, and also for **Bandol** and **Palette** in **Provence**. It is also planted in **Australia** and **California**, mainly for brandy production.

Trebbiano d'Abruzzo A dry white **DOC** wine of the **Abruzzi** region of **Italy**, made from the **Trebbiano** grape variety. Usually it is dull and best drunk cold. Occasionally it is complex and deep, with good ageing potential. Price is a good guide to quality. PRICE BAND: A–C.

Trebbiano di Romagna A white **DOC** wine of the **Emilia-Romagna** region of **Italy**. Usually it is clean, but dull and neutral. It can be dry, medium dry, or sweet, and still or sparkling.

Trentino The southern part of the Trentino-Alto Adige, Italy's northernmost wine region, the Trentino zone stretches along the Adige and Sarca valleys. The Trentino **DOC** comes in 20 different versions: 17 **varietals**, plus **bianco**, **rosso** and **Vin Santo**. Of the whites, bianco is a blend of **Chardonnay** and **Pinot Bianco** and the varietals are Chardonnay, **Moscato**, **Müller-Thurgau**, Nosiola, Pinot Bianco, **Pinot Grigio**, **Riesling Italico**, **Riesling Renano** and **Traminer Aromatico**. Traditionally, they were blended together more or less indiscriminately to make Trentino Bianco. However, today, with modern wine-making techniques, most producers have chosen to market their wines under varietal designations. Much Chardonnay, Pinot Grigio and Pinot Bianco is also used in sparkling wine production in Trentino. Rosso is a blend of **Cabernet** and **Merlot**, and the red varietals are Cabernet Franc, Cabernet Sauvignon, **Lagrein**, **Marzemino**, Merlot and **Pinot Nero**. Much of the region's wine, including much of the best, is sold outside the DOC system as **vino da tavola**. See **Casteller**; **Sorni**; **Teroldego Rotaliano**; **Valdadige**.

Trier A wine-producing city of the **Mosel-Saar-Ruwer** region of **Germany**. There are vineyards within the city boundaries, which come under the **Grosslage** of Römerlay, but the many **Einzellage** names are rarely used.

trocken The German term for dry wines, designed for drinking with food. The **residual sugar** level is controlled; up to 4 g per litre, or up to 9 g per litre if specifications of sufficient balancing acidity are also met. See also **halbtrocken**.

Trockenbeerenauslese A German and Austrian quality white wine category meaning 'selected dried grapes'. Individually selected, shrivelled, overripe grapes, usually affected by **botrytis**, are cut from the bunches, and pressed carefully. The minimum **must weight** is 150° *Oechsle* in Germany, but the fermentation usually stops when the **alcohol content** has reached only about 6%. This results in exceedingly sweet, rich, and luscious wines, with balancing acidity, and long ageing potential. They are most successfully made from the **Riesling** grape. See also **QmP**.

Trollinger   See **Schiava**.

Tronçais   Forest in France where some of the best oak is grown for making **barrels** for **ageing** wine. See also **Allier**; **Nevers**.

Trousseau   An alternative name, used in France, for the **Bastardo** grape variety, which is used with **Poulsard** to make the red wine of **Jura**.

Tursan   A VDQS wine from the foothills of the Pyrenees, in southwest **France**. The tough, tannic red and rosé versions are made from the **Tannat**, **Cabernet Sauvignon** and **Cabernet Franc** grape varieties. Charmless, strong-tasting white wines, with little aroma, are made from the **Baroque** grape variety.

Tuscany   A major wine-producing region of central **Italy**. Some of the country's best red wines are made here: **Chianti** (particularly Chianti Classico), **Brunello di Montalcino** and **Vino Nobile di Montepulciano**, all based on the

Sangiovese grape variety; **Carmignano**; and many **vini da tavola** based on Sangiovese, **Cabernet Sauvignon**, or a blend of the two. White wines can also be fine, although few reach the heights of the best reds. See **Bianco della Lega**; **Bianco della Val d'Arbia**; **Bianco della Valdinievole**; **Bianco di Pitigliano**; **Bianco Pisano San Torpè**; **Bianco Vergine della Valdichiana**; **Bolgheri**; **Elba**; **Galestro**; **Montecarlo**; **Morellino di Scansano**; **Moscadello di Montalcino**; **Parrina**; **Pomino**; **Vin Santo**.

Ugni Blanc See **Trebbiano**.

Ull de Llebre An alternative name, used in Catalonia, for the **Tempranillo** grape variety.

ullage The 'loss' of wine in bottle, owing to a faulty cork, or natural contraction. The level of wine in very old bottles can fall from the neck to the middle of the shoulder, or below. If below mid-shoulder, the wine is said to be 'badly ullaged', and should be regarded with some suspicion, because the risk of **oxidation** is high.

Ullage also refers to the air-space in a barrel, which should be kept to a minimum to prevent oxidation. Wine aged 'on ullage' in cask will develop **rancio** flavours.

Umbria A wine-producing region of central Italy. Umbria's most famous wine is **Orvieto**, usually a crisp, nutty, dry white for early drinking, but sometimes sweet. There is also high-quality white and red **Torgiano**, and good

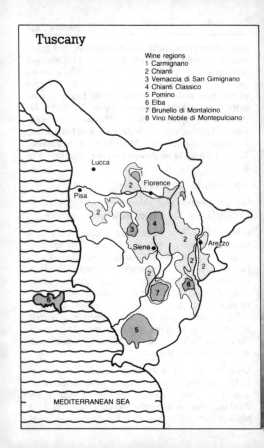

Tuscany

Wine regions
1 Carmignano
2 Chianti
3 Vernaccia di San Gimignano
4 Chianti Classico
5 Pomino
6 Elba
7 Brunello di Montalcino
8 Vino Nobile di Montepulciano

Lucca

Florence

Pisa

Arezzo

Siena

MEDITERRANEAN SEA

value reds from **Montefalco** (especially Sagrantino). See also **Colli Altotiberini; Colli del Trasimeno; Colli Martani; Colli Perugini**.

unbalanced A tasting term, used to describe a wine with an excess or deficiency of one or more elements, for instance, **acidity, tannin,** or alcohol.

Ungstein A wine-producing village in the **Rheinpfalz** region of **Germany**, producing full, fruity white wines. The vineyards come within the **Grosslagen** of Hönigsackel, Hochmess and Kobnert, and the **Einzellage** sites include Herrenberg, Nussriegel and Weilberg.

United States An important wine-producing country of north America. Wine is produced in many states, but most importantly in **California, Oregon** and **Washington State**. See also **Finger Lakes; Idaho; New York State; Texas**.

Ürzig A wine-producing village of the **Mosel-Saar-Ruwer** region of **Germany**, producing good-quality white wine, mainly from the **Riesling** grape variety. The vineyards come within the **Grosslage** of Schwarzlay, and the best **Einzellage** site is Würzgarten.

USSR See **Soviet Union**.

Utiel Requena A **DO** wine of eastern **Spain**, produced in a mountainous region just to the west of **Valencia**. Fresh, delicate, perfumed **rosado** wine is made from the **Bobal** grape, which

United States

1 Washington
2 Idaho
3 Oregon
4 California
5 Texas
6 New York State
7 Pennsylvania

is also used to make strong, flavourful, full-bodied reds.

Uva di Troia A good-quality red grape variety of southern **Italy**, grown particularly in the **Apulia** region.

Uva Rara An alternative name, used in the **Lombardy** region of **Italy**, for the **Bonarda** grape variety.

VA See **volatile acidity**.

Vaccarèse A red grape variety, one of 13 permitted in **Châteauneuf-du-Pape**. It produces wine fairly similar in character to that made from **Syrah**.

Vacqueyras See **Côtes du Rhône**.

Vaillons A **premier cru** vineyard of **Chablis**.

Val d'Arbia See **Bianco della Val d'Arbia**.

Valais See **Switzerland**.

Valcalepio A **DOC** wine produced in the Bergamo area of **Lombardy**, northwest **Italy**. The dry **rosso**, made from the **Cabernet Sauvignon** and **Merlot** grapes, can be of good quality. The **bianco**, from **Pinot Bianco** and **Pinot Grigio**, is usually quite ordinary.

Valdadige A **DOC** wine of the **Trentino** region of northeast **Italy**. A white **varietal** is made from **Pinot Grigio** and a red from **Schiava**. **Bianco** is a blend based mainly on **Trebbiano**, Nosiola and

Vernaccia, with the possible inclusion of some **Chardonnay**, **Pinot Bianco**, Pinot Grigio, **Riesling Italico** and **Müller-Thurgau**. **Rosso** and **rosato** are produced mainly from the **Lambrusco** and Schiava grapes, with occasionally **Lagrein**, **Merlot**, **Negrara**, **Pinot Nero** and Teroldego. PRICE BAND: A.

Valdeorras See **Galicia**.

Valdepeñas A **DO** wine to the south of **La Mancha**, central **Spain**. The region produces mainly whites, made from the **Airén** grape. However, it is most famous for its reds, sometimes oak-aged, from the **Tempranillo** grape (known locally as Cencibel, as in La Mancha). Traditionally, the Cencibel was diluted with Airén, but today the best examples are 100% Cencibel: deep, soft, fruity wines, capable of moderate ageing, and good value for money. PRICE BAND: A–B.

Valençay A **VDQS** wine produced in small quantities in the southeast corner of **Touraine** in the **Loire**. Fresh reds and rosés are produced mainly from the **Gamay** grape, with the possible addition of **Cabernet Sauvignon**, **Cabernet Franc** and **Merlot**. Crisp whites are made from at least 60% **Arbois**, **Chardonnay** or **Sauvignon Blanc**, with up to 40% Romorantin or **Chenin Blanc**.

Valencia A **DO** wine produced inland from the port of the same name, in eastern **Spain**. Most of the wine produced is dull, bland white, made from the **Merseguera** grape. Easy-drinking reds are made in the south of the region, mainly from **Garnacha** or **Monastrell**. A **mistelle**, called Moscatel de Valencia, is also produced, from a mixture of **Moscatel** juice and brandy.

Valgella See **Valtellina**.

Valle d'Aosta A small, alpine, French-speaking wine region of northwestern **Italy**. There is one **DOC**, Valle d'Aosta (or Valle d'Aoste), and red, white and rosé wines can be made from 22 different grape varieties. The wines are rarely seen outside the region.

Valle Isarco (also called **Eisacktaler**) A white **DOC** wine of the **Alto Adige** region of northeast **Italy**. Five pure **varietal** wines are produced: **Müller-Thurgau**, **Pinot Grigio**, **Sylvaner**, **Traminer Aromatico** and Veltliner. All are crisp, vibrant, fruity wines, with delicate aromas and good varietal character.

Valleé de la Marne A vineyard area in the **Champagne** region of **France**. It is planted mainly with the red grape varieties **Pinot Noir** and **Pinot Meunier**.

Valmur One of the seven **grand cru** vineyards of **Chablis**.

Valpolicella A red **DOC** wine from just north of Verona, in the **Veneto** region of **Italy**. It is produced from mainly the **Corvina**, **Rondinella** amd **Molinara** grape varieties. Most of the wine made is fruity, dry, cherry flavoured red for early-drinking, with a distinctive, slightly bitter finish. Quality ranges from poor and anonymous, to excellent. Often among the best are those described as Valpolicella Classico, indicating that they come from the original, 'classic' zone. Producers in the Pantena valley can add the name Valpantena on their labels. Single-vineyard wines are also usually above average. PRICE BAND: A–C.

Ripasso Valpolicella, which is re-fermented on the **lees** of Recioto della Valpolicella Amarone (see **Amarone**), is also nearly always better, richer and longer-lasting. See also **Recioto della Valpolicella**.

Valreas See **Côtes du Rhône**.

Valtellina A red **DOC** wine produced in northern **Lombardy**, **Italy**. The sturdy reds are based on the **Nebbiolo** grape. The best wines often carry the Valtellina Superiore DOC, which is further subdivided into four zones: Grumello, Inferno, Sassella and Valgella.

Even fuller-bodied wines are made by using partly dried grapes, known as *Sfursat* (or *Sforzato*). Nebbiolo grapes are dried before fermentation, when the naturally concentrated juice gives a minimum of 14.5% alcohol.

vanilla A tasting term, used to describe a vanilla-like aroma, usually derived from **oak** ageing.

varietal A wine made entirely (or almost entirely) from a single grape variety.

vat A general term used to describe a vessel in which wine is stored, or undergoes **fermentation**. They may be made of cement (sometimes resin-lined), wood or stainless steel.

Vaucoupin (also called **Vaucoupain**) A **premier cru** vineyard in **Chablis**.

Vaud See **Switzerland**.

Vaudésir One of the seven **grand cru** vineyards of **Chablis**.

Vaudevey A **premier cru** vineyard of **Chablis**.

VDQS (**Vin Délimité de Qualité Supérieure**) A part of the French system guaranteeing the origin of a wine from a demarcated area. Wines are placed into three main categories, of which VDQS is the middle category just below **AC**. In general, the laws of VDQS will lay down the following: the area entitled to the name; permitted grape varieties; density of vine plants; minimum alcohol levels; and yields. Occasionally regions are granted VDQS status with the expectation that they will later be promoted to AC.

vegetal A tasting term, used to describe a vegetable-like aroma, sometimes slightly rotting.

Veldenz A small village in the **Mosel-Saar-Ruwer** region of **Germany**. It produces good-quality white wines from the **Riesling** grape. The vineyards come within the **Grosslage** of Kurfürstlay, and the **Einzellage** sites are Elisenberg, Kirchberg, Mühlberg, Grafschafter, Sonnenberg and Carlsberg.

Velletri A **DOC** wine produced in the **Latium** region of central **Italy**. It makes mainly dry, fresh whites from the **Malvasia** and **Trebbiano** grapes. Warm, fleshy, dry red wines are produced from **Sangiovese**, **Montepulciano** and **Cesanese**.

velvety A tasting term, used to describe a textured, rich sensation of opulence.

vendange The French for harvest.

vendange tardive The French term used to indicate **late-harvest** wines, particularly in **Alasce**. Delaying the harvest allows the grapes to become very ripe and with high grape sugar levels. This usually results in sweet, concentrated wines, or completely dry wines, high in alcohol.

vendemmia The Italian for harvest.

vendimia The Spanish for harvest.

Veneto An important wine-producing region centred on Venice in northeast **Italy**. It is most famous for **Soave**, and the similar softly fruity whites **Bianco di Custoza** and **Gambellara**, as well as for **Valpolicella** and **Bardolino**, and for the fresh sparkler **Prosecco di Conegliano-Valdobbiadene**. See also **Breganze**; **Colli Euganei**; **Lison-Pramaggiore**; **Montello e Colli Asolani**; **Piave**.

Venezia-Giulia See **Friuli-Venezia Giulia**.

véraison A French term used to describe the change of colour which occurs during the maturation of the grape on the vine, when red-wine grapes change from green to reddish-black.

Verdelho A grape variety, grown on the island of **Madeira**, where it gives its name to a category of wine. Nutty, and only slightly sweet, Verdelho is the second driest style of Madeira, between **Sercial** and **Bual**. The variety is also used in making white **Dão** and white **Port**. In Australia Verdelho is used to make dry, characterful table wines. PRICE BAND: A.

Verdicchio A white grape variety grown mainly in the **Marches** region of **Italy**. It produces **DOC** wines in Verdicchio dei Castelli di Jesi, fresh, crisp, high-acid, good-value whites, and the similar, but much rarer, Verdicchio di Matelica. PRICE BAND: A.

Verduzzo Friulano A white grape variety native to the **Friuli-Venezia Giulia** region of **Italy**. There are two different types: *verde*, which produces dry, citrus-flavoured wines (e.g. **Aquileia**, **Latisana**, **Isonzo** and **Grave del Friuli**) *giallo*, or Verduzzo di Ramandolo, which makes sweet, golden-coloured dessert wines in **Colli Orientali del Friuli**. Verduzzo Trevigiano, used in the **Veneto** and **Piave**, is not related.

Vermentino A white grape variety grown in

Corsica and in Italy, in **Liguria** and **Sardinia**, where it makes the **DOC** wines in Vermentino di Sardegna and Vermentino di Gallura.

Vernaccia di Oristano A white **DOC** wine produced in **Sardinia** from the grape of the same name. The wine is similar in style to **Sherry** and is usually dry and rather bitter, although sweeter, fortified versions also exist.

Vernaccia di San Gimignano A dry white **DOC** wine produced in **Tuscany**, **Italy**, from the grape of the same name. The best examples are dry, full-flavoured and nutty whites. PRICE BAND: A–C.

Vernaccia di Serrapetrona A red, sparkling **DOC** wine produced in the **Marches** region of **Italy**, from the grape of the same name. The wine is usually sweet and softly fruity, but dry versions can also be found.

Vernatsch See **Schiava**.

Victoria A state and leading wine region of **Australia**. It produces a wide range of styles: sparkling wines from the **Great Western** region; red and white **varietals**, particularly **Pinot Noir** from **Geelong**; **Sémillon** and **Shiraz** from the **Murray River Valley**; excellent red and white varietals from the cool-climate **Yarra Valley**; and luscious liquer wines from **Rutherglen**.

vieilles vignes A French term sometimes found on labels, which indicates that the wine was produced from grapes grown on old, well-established vines.

vigneron The French term for vine-grower.

vignoble The French term for vineyard.

Vila Nova de Gaia See **Port**.

vin The French word for wine.

Vin de Corse An **AC** wine of the French island of Corsica. Most of the wine produced is red, from a variety of grapes including **Nielluccio**, Sciacarello and **Grenache**. The small amount of white wine produced is made mainly from **Vermentino**. The names of better areas – Calvi, Coteaux du Cap Corse, Figari, Patrimonio, Porto Vecchio and **Sartène** – can be appended to the Vin de Corse AC. See also **Ajaccio**.

vin de garde A French term used to indicate a wine considered capable of improving with **ageing**.

vin de pays A part of the French system guaranteeing origin from a demarcated area. Wines are placed into one of three categories, of which *vin de pays* is the lowest (below **VDQS**). In general the laws of a *vin de pays* region are more flexible than for **AC** and VDQS.

Vin de Savoie The general **AC** for wine of the **Savoie** region of France. Most of the best wine is made from the **Altesse** grape, producing dry, full-bodied, spicy, aromatic whites. **Jacquère** is widely planted, producing dry, biting white wine, which is best used as a base for sparklers. Dense, deep-coloured, austere reds are made from **Mondeuse**, plus some **Gamay** and **Pinot Noir**. Certain **crus** can add their village names to 'Vin de Savoie', notably **Apremont**, **Arbin**, Chignin, Cruet, Jongieux, Marignan, **Montmélian**, and Ripaille. See also **Crépy**; **Seyssel**.

vin de table The lowest category of French wine, with no indication of geographical origin. It comes below the **QWSPR** (quality wine) designations **vin de pays**, **VDQS** and **AC**.

Vin Délimité de Qualité Supérieure See **VDQS**.

vin doux naturel The French term for a sweet wine, produced by adding alcohol (in the form of grape spirit) to partially fermented **must**. See **Beaumes-de-Venise**; **fortified wine**; **Maury**; **Muscat de Beaumes-de-Venise**; **Muscat de Frontignan**; **Muscat de Lunel**; **Muscat de Mireval**; **Muscat de Rivesaltes**; **Muscat de Saint-Jean-de-Minervois**; **Rasteau**.

vin gris The French term for a very pale pink-coloured wine.

vin jaune A highly distinctive white wine produced in the **Jura** region from the **Savagnin** grape. Its distinctive dry, assertive, nutty flavour derives from long barrel ageing under a layer of yeast cells, similar to **flor** in **fino** Sherry. It is produced in the ACs of **Arbois**, **L'Etoile**, **Château-Chalon** and **Côtes du Jura**. PRICE BAND: D–E.

vin mousseux A French term for sparkling wine.

Vin Santo A style of wine produced in **Italy**, particularly in the **Tuscany** region where it is made from the **Malvasia** and **Trebbiano** grapes. The grapes are semi-dried before pressing, and the **must** is then placed in small, sealed barrels for fermentation and maturation. The wine remains in barrel, often stored in a roof space, for at least three years. The result is a golden, concentrated, aromatic wine, ranging from very sweet to quite dry. Quality is highly variable. A large amount of *Vin Santo* is produced for private consumption. PRICE BAND: B–D.

viña The Spanish word for vineyard.

vinho The Portuguese word for wine.

Vinho Verde An **RD** wine of northern **Portugal**. Most of the wine produced is a harsh, austere red, but in export markets the white is much better known, made from several grapes including **Alvarinho** and **Loureiro**. At its best this is a crisp, high-acid, bone-dry, refreshing wine; although too often it is off-dry and flat. It is best drunk as young as possible. PRICE BAND: A–B. (Vinho Verde is only green in the sense of the tasting term **green**.)

vinification The making of wine. Usually the term is used loosely, to cover every stage of winemaking from **fermentation** through to **maceration**.

vino The Spanish and Italian word for wine.

vino da tavola The Italian term for table wine. In theory it is the lowest quality designation, below the **QWPSR** (quality wine) designations **DOC** and **DOCG**. In practice some producers, notably in **Tuscany**, produce high-quality (often highly-priced) table wines in order to avoid what they see as restrictive DOCG regulations, particularly in relation to permitted grape varieties.

vino de color The Spanish term for the colouring agent used to make brown **Sherry** and **Málaga**. It is made by re-fermenting a mixture of **arrope** and grape juice.

vino de mesa The Spanish term for table wine.

Vino Nobile di Montepulciano A red **DOCG** wine produced in the Tuscany region of **Italy**. It is made mainly from the **Prugnolo Gentile** grape (a **clone** of **Sangiovese**), plus some **Canaiolo**. The wine has similar characteristics to **Chianti**, although until recently quality has lagged behind the best examples of Chianti Classico. This is beginning to change now, as Vino Nobile producers are improving all the time, and a distinctive style is emerging, more spicy and full-flavoured. PRICE BAND: B–C. See also **Rosso di Montepulciano**.

Vinsobres See **Côtes du Rhône**.

vintage In general, the year in which the grapes used to make a wine were harvested. In most wine-producing regions, climatic conditions can vary considerably from one year to the next, leading to good and and bad vintages. However, with modern winemaking techniques good producers should be able to make acceptable wines every year. Vintage has special significance in **Champagne** and **Port**.

Vintage Character See **Port**.

Vintage Port See **Port**.

Viognier A white grape variety grown almost exclusively in the northern **Rhône**, where it is used to make the white wines **Condrieu** and **Château-Grillet**, and sometimes (as a minor ingredient) the red wine **Côte Rôtie**.

Visan See **Côtes du Rhône**.

viscous A tasting term, used to indicate a heavy, dense wine, often with persistent **legs**.

viticulture The cultivation of vines.

Vitis vinifera The species of vine from which most wine is made. In most regions, however, the *vinifera* vine is grafted on to rootstock of *vitis* species native to America, such as *Vitis labrusca*, because of their resistance to **phylloxera**.

Viura See **Macabeo**.

volatile acidity (VA) The winemaker's term for the class of chemical substances, principally **acetic acid**, formed in wine by the **oxidation** of **alcohol**. VA is present in most wines in trace quantities, but in excess it is a fault, giving the wine an unpleasant **acetic** taste.

Volnay A red **AC** wine of the **Côte de Beaune** area of **Burgundy**, made from the **Pinot Noir** grape. Most of the wines are quite light in weight, but are intensely perfumed with enticing red fruit aromas. The **premier cru** wines generally have more weight, and need more time in bottle to develop their fleshy, complex, violet-scented character. PRICE BAND: C–D.

Vosgros A **premier cru** vineyard of **Chablis**.

Vosne-Romanée A red **AC** wine of the **Côte de Nuits** area of **Burgundy**, made from the **Pinot Noir** grape. The straight AC wine is usually of good quality, perfumed and elegant, and the **premiers crus** can match the quality of some other Burgundy **grands crus**. The *grands crus* of Vosne-Romanée are among the greatest red wines in the world. The very best are **La Tâche**, **Romanée-Conti** and **Richebourg**, followed by **Romanée** and **Romanée-Saint-Vivant**. The *grands* *crus* **Echézeaux** and **Grands-Echézeaux** are generally considered as part of Vosne-Romanée, although technically they are attached to **Flagey-Echézeaux**.

Vougeot An **AC** wine of the **Côte de Nuits** area of **Burgundy**. Most of the wine produced is red, from the **Pinot Noir** grape, and at its best is plummy, rich and quite good value. A small amount of reasonable white is produced from **Chardonnay**. PRICE BAND: C.

The village of Vougeot is most famous for its **grand cru** red wine, **Clos du Vougeot**.

Vouvray A white **AC** wine of the **Touraine** area of the **Loire**. The wines are produced in similar styles to **Montlouis**: dry, **demi-sec**, **moelleux** and sparkling wines, all based on the **Chenin Blanc** grape. The dry wines are usually quite austere and high in acid, particularly in their youth. *Demi-sec* is the most consistently successful style, and the Chenin Blanc grape can develop great complexity with bottle age, with the aroma and taste of quince, apples, nuts and honey. The sweetest, *moelleux* wines are made only in very good years. The sparkling wines, usually dry and made by the **méthode champenoise**, can be very good value for money. PRICE BAND: A–C.

VQPRD (Vin de Qualité Produit dans une Région Déterminée) The French term for QWPSR.

Wachenheim An important wine-producing village of the **Rheinpfalz** region of **Germany**, producing fine, full-bodied white wines, from the **Riesling** and other grape varieties. The vineyards come within the **Grosslagen** of Mariengarten, Schenkenböhl and Schnepfenflug, and the best **Einzellage** sites include Goldbächel and Gerümpel.

Washington State A wine-producing state of the Pacific northwest of the **United States**. Washington enjoys a warmer climate than its neighbour **Oregon**, producing good-quality **varietal** wines, particularly whites from the **Chardonnay**, **Sémillon** and **Riesling** (unfashionable, but often excellent) grape varieties, and reds from **Cabernet Sauvignon** and **Merlot**. See also **Yakima Valley**.

wein The German for wine.

weingut The German term for a wine-producing estate. If the word *weingut* appears on the label, it implies estate bottling.

Weissburgunder (also called **Weisser Burgunder**) The German name for the **Pinot Blanc** grape variety.

Weissherbst The German term for a pale pink wine, usually – and most successfully – produced from the **Spätburgunder** grape variety.

Welschriesling A white grape variety, producing medium-quality wine, not to be confused with the 'true' **Riesling**, (or Rhine Riesling). It is grown in **Yugoslavia** as **Laski Rizling** (or Laskiriesling), in the **Burgenland** region of **Austria** as Wälschriesling, in **Hungary** as **Olasz Rizling**, and in northern **Italy** as the **Riesling Italico** (especially in the **Friuli-Venezia Giulia**, **Veneto**, **Oltrepò Pavese**, **Trentino** and **Alto Adige** regions).

Western Australia An important wine-producing state of **Australia**, including the **Great Southern** area. It produces good-quality **varietal** wines made from the **Cabernet Sauvignon**, **Shiraz**, **Chardonnay** and **Sauvignon Blanc** grape varieties. **Margaret River**, with its temperate climate, produces high-class Cabernet Sauvignon, and successful **Sémillon**, Chardonnay and **Pinot Noir**. The hot-climate **Swan Valley** produces mainly **big** white wines, from **Chenin Blanc** and **Verdelho**, and some reds from **Shiraz** and Cabernet Sauvignon.

wine The fermented juice of the grape.

Winkel A small but important wine-producing village of the **Rheingau** region of **Germany**. It produces very good quality, powerful, long-lived white wines from the **Riesling** grape variety. The vineyards come under the **Grosslagen** of Hönigberg and Erntebringer, and the best **Einzellage** sites include Hasensprung, Gutenberg, Jesuitengarten and Schlossberg.

winzergenossenschaft The German term for a wine-producing co-operative.

Wonnegau The southernmost of the three **Bereich** subregions of the **Rheinhessen** region, **Anbaugebiet**, of **Germany**, producing sound, everyday white wine.

wood A tasting term, sometimes used as an alternative to **oak**, to indicate the presence of the flavours that result from **ageing** a wine in wooden barrels.

woody A tasting term, used to describe the unpleasant taste of wine that has received excessive **ageing** in old or dirty barrels.

Württemberg One of the 11 **Anbaugebiet** quality wine regions of **Germany**, with vineyards on the banks of the river Neckar and its tributaries. Most of the wine produced is white, from the **Riesling**, **Müller-Thurgau** and **Kerner** grape varieties. Light reds (and **Weissherbst** rosés) are produced from **Trollinger**, **Spätburgunder**, **Limberger** and **Portugieser**.

Xarel-lo A white grape variety of **Spain**, grown throughout Catalonia, particularly in **Penedès**, **Tarragona**, and **Alella**. On its own it produces rather neutral wine, but it contributes body to blends (with **Parellada** and **Macabeo**) in sparkling wines. See **Cava**.

Xérès The French name for **Sherry**. The name of the Sherry **DO** is unusual, in that it is trilingual: Jerez-Xérès-Sherry.

Xynomavro A red grape variety of **Greece**,

planted particularly in Macedonia in the north where it produces increasingly good red wine in Naoussa.

Yakima Valley An **AVA** wine-producing region of **Washington State** in the United States. Traditionally **Concord** grapes were grown here, but the valley now produces good-quality **varietal** wines including **Cabernet Sauvignon**, **Merlot**, **Sauvignon Blanc** and **Sémillon**.

Yarra Valley An important wine-producing area within the state of **Victoria** in **Australia**. It enjoys a cool climate and produces excellent red and white **varietal** wines and blends, from grape varieties including **Cabernet Sauvignon**, **Shiraz**, **Merlot**, **Gewürztraminer**, **Riesling**, **Chardonnay**, and perhaps the star of the Yarra, **Pinot Noir**.

yeast A group of bacteria which is responsible for producing the enzymes which promote **fermentation** of grape juice, the conversion of grape sugars into alcohol, with heat and carbon dioxide by-products. Wild yeasts occur naturally on the outside of grape skins, and these will start fermentation soon after the grapes are crushed. Some winemakers prefer to get rid of the natural yeasts using **sulphur dioxide**, and then start the fermentation with cultured yeasts produced in a laboratory.

yeasty A tasting term, used to describe the distinctive smell of yeast found in wineries during fermentation. It is usually indicative of a fault in wine, but yeasty is often confused with 'bready', a desirable characteristic in **Champagne** and some **Chardonnay**-based wines.

York Mountain An **AVA** of **San Luis Obispo** county, **California**.

Yugoslavia A wine-producing country of eastern Europe, producing a large quantity of wine. Much of it is **Laski Rizling**, made from the **Welschriesling** grape variety, rather bland, characterless, sweetish wine, which sells very well in the UK. **Varietal** wines from Dalmatia, Slovenia, Serbia, Istria and Macedonia, made from native and 'foreign' grape varieties, have potential, but it is not being realized yet.

Zell A **Bereich** subregion of the **Mosel-Saar-Ruwer** region of **Germany**, extending from the village of Zell northeast to Koblenz. There is a high proportion of **Riesling** planted, producing good-quality white wines, although lacking the elegance of those from the *Bereich* of **Bernkastel**. Most of the wine is sold under the famous **Grosslage** name of Schwarze Katz (Black Cat), or the *Bereich* name.

Zeltingen-Rachtig A wine-producing village of the **Mosel-Saar-Ruwer** region of **Germany**, producing good, well-balanced white wines, mainly from the **Riesling** grape variety. The vineyards come under the **Grosslage** of Münzlay, and the **Einzellage** sites are Schlossberg and

Sonnenuhr (the best two), Deutschherrenberg and Himmelreich.

zestful A tasting term, used to describe a fresh, lively wine, with a good balance of crisp fruit and acidity.

Zierfändler A white grape variety of **Austria**, which along with **Rotgipfler** is used to produce the heady, spicy, rich wine Gumpoldskirchner.

Zinfandel A red grape variety grown almost exclusively in **California** (although it may be related to the **Primitivo** variety of **Italy**), producing a wide variety of styles from 'white' Zinfandel (which is, confusingly, pink) to **fortified** port-like wines. But it is at its best in full-bodied, tannic reds, with rich, spicy, concentrated blackberry flavours. It is underrated, and often good value for money.

Zitsa A white semi-sparkling or sparkling wine of western **Greece**, produced in high-altitude vineyards around the village of the same name, from the **Debina** grape variety. The wines are light and appley flavoured, of good quality, and getting better as producers install more modern wine-making equipment. PRICE BAND: B.